Todd's smile was full of mischief. "Dad, you remember Cara Bentley, my client?"

"Ah," he said. "Of course I remember the...client. Come in. Come in." He turned to walk back into the house, assuming we would follow.

I poked Todd in the ribs. "You've got to stop introducing me as your client," I hissed. "I'm beginning to think I'm going to get billed for all the extra hours we spend together."

He turned a broad grin on me. "Of course you're getting billed for all those hours. How else can I ever afford the cabin I want on that lake in Canada?"

I quirked an eyebrow. "If you think I'm paying so you can flee the country to get away from me, you're much mistaken, guy."

Suddenly Todd's grin faded and his eyes darkened. He slipped his arm around my waist and spun me effortlessly until I was standing with my back against the side of the cottage. He placed a hand against the wall on either side of my head, trapping me. Not that I was trying to escape.

"Todd," I said breathlessly. "Your father's waiting."

He ignored me. Well, he actually ignored what I said. Me he paid lots of attention to as he leaned over and kissed me.

As kisses go, I don't know how it would rate on a scale of one to ten. I haven't had lots of experience, so I can't make a sound judgment. But I do know that as far as I was concerned, and I am, after all, the one who counts, I felt it all the way to my toes.

It was a discreet cough that pulled us apart. We turned to see Todd's dad standing at the door watching us.

"Toddy, I must insist you stop ravishing your...*client* on my front porch. What will my neighbors think? I have a reputation to consider." And he turned and walked inside.

A PALISADES CONTEMPORARY ROMANCE

The DOCUMENT

GAYLE ROPER

PALISADES

THE DOCUMENT
published by Palisades
a division of Multnomah Publishers, Inc.

© 1998 by Gayle Roper
International Standard Book Number: 1-57673-295-9

Cover illustration Corbert Gauthier
Design by Brenda McGee

"Generation to Generation" used by permission of Greg Hytha

Printed in the United States of America

For information:
MULTNOMAH PUBLISHERS, INC.
POST OFFICE BOX 1720
SISTERS, OREGON 97759

Library of Congress Cataloging-in-Publication Data:
Roper, Gayle G.
    The document / by Gayle Roper.
        p. cm.
    ISBN 1-57673-295-9 (alk. paper)
    1. Amish—Pennsylvania—Fiction. I. Title
PS3568.068D63   1998   98–30771
813'.54—dc21   CIP

98 99 00 01 02 03 04 — 10 9 8 7 6 5 4 3 2 1

With affection for
Bob and Linda
and
Rick and Eileen
and all the other parents
involved with us in
the adventure of adoption

∿

God sets the lonely in families…

PSALM 68:6A, NIV

Generation to Generation

Words and Music by
Greg & Linda Hytha

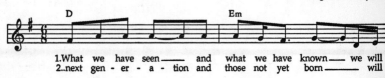

1.What we have seen____ and what we have known____ we will
2..next gen - er - a - tion and those not yet born____ will

tell of the praise____ wor - thy deeds He has done____ of His
know of the praise____ wor - thy deeds of the Lord____ and in

pow - er and won - ders His sta - tutes and laws____ He com -
turn they will tell____ of their God to their chil - dren____ and

man - ded we teach to____ the child - ren____ so the
praise Him in one____ ac -

cord   so the child - ren will trust____ in the

God of their fa - thers   re - mem - ber - ing —— praise - wor   thy

deeds He has done—   they will   keep His com-mands —— as His

sons and His daugh-ters ———— with   hearts that are   faith - ful to God—

—   from   ge - ne-ra - tion to—— ge - ne - ra —— tion   we will

tell   of   the praise—— wor - thy deeds—— of the Lord—   from

ge - ne - ra - tion to——   ge - ne - ra - tion   we will

tell   of   His   pow - er   and wo - ders————

Generation to Generation
-2-

Biemsderfer Family Tree

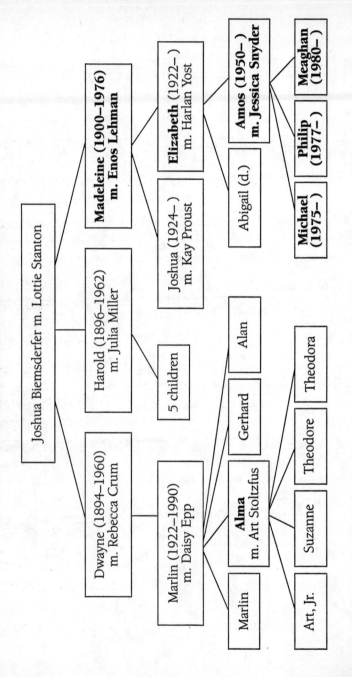

ONE

When I look back on the three-month period that effectively and thoroughly changed the course of my life, I sometimes wonder which event had the greatest impact. Was it the finding of Pop's papers? Perhaps the vengeful and terrible things that happened as a result of following what I found in those papers to its logical conclusion? Or was it Todd backing me against the wall of his father's retirement cottage and kissing me within an inch of my life?

Maybe the best answer is all of the above, though it could be argued that without Pop's papers, without The Document, nothing else of import would have happened.

I took The Document very seriously because I hate surprises. I have all my life. I find great security and comfort in knowing what's going to happen and when.

"You've got no sense of adventure," my brother, Ward, always says in great disgust. Ward is six feet tall, handsome in a Mel Gibson sort of way, and has enough energy to make me tired just hanging out with him. "Surprises are what make things fun."

"For you maybe. I say: Remember Disney World."

"Remember Disney World" is my personal battle cry whenever I need to remind my family that I'm different.

Mom and Pop, our grandparents with whom we'd lived since the death of our parents, had planned a surprise vacation to that magical place the fall I was nine and Ward was seven. We kids didn't know we were going anywhere until we got up one morning and Pop drove us to the airport instead of school.

I couldn't handle the spontaneity. I became cranky, moody, and an all-around pill, and we hadn't even checked our baggage yet.

"You didn't tell me," I cried to Mom as we sat on the bed in our beautiful room at the Grand Floridian. Pop and Ward had gone down to the lobby to listen to the pianist—or, more likely, to get away from me. "You've got to tell me! I need to know ahead of time!"

That night as I cried myself to sleep, despairing that no one understood, I heard Pop tell Mom, "We will never surprise her again. Do you understand?"

Well, in spite of his dictum, which, incidentally, neither of them kept, I found a surprise unlike any I'd ever known that day in June—a surprise that changed my life. I'm still reeling all this time later.

The day of the surprise Pop had been dead only two months. We knew he was dying, an old man of eighty-two who had been in great pain for several years with the twin demons of a deteriorating spine and emphysema. He knew God and loved God, and his death was a release and a relief to all three of us: Pop, Ward, and me. Mom had died three years earlier.

But Pop's death was one time when my much touted anticipation did little to prepare me. The emptiness both in my heart and in the house yawned before me like a great chasm. I knew I had to climb down into that pit of sorrow to be able to climb out the other side to normality, whatever that would be without Pop.

I got through the first month after his death by finishing my latest book. I had a deadline looming and I wrote nonstop, all hours of the day and night. I schlepped around in sweats or my nightgown, ate junk food and home-delivered pizzas, and emerged only long enough to go to church on Sunday. My characters lived such full lives that most of the time I was able to ignore the emptiness in mine.

But eventually the book reached its conclusion, I sent it off to my publisher, and I came back from the post office to that empty white Victorian in Haddonfield, NJ. In the past, every time I finished a book, Pop and Mom, then just Pop, took me out to a fancy restaurant for a spare-no-expense dinner.

"To Cara, the great American novelist," Pop would always toast me with his warm, magnetic smile. I knew he knew I wasn't that good, but he was acknowledging that I was succeeding in a field where many failed, even if he thought the field I was competing in was lesser somehow. I also knew he never read my books, but I didn't take it personally. He never read anything but the Bible, the *Wall Street Journal,* and business magazines. It was the dinner and the toast that told me that even though he couldn't comprehend that I actually liked writing, he was proud of me.

Suddenly, as I entered the silent, still house after my trip to the post office, it hit me that there would be no dinner, no toast, ever again. It was now just me and my microwave.

Pain unfurled in my chest, a black banner expanding, filling my lungs until I could barely breathe. The weight and mass of my distress gripped my heart so tightly I felt I had to push on my ribs to make certain my heart continued to beat, sort of self-administered CPR.

I don't know how long I lay on the sofa in the living room trying to survive the pain, but the bright June day had become dusky by the time Rainbow climbed on me and began kneading her little feline feet into my chest. She stood over my face, staring down at me in her slightly haughty, intimidating way.

"Don't let her push you around, Cara," Pop told me the first time Rainbow stared me down and got an extra can of cat food. "She'll be a bully if you let her. Remember, you're bigger. You're the boss."

The problem was that no one had told Rainbow that bigger meant boss. We had to keep reminding her.

I grabbed her and hugged her tightly, today's reminder. Her silky orange, black, and white fur soothed me with its touch.

She struggled against my hug, broke free, and jumped to my feet, waiting at a safe distance for me to get up and let her out. When I didn't, she climbed back up me, each step a little nail driven. This time when she reached my face, she put her nose on mine.

I sighed, surrendered, and sat up. She jumped to the floor. She had been Pop's cat, sitting on his lap purring, lying on the back of his chair, one paw on his shoulder, sleeping beside him in the king-sized bed he and Mom shared. She had only recently stopped her intense grieving for Pop, and I had become the focus of her attention. I think I alleviated her grief somewhat just because I was present. I know she made me feel better.

I got up from my sofa and let Rainbow out into the backyard. She immediately ducked behind Mom's rosebushes and relieved herself. She was back at the door in less than a minute.

"Life would be easier for all of us if you'd use your litter box," I told her as she sat to clean her paws after her excursion into the dirt. As always, she ignored me. My consolation was that on the litter box issue at least, she'd also ignored Pop.

Pop was John Seward Bentley, Jr. That we called him Pop and our grandmother Mom was Pop's little joke. After World War II, he had opened a small store that sold electrical appliances, and though the store had grown into Bentley Marts, a large, privately held chain of forty-five stores in the Mid-

Atlantic states, he always liked to joke that he and Mom owned a Mom-and-Pop store.

Ward (John Seward Bentley IV) was a lot like Pop. Driven. Type A. They moved quickly, thought at lightning speed, and had five projects going at any given time.

"Cara," both Pop and Ward would tell me, "you've got to get out of that novel and into life!" Or away from that computer. Or that movie. Or that how-to-write book.

Sometimes I thought Mom, no slouch in the personality pool herself, almost understood that to me that novel, that movie, that manuscript I was working on—they were life. The characters fascinated me. The plotlines struck my imagination. The juxtaposition of purposes, ambitions, and loves filled my mind as I wondered how that character would react if he trusted God instead of himself or how that villain would change if eternal issues ever filled his thinking.

Here I was, a thirty-year-old woman who wrote inspirational romances, earned a comfortable income from them, shared a home with her grandparents, and lived mostly in her mind. I was happy with myself like that, but no one else seemed to be.

"Cara, baby," Pop would chide me in his booming voice. "You've got to live life large! You're a Bentley!"

I tried for years to follow his advice, but I finally accepted that I'm not the live-life-large type, Bentley or not. I'm more like gentle rain to my family's cyclones. But I enjoyed their whirlwind style because it kept life at 356 Harris Avenue vibrant and interesting, even if it occasionally made me cranky with surprises.

During Mom's final illness as her strength ebbed and she neared death, it hurt me to see her once brilliant inner light dim, then flicker, then burn out completely. It was a great mystery to me that body and personality were so interconnected that the diminishing of one caused the lessening of the other, the extinguishing of one caused the cessation of the other.

"How, God," I asked more than once, "did you intertwine these two distinct entities into one human? How are we personality and body, emotional and physical? And how is it that we can't be one without the other? And what about the spiritual aspect of an individual? How did you plant that in us?"

"Cara," Mom would say as she lay wasting away on her pillows, "come sit by me." She'd pat the space next to her, and I'd climb onto the great bed and hold her frail hand.

"Cara, you are beautiful." Her eyes held love and something like pity.

"Mom, please." It always embarrassed me when she said that because I looked in the mirror every day. I knew what I looked like.

"You are! You have glorious hair."

I had brown hair with a golden sheen to it, but it was just hair that I combed straight back from my forehead. There were little wisps that worked their way free around my face in spite of my best efforts to restrain them with extra duty hair spray. I dealt with the heavy mass by clasping it back out of my way with a barrette at the nape of my neck or making a quick braid.

"And your eyes!"

"Mom, they're just brown eyes, like millions of other eyes."

"And your smile! If you'd just smile more, Cara, love. You've always been such a solemn little thing."

"I'm hardly little, Mom," I said, ignoring the smiling bit. I knew I'd never convince her that I was an optimist, but I was. I knew the sun was going to come up tomorrow and I reveled in it. I just didn't want to go out and smile at it; I wanted to write about it. "I'm five foot eight."

"And all glorious legs," she said.

"I can tell you haven't tried to buy blue jeans lately."

"Cara, don't do that!"

"What?"

"Mock yourself like that. Just because your heroines all have auburn hair and emerald eyes or raven hair and violet eyes, you think you're plain. Well, you're not!"

"I love you, Mom." And I'd kiss her and she'd sigh.

"You need a man, Cara."

"Mom, how politically incorrect! I manage alone quite nicely."

"I have never doubted your ability to cope, my dear. I just hate to see you so solitary."

"I'm not alone," I'd say. "I have you and Pop."

As she became desperately ill, she would grasp my hand and murmur, "Cara, love. Please." She whispered those words to me when I bent to straighten her pillow or brush back her hair, when I gave her medicine or helped her to the commode. In fact, they were the last words she said to me before she died. I knew what she really meant: "Cara, for Pete's sake, get a life! You're a Bentley!"

I loved that she cared. I loved that she and Pop worried, that they despaired of me. It made me feel warm and toasty that though they didn't understand me one bit, they wanted me to be happy. But it didn't make me change my pleasant, bystander life.

After Pop died, Ward took up Pop and Mom's mantle in more ways than the management of Bentley Marts. He was constantly after me.

"I don't care what you do or where you go, Cara. Just do! Go! You're a—"

"I know. I'm a Bentley." I put my hand on his shoulder and said as firmly as I could, "But I don't want to go anywhere,

Ward, and I'm doing what I love."

"Sitting in one room all day writing?"

I nodded. "I meet the most interesting people that way."

He frowned at me, his choleric nature totally unable to comprehend a phlegmatic woman like me. But that didn't stop him from trying to make me see the light.

"God doesn't like us to be so introspective," he told me as he paced the room. "That's why the Bible is full of one another verses."

I blinked. "What?"

"You know—love one another, encourage one another, do good to one another."

I had no answer for that comment, but I gave it my best try.

"I go to writers conferences," I said, "and to Romance Writers of America and Christian Booksellers conventions. I deal with others all the time."

"Right," he said, unimpressed. "And when you go to these places, you hang around all day with other recluses just like yourself."

I thought of the wild and wonderful personalities of many of the writers and editors I knew. Recluses hardly fit the bill. I thought of the panels I sat on and the classes I taught and the fascinating conversations I had. In reality I did quite well with people. After all, I'd lived all my life with Pop and Mom and Ward. I knew all about people skills, and I loved my times on the dais or in the spotlight. But I was always happy to come home and be alone again. In fact, I needed to come home and be alone.

But Ward never saw me do anything but write. He naturally assumed I had serious limitations.

He and his wife, Marnie, a delightful, sparkly blond, lived fifteen minutes away from me in Washington Township. They had a large and wonderful new house with windows and gables and a stone front and a huge yard for John Seward Bentley V to run around in—as soon as he was old enough to run.

"Cara," Marnie said when they dropped in one day to check on me, "don't stay in this huge old house!"

"But I like it here," I said for the hundredth time as I watched my brother begin his now-routine tour of the place.

"Just checking," he mumbled as he slid through the doorway to the kitchen.

"It's not going to fall down," I said.

He made a soft grunt, obviously expecting exactly that, now that there wasn't a man living here. As Marnie and I talked, I heard him go down to the basement to check the furnace. I heard him trying the locks on the back door. I heard him climb to the second and third stories, moving from room to room, methodically going over some mental checklist he'd created.

I felt a bit like Rainbow must when I hugged her too tightly.

Marnie laid her hand on my arm. "This place is too big for you, Cara. There's too much upkeep. We worry about you, all alone up here."

I smiled and said nothing, though I thought, *Et tu, Marnie?*

"You need to buy a nice condominium near us. Johnny will want Aunt Cara nearby."

I thought that Johnny couldn't have cared less, but I knew that Marnie, with all her heart, vitality, and charm, was as concerned about me as my little brother. I just couldn't imagine why they'd even think I would want to leave the house that had been my home almost all my life. I loved the high-ceilinged rooms, the wraparound porches, the gingerbread trim, and the tall, nearly impossible-to-decorate windows that let the late spring light stream in.

"I think maybe I'll paint the outside," I said to Marnie as I rocked sweet-smelling Johnny softly in my arms. It was my way of saying that I wasn't moving. "Maybe I'll use a tri-color scheme like the Victorians down in Cape May. How about powder blue with mauve and white? Or taupe with forest green and a real pale beige? Or maybe two colors—a soft yellow with white?"

She didn't say anything as she sank into Mom's favorite chair, but her kind face was full of worry. About me.

"That's not a rush decision," I said hastily, acting as if the painting were the issue that concerned us. "Mom and I were talking about it just before she became ill for the last time, and I've continued to think about it ever since. Three years of thinking means it's not an impulse, right?" I looked at her with feigned innocence.

"Cara, I don't care if you paint the place purple with fuchsia and lavender," she sputtered. She jumped to her feet and began to pace, her arms shooting in all directions in her agitation. "It's the place itself that concerns me, and you here in it alone. You're letting life pass you by!"

"Oh, Marnie." I gave her a warm hug, Johnny squeezed between us in a loving nest. She hugged me back, perhaps too ardently, because Johnny began to squirm. Without thinking, both of us bent and kissed him, me on the top of his bald little head, she on his chubby cheek. One thing in life was certain: Johnny would never lack for love. He was a Bentley.

I smiled at my sister-in-law. "I think you're forgetting one basic thing. I don't like changes. No, I hate changes. I've had too many recently, and I'm not facing another by moving. Let me get used to Pop being gone." I smiled ruefully. "I mean, I'm still struggling over Mom's death three years ago."

When Ward, Marnie, and Johnny left, it was with warm

hugs and kisses but no understanding. Bentleys are supposed to be doers!

To some extent Mom and Pop and Ward and Marnie were right about me. I was letting life pass me by. I was a recluse. But I was a happy recluse—until that June day.

I wandered from room to room, Rainbow trailing behind. As I walked through the dining room, I thought of the time way back near the end of the lean years when Pop had decided he and Mom could afford new wallpaper, though they had to hang it themselves.

"Tess, straight! It's got to be straight!"

"Don't you give me straight, John Seward Bentley, until you match that pattern like you're supposed to! And look! You cut that piece too short!"

I remembered the fat little paperhanger who had finally been called, a man I had looked upon as a marriage saver. And I remembered Mom and Pop standing in the freshly hung room, arms about each other, smiling in shared pleasure that they could finally afford something as wonderful as new wallpaper and a paperhanger.

In the kitchen I saw the stove Pop had gotten Mom even as she lay too ill to cook on it.

"It's the new kind with no burners," he told her as he kissed her pale cheek. "It'll save you cleanup time."

The pain on his face as he leaned over her told me he knew she'd never use it. He just needed to do something concrete for her, something to bring some sort of control to a situation beyond his control.

"John," she whispered, knowing full well that the gift was a Band-Aid on a hemorrhage, "I love you."

I came to Pop's office with its walls of plaques and commendations and awards for his years of business achievement and

19

community service. I looked at the neat, cleared desktop holding only his pictures of a young Mom and the last one taken of the whole family before her illness. I knew the drawers were ordered or empty too. Ward and Mr. Havens, Pop's lawyer, had taken all the clutter away. Pop's stacks of magazines, papers, bank statements, investment profiles, and motivational quotes had driven Mom crazy.

"John," she'd storm, hand on her hip, "you have the most unsightly, pack-rat habits of anyone I know. One of these days I'm going to clean up this mess, and then you'll be sorry."

"Tess," Pop would answer, "did I ever tell you how beautiful you are when you're angry?"

"Don't you beautiful me, John Seward Bentley!" she'd say. "Clean up your room!"

"Or you won't give me my allowance?" he'd say, walking up behind her and nuzzling her neck.

"John, stop that! The children are watching!" But her frown, never very seriously in place to begin with, showed signs of severe strain.

"Let them," he'd say. "And they'll know what God meant marriage to be." He'd turn her in his arms and kiss her thoroughly, and she'd cuddle against him, smiling happily.

Maybe they are why I write romances, I thought. I have seen what real love is.

Once about ten years ago, I'd gone to Mom and Pop's bedroom. I needed to talk to Mom about something long forgotten. I knocked on the door and she called, "Come in."

I opened the door to find her and Pop cuddled in the middle of their huge bed, her gray head resting on the grizzled gray hair of his bare chest.

"Oh," I said, blushing. "I'm sorry!" I started to close the door.

"No, no, Cara," Pop called. "Don't go."

I hesitated, feeling I was intruding, knowing I was intruding.

"I called for you to come in, Cara, love," Mom said, "because I want you to know that love, true love, doesn't die with the years. Gray doesn't mean gone." And she rested her hand on Pop's chest. He grinned at me like a young man.

I shook my head in false disdain. "You two are such a bad example to an innocent young woman like me."

"She needs more proof, Tess," Pop said. And he bent over and kissed Mom a great smacker.

"I love you guys so much," I whispered as I closed the door. All day I couldn't stop smiling.

Now I started crying, and the tears wouldn't stop. They rolled over my lids and down my cheeks in a rain of loss.

God, how can I survive this aloneness?

The thought brought an intense, thrumming anxiety. My heart began to pound and my hands shook as I clasped them to my chest.

Always before I'd been alone by choice, alone surrounded by loving people. Now I was alone, period.

I was almost in a panic as I ran to the linen closet and pulled out a box of tissues. I tore it open, grabbed a fistful, and began mopping my face, but the tears kept coming. I returned to the living room with the tissue box under my arm, Rainbow padding behind me. I sank to the floor and, knees bent, laid my head on them. I sobbed and sobbed.

A tentative paw patted my thigh, and Rainbow whimpered.

I reached out and swept her into my lap. For once, she stayed.

"Oh, baby, what are we going to do?"

She had no answer, but she lay still, letting me stroke her and bury my face in her fur. Finally though, she could bear it no longer, and she hopped down. She stalked under Mom's drop-leaf table and began rubbing her head against the box Mom always kept tucked under there.

"So I can enjoy these things any time I want," she always said as she reached down and pulled out the generations of photos lying there.

I crawled to the box and tugged it from its hiding place. It suddenly became my life preserver. I could do better than go to dinner with Pop and Mom tonight. I could live our lives together over again.

The first picture I pulled out was a very old sepia one of Pop's parents, the first John Seward Bentley and his wife, Mabel, seated in a stiff, formal pose from the early twentieth century. In great contrast, the next photo I pulled out was an informal picture from Ward and Marnie's wedding five years ago. The sun was shining, the warm June breeze was blowing Marnie's veil out behind her, and everyone was smiling. Mom, three months short of beginning her final, fatal struggle, wore a midnight blue dress that looked stunning with her white hair. Pop's great chest strained his starched shirt and tux. Marnie was radiant and Ward handsome, though they looked impossibly young.

Even I looked good in the rose gown Marnie made me wear instead of the beige I wanted. Marnie had also insisted I "do something with that hair!" The result was an elegant chignon at the base of my neck instead of the usual ponytail, softened by curls about my face. The baby's breath and roses tucked in my hair made me look alive in a way my usual slicked-back look never did.

I smiled through the mists blurring my vision.

For two hours I cried as I looked at black-and-white photos of Pop in his World War II army uniform, of Mom, her hair in a forties pompadour, holding the young Trey (John Seward Bentley III, my father), of my great-grandparents standing in the front yard of this very house when it was brand-new, the trees and shrubs so small and unformed.

I found a picture of Ward and me standing with Mickey Mouse on that long-ago vacation. Ward stood tall and proud and beaming. I looked furious, as though Mickey Mouse had just told me a dirty joke.

I pulled out a black-and-white of my mother and father who smiled at me from the beach at Ocean City, NJ. It had always saddened me that I couldn't remember a single thing about them. In fact, I didn't even think of them as my mother and father. They were Trey and Caroline, the names Mom and Pop always called them when they spoke of them. With a jolt I realized that I was now older than my parents had ever been. They were twenty-nine when they died.

I reached blindly into the almost empty box, and my fingers closed over an envelope. The old-fashioned, Palmer method handwriting on the front read "John Seward's papers."

Curious, since I thought Ward and Mr. Havens had all Pop's papers, I opened it. I took out the topmost page and unfolded it.

Commonwealth of Pennsylvania, it read across the top in a swirl of Gothic letters.

In the Court of Common Pleas, No. 2, of Lancaster County in re: Adoption of Lehman Biemsderfer, June 1918. Be it remembered that I, Herman F. Walton, Prothonotary of the Courts of Common Pleas, No. 2, of Lancaster County, do hereby certify, that the following is the true and correct copy of the decree:

entered by the said court in the above case, to wit:

Now, the 20th day of August A.D. 1918 the court, upon

consideration of the foregoing petition, being satisfied that the welfare of the said Lehman Biemsderfer will be promoted by the adoption prayed for in said petition, do upon motion of A. R. Furst, Esq. for petitioners, grant the prayer of said petition, and do order and decree that the said Lehman Biemsderfer shall assume the name of the adopting parents, and be hereafter known and called by the name "John Seward Bentley, Jr." and shall henceforth have all the rights of a child and heir of the said John Seward Bentley and Mabel Brooks Bentley, equal with any other children they may have, and shall be subject to the duties of such children in accordance with the provisions of the Act of Assembly in such cases made and provided.

In testimony whereof, I have hereto set my hand and affixed the seal of the Court, this 20th day of August in the year of our Lord one thousand nine hundred and eighteen.

The red raised seal of the Court of Common Pleas of Lancaster County decorated the lower left-hand corner of the paper while the signature of Herman F. Walton, the prothonotary, filled the right.

Stunned, I stared at the paper. When I could finally find my voice, I turned to Rainbow.

"Baby," I said in disbelief. "We're not really Bentleys!"

TWO

I pulled at the other documents in the envelope and found a receipt dated August, 1918.

Received from Mrs. Bentley, six and 00/100 dollars: Cost of adoption papers.

The receipt was signed by a (Mrs.) C. A. Yule.

Six dollars. Pop cost six dollars. Pop, who made millions, cost six dollars.

There was one more letter in the envelope. I opened it and found a personal letter to my great-grandmother from Mrs. C. A. Yule, written on the stationery of The Children's Home Society of the City of Lancaster: For the Relief of the Poor and the Care of Destitute Children.

My dear Mrs. Bentley,

I am enclosing herewith the certified copy of the decree of adoption, which finishes up the case.

When visiting the mother of your dear little boy, she asked me as a last request if you would give me a picture of Lehman for her. She felt that having it would do much to make her live as she should. She is doing so well. We are proud of the effort she is making. I shall appreciate it very much if you could send me the picture very soon.

I am glad you were able to get away for a little while. I'm sure John Seward had a lovely time playing in the sand at the shore.

I sincerely hope the dear baby will grow up into the kind

of man you will have reason to be proud of. You are doing a very noble thing indeed in taking a baby to rear as you would one of your own. There is no telling what this will mean to his future.

I stared at the three papers and felt my world tilting under me until I felt I would slide off into—I was so stunned I didn't even know where I would slide to. I didn't know anything anymore.

Pop wasn't a Bentley! He was a—I grabbed the papers again. He was a Biemsderfer. What kind of a name was that, for Pete's sake! Biemsderfer Marts somehow didn't have the same ring.

Rainbow climbed across me and jumped into the picture box, settling down very comfortably on the few remaining snapshots. She looked so comfortable, so content, so in control.

Five minutes ago, I was in control, too. Eaten up with grief, certainly, but in control. I knew who I was, who my family was, where we all came from. Now I had no idea who we were.

"What do you mean, you don't know who we are," Ward asked me two days later when I drove to their house in a snit. "Of course you know who we are. I'm Ward Bentley. You're Cara Elizabeth Bentley."

"But who's that? Before I found these papers," I indicated them lying on his and Marnie's curly maple kitchen table, "I knew who I was based on who the other people in my life were. I was your sister because you were my brother. I was Marnie's sister-in-law because she was married to you, my brother. I was Pop and Mom's granddaughter because they were the parents of my parents, Trey and Caroline. I was a Bentley because we were

26

all born Bentleys. But now I know we weren't. Now we're not who we seemed, so I'm not who I seem."

Ward stared at me, his disbelieving blue eyes the same shade as the knit shirt he wore. His brows were drawn in a frown and his lips pressed together. I knew exactly what he was thinking about my reasoning powers, and I knew it wasn't very nice. I also knew he'd have no hesitancy about telling me what he thought, so before he could speak, I plowed on.

"Did you know about this?" I waved the adoption certificate in his face.

He nodded.

"You did?" I was floored.

He shrugged. "I've known about it for years."

I stared at him, then looked at Marnie. "Did you know?"

She nodded. "Ward told me when we were dating, and I talked with Mom and Pop about it a couple of times over the years."

Stunned, I stared at the sheet in my trembling hand. It shook so much I looked like I had palsy. "How come I never knew?" My voice trembled almost as much as my hand. "How come no one ever thought to tell me? Didn't anyone think I might just deserve to know?"

"Cara, for heaven's sake," Ward said, torn between exasperation and sympathy. "It's no big deal."

"No big deal? Are you serious? Ward, you're an intelligent man. Surely you see the implications here."

Ward looked at Marnie like he was missing something, then back at me. "This is one of those times when I can't possibly respond correctly, isn't it? If I say no, I don't see the implications, then I'm stupid and insensitive, right? If I say yes, I see the implications, than I'm a heel because I never discussed them with you."

"Just answer the question, Ward. There's no trick here."

He didn't look convinced, but he bravely said, "No, I don't see the implications."

I looked at him, flabbergasted. "I can't believe it."

"See," he said to Marnie. "I knew I'd get it wrong."

"Don't you care that Pop was adopted?" I asked.

"No," he said cautiously. He wasn't used to my being anything but docile, and I was unnerving him. "I think it's kind of nice."

"Of course it's nice, but that doesn't have anything to do with anything. You honestly don't care?"

He shook his head. "No. It's no big deal."

"Ward!" Shaking my head at my brilliant but dense brother, I turned to my sister-in-law. "Marnie, do you see the implications?"

"Oh yes. I see implications, but I don't think they matter."

"Of course they matter. If they're there, they matter," I said stubbornly.

"Three generations have passed," Marnie said. "The implications are minimal."

"What implications?" Ward shouted. "There are no implications. Pop was adopted, period. That's all there is to it. No more. No less. You just don't like the surprise of it all. That's why you're so grumpy and out of sorts."

"You're darn tootin' I don't like the surprise," I shot back. "Doesn't it bother you that you built your whole identity on being a Bentley and we're not even Bentleys?"

"Of course we're Bentleys," he said. "We're the children of Trey and Caroline Bentley."

"And Trey was the child of John and Tess Bentley," I continued. "And John was the child of—who?"

"Of J. S. and Mabel Bentley," Ward all but shouted.

"No," I said. "No, he wasn't. He was some other couple's child."

"Only biologically," Ward said. "Not in any way that truly counted."

"But biologically counts," I said.

Marnie nodded. "Nature versus nurture. It's one of the implications."

Ward looked at Marnie in mild disgust. "You're a big help."

"You're right." I smiled at her. "Pop got his bombast from someone, but not J. S."

"Well, who cares now?" Ward asked. "I got mine from him and Trey. That's all that matters."

"No, it's not. At least not to me." I looked from one dear face to the other, knowing I was about to upset them even more. "That's why I'm going to Lancaster to see what I can find out about Lehman Biemsderfer."

I expected Ward to be angry, not sarcastic.

"Oh, right," he said, all but laughing in my face. "What do you expect to do—open the phone book, look up the name, and walk up to a house? And when they answer, you say, 'Hi, I'm Cara, your long lost cousin several times removed. Aren't you glad to meet me?'"

"Of course not," I said. "I'm sure it won't be that easy. That's why I'm going to move there for a while."

Now Ward hit the ceiling.

"Are you crazy? You can't go running halfway around the world on your own!" he said, alarm in his eyes.

"Phoo. It's only an hour and a half from here, Ward. Besides, I thought you wanted me to get out and get involved in life."

"But not in a wild goose chase like this!"

"Why not?"

He stared at me through slitted eyes before he came up with his answer. "Because."

I rolled my eyes. "You'd better come up with some better reasons than that before Johnny gets old enough to challenge you." My face got stony. "And you'd certainly better come up with a better reason than that for me."

"You can't do it, Cara." He stood up and began to pace. "It's not safe for a single woman alone in today's world."

"I'm a woman alone whether I'm in my house or in Lancaster."

He ignored that obvious point of logic because it was in my favor, then he sank back in his chair and leaned across the table toward me. "So come to Washington Township and live in one of those new condos about a mile from us. They're just the thing for you."

I shook my head. "I don't want to."

"Sure you do. They're roomy and beautiful and have two bedrooms so Johnny can come spend the night."

Obviously they'd checked them out for me. "I don't want to."

"They have great landscaping and each unit has a large back porch and there's a Jacuzzi tub in the master bath to work out the kinks after a hard day at the computer."

"I don't want to, Ward," I said slowly and through clenched teeth.

My brother stood, leaned forward on his knuckles, and stared me in the eyes. "I don't care what you want, Cara. You can't go running off like this! You're coming to Washington Township."

I'd been working hard to keep my emotions under control because I feared the tears that were so close to the surface these days. I wanted to seem like the same nice, sane girl I'd always been. But at that moment I lost my control.

"You're nothing but a bully!"

He blinked and pulled back. "I am not," he said indignantly.

"Yes, you are. You always have been. You've been ordering me around all my life. 'Cara, do this. Cara, do that. Cara, go here. Cara, go there.' Well, it's time to back off, you dictator you!"

Ward actually looked hurt as he defended himself. "I am not a dictator. I only have your best interests at heart. Tell her, Marnie." And he looked to his wife for support.

"She's right, sweetheart," Marnie said. "You can be a dictator."

He stared in disbelief. "You never told me that before."

"That's because I never let you bully me." She smiled gently at him.

"I never try."

Marnie and I looked at each other. "Yeah, right," we said in unison.

"Ward, honey," Marnie said. "You run a major corporation with I don't know how many hundreds, maybe thousands of employees. You give orders all day. When you come home, you sometimes forget I'm not an employee. I have to fight back. I just don't have to worry about my job security."

"Oh no?" he said archly.

She shook her head. "If you fired me, you'd never find your socks, let alone a new bar of soap for the shower." She smiled at him serenely.

I had to hand it to Marnie. She knew how to handle my brother with her own special combination of love and spirit. And I was proud of Ward that he'd seen through the blond curls and slim little figure to the quality lady inside.

"Is my bossiness what that hands-on-your-hips, feet apart, don't-you-tell-me attitude that I see every so often is all about?"

"Balance of power, honey. There are times I have to fight for it."

31

"But Cara's never fought me before," he said, turning bewildered eyes on me.

"No, she hasn't," Marnie agreed. "She's dealt with you by ignoring you. This is the first time she's ever cared enough about something to face you down. She's dealt with all you high-powered Bentleys by keeping her head low, and her mouth shut, and doing her own thing. She's as much a control freak as the rest of you; she's just less noisy and more polite. You, on the other hand, are as obvious as a bull in the middle of the proverbial china shop." She looked placidly from one of us to the other.

Ward leaned over, clasped her by the back of the neck with a warm, possessive hand, and kissed her. "See why I married her, Cara? She is so smart!"

"Yes, I am," Marnie agreed and grabbed his hand as he released her. "So listen to me. You've got to let Cara go, and with your blessing."

I was going, blessing or not, but I didn't think this was the best time to say so.

"Marnie." His eyes pleaded for her to back down.

She patted his arm. "Be wise, Ward."

He threw his hands in the air in surrender. "Okay, okay. But I don't have to like it, you know."

"Thanks, Ward, ever gracious in defeat," I said, surprising myself with my sassiness. "And you don't have to worry about me. I won't get attacked by thieves and robbers. Or held hostage by bad guys. And I promise I won't let anyone slit my throat."

"Funny," Ward said. "But they're not the dangers I see for you."

"And what are they?"

"You've made yourself this sweet, cozy little world, Cara.

32

Only good things happen there. True love always wins there. And if something goes wrong, well, you just rewrite it."

Now it was my turn to sit back in my chair and stare. "Ward! That's not so." I blinked against the surge of tears.

Marnie got up, came over to me, and hugged me. She knelt beside my chair and took my hand. "What he says is true, Cara. Your life with your writing is more real to you than we are. And you can control your writing. The trouble is, you can't control life, especially in a quest like the one you're setting for yourself."

My tears fell as Marnie's comments breached what little restraint I still possessed. What she said wasn't true. It couldn't be true. It mustn't be true. But I knew deep inside that in many ways it was. I'd always lived a large portion of my life in books, either ones I wrote or ones I read.

Still I fought her gentle condemnation because agreeing out loud was unthinkable. I couldn't be that vulnerable anywhere but on the written page. And there my characters expressed my thoughts for me and my carefully constructed plotlines made it all come out right.

So I, Cara Elizabeth Bentley, scion of the oh so clever John Seward Bentley (or whoever he was) and sister of the dictator, Ward Bentley, reverted to breeding and fought.

"I didn't come here to be analyzed, Marnie," I said as I wiped wildly at my face. "I came here to find support from those I love."

Even to my own ears I sounded like a prig. Marnie dropped her eyes and my hand, got to her feet, and went back to her chair.

"Cara," Ward said, warning in his voice. "Marnie is the one who has supported you."

"That's right," I said, desperate, unwilling to admit he was right. "Stand up for your wife and dump on your sister."

Ward opened his mouth to let me have it, but Marnie gave him a look that snapped it shut again. There was a long, uncomfortable silence.

Suddenly Ward sat up and said, "Aha!"

My shoulders immediately tensed. An *aha* could only mean I needed to look out.

"You just made the strongest argument I can think of against the need to find out about your extended family or whatever they are," he said.

"*Our* extended family," I said, shaking my head, not following.

"You want to find family, right? Well, I ask you, what makes family?" It was Ward at his worst, full of his own ideas. "Love. That's what makes a family. You came to get support from those you love. You said so yourself. We're your family because we love you."

I knew there had to be flaws in his logic, but he was talking so fast I didn't have time to pounce on them. Writing gave me the time to find the holes in logic and restructure to fill them. Real life was certainly more complex.

Ward continued, still full of himself. "You think I support my wife over you. I don't, but if I did, does that mean I love her more than you? Yes. I do love her more than you or at least differently. I love her more than anyone on the face of the earth. She makes my life sing. She's the grace that makes me a decent person instead of that dictator you mentioned. I look at her sometimes and my heart just swells. I don't know how I could be so blessed that she chose me."

He looked from Marnie to me, ready to make his big point. "And she and I—we're not even related!"

He sat back, looking so proud of himself for finding such a

34

grand argument that Marnie and I both burst out laughing. She also ran to him, threw herself in his lap, and gave him a hug to end all hugs.

"That was about the nicest thing you ever said," she whispered. He wrapped his arms about her and gave her a great kiss.

"I hope you're not related," I said, "or that kiss would be illegal in all fifty states."

They didn't appear to hear me, so I got up and wandered down the hall to Johnny's room. I needed quiet to think about what Ward had just said. I also needed to get away from the sight of their love, which every day was growing to be as dense and sturdy and full of joy as Mom and Pop's.

While I wasn't exactly unhappy as Cara Bentley, spinster, I knew there was a world out there I was missing. Mostly I was satisfied enjoying it vicariously in the stories I created, but even someone as reserved and introspective as I was knew there was a world of sharing, of giving, of touching, of passion I knew nothing about.

It wasn't too bad watching that kind of love in Mom and Pop. They were supposed to love each other like that. But watching it in Ward and Marnie sometimes hurt. After all, he was my little brother. How did he get to be so cherished and so cherishing while all I did was watch? How had I gotten passed over?

I walked into Johnny's room and stood beside his crib. In spite of my melancholy, I had to smile at his pudgy body curled in sleep. I leaned over and brushed my finger down his soft cheek and ran my hand over his bald little head. He sighed, stuck his thumb in his mouth, and began to suck it noisily.

And as I looked at him, I suddenly saw the hole in Ward's

grand argument about family. A song based on Psalm 78 flashed through my mind:

> *From generation to generation*
> *We will tell of the praiseworthy deeds of the Lord.*
> *From generation to generation*
> *We will tell of his glory and wonders.*

I sat down in Johnny's rocking chair and got very still.

That's it, isn't it, God? It's the bond of blood and sinew and intellect passed from generation to generation. It's the genes of the parents passed on to the child. It's heredity and patrimony and getting and begetting. It's the Biemsderfers in Lancaster.

"Cara," Marnie's soft voice called from the doorway of the room. "Ward wants to see you."

I rose and walked to her. As I slipped my arm about her waist, I said, "I'll just bet."

She smiled. "He loves you a lot."

I nodded. "But I have to do this."

"I know. So does he. It's just never struck him—or you for that matter—how much of a Bentley you really are under that seemingly passive exterior."

We entered the kitchen where Ward was busy microwaving popcorn. When it stopped popping, he rescued it from the oven and dumped it into a cream-colored earthen bowl. He put it in the center of the table, then fussed about getting napkins, glasses, and drinks. Finally we were all settled and he looked at me.

"Cara, Marnie's right. I have no right to try and stop you from making your life's choices. I think this isn't a wise choice, but it's also not wrong. So I say go, search, see what you find. Just know we're always here. Always. We are your family."

I looked at Ward through tears. "Thanks," I managed. I looked from him to Marnie. "I don't know what I'd do without you two."

"But there is one thing," Ward continued.

I should have known.

"Don't tell people who you are."

"What?"

"Don't tell them who you are. You keep forgetting that you're a rich woman, Cara. Pop has left us more money than most people dream of."

He was right. I did tend to forget. My own career was successful enough that I rarely thought of the money I had as a result of Bentley Marts. But then I'd never needed to. It was just there.

"I'm not looking for a husband here," I said. "You don't have to worry about some gigolo or fortune hunter."

I thought I heard him mutter, "I wish," under his breath, but since I couldn't be certain, I said nothing.

He continued. "People will try to ingratiate themselves for all the wrong reasons if they know who you are. I don't want long lost relatives trying to claim you for any reason other than that they want to be your relative."

"It's your cozy-world syndrome," Marnie said. "He's trying to protect you from it."

I looked at them both and shook my head. "I'm really not as dumb as you think, you know."

They both looked skeptical.

"Do we have a Bentley Mart in Lancaster?"

"Just east of town in the strip of stores and malls that line Route 30. But Bentley isn't that unusual a name. I don't think anyone will make a connection."

I poked around in the popcorn bowl, looking for one last

piece but finding only unpopped kernels. I had to agree that Ward had a valid point on the money issue. I looked up and nodded.

"I see your point, Ward. I won't tell anyone who I am."

He seemed to breathe more easily. Marnie beamed as she looked from one of us to the other.

I hugged them both, then pulled my beige jacket from the front hall closet where Marnie had stashed it. It was time to return home to Haddonfield and prepare to set off on my quest, as Marnie called it.

And that's how I found myself living in a motel in Bird-in-Hand, Lancaster County, and sitting across a vast cherry desk from my stiff but handsome new lawyer, Todd Reasoner.

THREE

I got Todd Reasoner's name from Mr. Havens, our lawyer, when I visited him the day after I spoke with Ward and Marnie.

"So you plan to do an adoption search?" Mr. Havens asked, careful to sound dispassionate. He was a spare little man who somehow commanded great attention and respect. I think it had something to do with the way he carried himself, exactly like the ex-Marine he was, and the absolute authority with which he always spoke. It was like a real-life equivalence of the old ad: When Dean Havens speaks, people listen.

I nodded. "I want to find out what my heritage is, what our heritage is."

"Do you have a medical reason for seeking this information?" He seemed genuinely concerned. "I never heard John mention any medical problems, but that doesn't mean there wasn't or isn't one."

I shook my head. "No medical problems that I know of. I just want to know who we are if we aren't Bentleys."

"Cara, my dear, I think a search going back three generations is most likely doomed to failure." He made his observation gently, but its effect was to stiffen my backbone even more.

"Maybe. Maybe not." I smiled with a sweetness I didn't feel. I was tired of people telling me what to do—or rather what not to do. "I just know I feel compelled to try."

He nodded. "I wish you well. You understand that you'll need a member of the Pennsylvania bar to assist you, since state laws differ on adoption and the accessibility of pertinent information and records."

I raised an eyebrow. I hadn't even considered the very real need to find a Pennsylvania lawyer, but I quickly saw the sound reasoning in Mr. Havens's comment. I thought of the yellow pages and all those lawyers smiling charmingly out of the full-page ads. The thought of picking one to be my attorney was daunting. "Can you recommend someone in the Lancaster area?"

He spun his chair and stared out his window at the ancient willow tree with its feathery branches touching the ground. I sat and waited while he went through his mental Rolodex. After a minute he turned back to his desk, grabbed the phone, and pushed a couple of buttons.

"Martin, come in here a minute, please." He hung up immediately, the prerogative of the senior partner who assumed—and received—unquestioned compliance.

Immediately there was a knock on the door, and a young man poked his head in. "Yes, Mr. Havens?"

"Come in, Martin."

Martin, wearing bright red suspenders to hold up his navy slacks, smoothed his red-and-blue rep tie as he walked to Mr. Havens's desk.

"Martin, this is Cara Bentley. Cara is moving to the Lancaster area for a while and will need legal advice while there. You graduated from Dickinson Law School. That's in Carlisle, PA, my dear," he said in an aside to me. He turned back to Martin. "You must know some lawyers who have begun practicing in Lancaster."

Martin nodded. "I can think of three who graduated with me who practice either in Lancaster City or close by. Paul Adamson is associated with a large firm in the city. Allison Fleet is the junior partner in a three-partner practice in Manheim, just north of Lancaster, and Todd Reasoner is a sole practitioner in Bird-in-Hand, a small town just east of Lancaster."

"Which one do you recommend?" Mr. Havens asked.

"If I may, what kind of work is needed?"

"Legal advice on an adoption search," I said.

"Paul's firm is located right near the courthouse and has the prominence to help someone high profile like you, Miss Bentley."

I shook my head. "No one is to know who I am." I explained Ward's fear and request for anonymity. "So I'm doing this as Cara Bentley, writer. I don't want flash and prestige. I want competency."

"Then I recommend Todd Reasoner. He's more than able, has excellent credentials, sailed through the bar exams when the rest of us were sweating bullets, and is conscientious to a fault. He's very religious, but I mean that in the good sense that it makes him want to do everything right."

I nodded. "He sounds like the man for me."

As soon as I got home, I called to make an appointment, hoping I could see him immediately. His fire-eating dragon of a receptionist/secretary soon disabused me of that idea.

"Mr. Reasoner will be in court until Thursday," she said in a doomsayer's voice that could comfortably announce the end of the earth. "But I believe he could see you on Friday at three o'clock."

"Not sooner?" I was used to Mr. Havens seeing any of us whenever we asked. Not that I'd ever asked much, but I knew Pop and Ward saw him at their convenience. Of course Bentley Marts had Mr. Havens on a retainer and was undoubtedly his biggest client. Todd Reasoner, Esq. had no reason to revamp his schedule for Cara Bentley, spinster.

I spent the intervening days closing up the white Victorian in Haddonfield, stopping the paper, and having the mail held until I had a forwarding address. I packed my clothes and laptop and contacted my agent, Jo Wilkes.

"You're taking a vacation, Cara?" Jo said, amazed. I knew I should have e-mailed her instead of calling. She'd been after me to get a life almost as ardently as Pop and Ward. "That is absolutely wonderful!"

"Just a short break. Nothing special. I'm moving to the Lancaster, PA area."

"Great," she said too enthusiastically. "You can play tourist while you look for settings for future novels. People love that Amish stuff, you know." She pronounced the word *Amish* with a long A.

"It's Amish, short A," I said.

I could hear her mental shrug. "Just don't become one," she told me. "You don't have time. You have a December 1 deadline on that next romance. And I need something in writing to present for your next series. I've got three houses that I want to bid on you." I could hear the grin in her voice. "You are getting yourself quite a fine reputation, Cara. We want to capitalize on it."

I grunted. The last thing I wanted to do now was work up a book proposal. Unless, I thought, I write a novel about an adoption search.

It took me a while to find a motel that would let me bring Rainbow with me, but I certainly wasn't going to leave her behind. She needed to be with family as much as I wanted her comforting presence. I finally found the Horse-and-Buggy

Motel located right in Bird-in-Hand, just down the street from Todd Reasoner's office. I booked a room for several nights, figuring I could decide how long I wanted to stay after I got into the search and saw how difficult or easy it would be.

Thursday night Rainbow and I sat on my bed and stared across the parking lot and the street at the pair of horses and buggies standing in the golden light of evening, waiting to take tourists on a ride through Amish farm country. A woman with a white head covering and a light blue patterned dress stood by the first horse and buggy, talking to some tourists who had just climbed inside. In a minute she was up on the front seat and the buggy moved onto Route 340.

Was she an Amish lady? Did Amish ladies give buggy rides to tourists? Didn't they sort of keep to themselves? I realized then how little I knew about this most interesting and obvious of subcultures in Pennsylvania and maybe in the whole country.

I'd been so single-minded about the adoption search that I'd never even considered the rich cultural aspect of Lancaster County, in spite of Jo's comment.

I reached out and stroked Rainbow under the chin. "I guess I ought to do some sightseeing."

Rainbow responded by curling up on the pillow and going to sleep. The trip had been very tiring and unnerving for her, and she'd spent the entire drive yelling for help. That's exactly what her plaintive call sounded like: "Elp! Elp!" In high soprano.

I abandoned Rainbow in the room and walked to the motel office. Against one wall was a large rack of tourist brochures. I took one of everything and carried them back to my room where I spread them on the bed. I found I could do everything from going to an amusement park to enjoying outlet shopping to touring a genuine Amish farm to visiting a farmers' market to eating seven sweets and seven sours (whatever they were) to visiting a wax museum to seeing a play at a Christian theater called Sight and Sound to hearing a lecture at a reconstruction of the tabernacle of the Old Testament.

How in the world would I find out what was genuine to the area and what was tourist fluff?

I left the brochures on the bed and went for a drive. I followed twisting two-lane macadam roads wherever they led me, figuring I could always find my way back to Route 340 if I asked enough people and looked desperate enough. I rolled down the car windows and enjoyed the sweet, heady scent of the wild honeysuckle, the clean aroma of freshly mown grass and the distinctive smell of that farm country staple, manure. I eyed the fields of tobacco, tomatoes, alfalfa, and corn, glowing golden in the slanting light of the evening sun. I found myself filled with expectancy and a warm sense of purpose, a somewhat surprising feeling considering all the changes I had forced on myself.

Maybe the rosy inner glow was because I had caused at least some of the changes myself instead of someone forcing them on me. I had chosen to search. I had chosen to move. I squinted into the setting sun and felt almost happy for the first time in a long while.

I rounded a curve and slowed suddenly and dramatically for a closed buggy, gray and fragile, plodding slowly ahead of me. I inched along at a snail's pace in its wake, staring at the red reflective triangle on its lower back and the red rectangular reflectors placed at intervals all about its outer edges. What was protocol here on these winding roads where often nothing was visible around a steep curve? Did I just take the risk and pass the thing? Or did I have to trail along at one horsepower until it turned into some farm somewhere?

As I contemplated this quandary, a car zipped up behind

me, slowed momentarily, then sped around both me and the buggy. Question answered, I hit the gas and followed his example. After all, he had a Pennsylvania license plate. He must know what he was doing.

I ambled on, each bend in the road opening another vista of patchwork fields, farmhouses, barns, and silos. The overwhelming color was green: emerald, celadon, olive, lime, forest. Fields of burgeoning crops, copses of maple, beech, and pine, lawns and gardens and vines. I sighed. I'd never realized before how soothing green was.

I rounded a curve and hit my brakes, jarred out of my near stupor by the delightful sight before me. I stopped and watched in wonder.

A small Amish girl of about ten stood in the middle of the road, her small face screwed up in concentration as she drove an ungainly herd of Holsteins across the road from pasture to barn. She waved a stick to encourage the beasts, but they seemed unaware of the stick or the child, plodding patiently across the macadam to the safety and release of the barn and its milking machines.

The girl, her hair pulled back into a bun at the base of her neck in imitation of her elders but lacking their *kapp,* ignored me and the two cars waiting from the opposite direction. One of the cows stepped out of line, and she calmly and authoritatively whapped her on the flank. The cow immediately fell back in place.

The last cow meandered out of the meadow, and I saw for the first time a boy in black breeches and white shirt, his straw hat pushed back on his head, bare feet flying. He was encouraging the cows from behind by waving his arms and shouting at them. As the last of the beasts passed out of the pasture and through the gate, he pulled it closed. Climbing up on the bottom rung, he carefully fastened a rope about the top rail of the gate and the adjoining fence. He leaped gracefully to the ground, raced into the road after his sister and his herd, and turned to grin at me. I grinned back and waggled my fingers. He ducked his head shyly, ran to the gate into the farmyard, and pulled it shut behind him.

That night I dreamed of towheads in straw hats, buggies pulled by graceful horses, and barefoot little girls wielding big sticks. It was the soundest night's sleep I'd had since Pop died.

I arrived at the office of Todd Reasoner, Esq. at 2:55 the next afternoon. I walked to the receptionist's desk, noted her name-plate, and extended my hand.

"Hello, Mrs. Smiley. I'm Cara Bentley."

I admit that I've gotten used to a certain response to my name. Those who know Bentley Marts hop to attention as though I actually had something to do with their success, and readers frequently know who I am, too. Mrs. Smiley, however, turned her dour face toward me, and I felt as if I were not only tardy but had brought in a significant helping of manure on my shoe.

"How do you do," she said frostily, letting my hand hang suspended in space while her fingers remained on her computer keyboard. "Mr. Reasoner will be with you shortly. Please have a seat." And she tipped her head toward the pair of paisley upholstered chairs against the far wall.

I took a seat, crossing one beige linen-clad knee over the other, tucking my legs back under the chair out of the way. I felt I should sit at attention and wondered if everyone who waited under the gimlet eye of Mrs. Smiley reacted that way. I don't think my shoulders had been thrown back so rigidly since inspection at Camp Sankanac when I was a kid.

Maybe she disapproved of slacks, I thought, but certainly mine were loose enough to be modest, and my beige silk shell had plenty of slack. Still, I'd seen more dresses in my two days in Bird-in-Hand than I'd seen in years. Then again, maybe her problem was an aversion to beige. Or maybe to me. Maybe to everyone.

Ignoring me, she bent her carefully permed-and-sprayed gray head over her work, her sensible blue dress buttoned to the neck, unrelieved by jewelry or scarf. I could see her low-heeled blue pumps under the desk, pressed neatly side by side. Her wire-rimmed glasses hung about her neck on a silver chain, and she suddenly grabbed them and pushed them onto her nose. She sniffed, set a folder of papers on her right, and began typing. Her fingers were beautifully manicured with hot pink nails that danced over her computer keyboard, creating a rhythm and beauty completely at odds with the sterility of the rest of her.

Ah, God, I thought, not for the first time, *you did the most amazing thing in creating people. They are so unbelievably fascinating!*

And writerlike, I began to create a persona for Mrs. Smiley that explained her hauteur and her nails. Somehow I knew she wouldn't like my giving her a husband who left her for a younger woman who wore hot pink, low-necked tops and slacks instead of nails, nor would she want the pudgy professor who pursued her now, trying without success to find the hot pink part of her that allowed the nails.

After carefully ignoring me for an eternity of five minutes, Mrs. Smiley rose, looked suspiciously at me, and beckoned. "Mr. Reasoner will see you now."

I unfolded my legs and followed her to a door where she

paused and knocked softly. When she pushed open the door, she stepped aside for me. As I walked past her, she said, "Miss Cara Bentley, sir," for all the world as though she were announcing me to the queen.

Todd Reasoner rose, a smile of professional welcome on his handsome face. At least I thought it was a handsome face. Maybe it was the last five minutes in Mrs. Smiley's presence or years of talking with little, brittle Mr. Havens, but I perked up at the sight of my new attorney.

He glanced quickly at Mrs. Smiley, smiled absently, and said, "Thank you." Her cheeks turned almost as pink as her nails as she bobbed her head in his direction. I watched in fascination.

She's smitten, I thought. Who cares that he's twenty or thirty years her junior. She thinks he's wonderful. The son she never had? Or the man she always dreamed of?

I looked at Todd Reasoner again and understood why she was so taken with him. It might have been the curly brown hair or the deep brown eyes or the neatly tailored tan suit over a white shirt and tan tie with incredibly narrow brown diagonal stripes. But I thought it was probably the shoulders, broad enough for one of my heroines to swoon against quite effectively, or the jaw, so strongly hewn that I could cut my finger on it, were I ever fortunate enough to get a chance to touch it.

He came out from behind his desk as Mrs. Smiley withdrew and indicated a seat in a padded leather chair. "Miss Bentley," he said politely as I took the proffered seat. He then retreated behind his desk to his own padded leather chair.

As he took his seat, I glanced around the room. On the wall were the obligatory diplomas, matted and framed, a B.A. from Ursinus College and a J.D. from Dickinson Law School. I saw proof he was a member of the Pennsylvania Bar, the frame of this document a magnificent cherry with several gold strips worked into the wood lest anyone miss its import.

A pair of what appeared to be original watercolors hung on the wall to my right, lovely renditions of Lancaster County farms without any cloying Amish cuteness. Beneath the pictures was a cluster of comfortable seating, a sofa and two wing chairs. A beautiful quilt, a kaleidoscope of animals tumbling from an ark marooned on Mount Ararat, hung on the wall behind Todd. A fern, a philodendron, and a hearty croton sat on a credenza under a window.

"How may I help you, Miss Bentley?" Todd Reasoner asked, and I turned my attention to him. Such a hardship.

"I'm beginning an adoption search, Mr. Reasoner, and I need clarification on Pennsylvania laws concerning the accessibility of records."

He nodded. "For yourself?"

"Well, sort of," I said. "I'm seeking the information for my curiosity, but the person whose records I'm seeking is my grandfather."

He arched an eyebrow. "How old is your grandfather?"

"Well, he was eighty-two when he died."

"Eighty-two? And he's dead?"

I nodded, swallowing. It still hurt so deeply.

"When did he die?"

"A couple of months ago. It's only since his death that I learned he was adopted."

I reached into my purse and pulled out the envelope I'd found among the photos. I drew out the Certificate of Adoption, opened it, and passed it across the desk.

Todd read it without comment. I took out the letter requesting the picture of Pop and the six-dollar receipt and passed them over, too.

"I'm hoping these documents will help me gain access to the original documents where I can find the names of Pop's birth parents."

Still he said nothing.

"Right?" I prompted.

Todd began shaking his head. "Pennsylvania guards its adoption records very carefully. In fact they are locked in a safe for protection. It would be very difficult for you to gain access to your own adoption records. To gain access to someone else's is virtually impossible."

I frowned. "There must be a way."

He shrugged. "If there is, I don't know it offhand. But I am not an expert on adoption law. I'll have to research this whole issue before I can give you my final thoughts and recommendations."

"And how long will that take?"

I must have sounded more confrontive than I'd meant to because he sat up straighter and in a cool voice said, "I can have the information for you by midweek."

I looked at Todd Reasoner thoughtfully. Mr. Havens would have had it for me by tonight or tomorrow at the latest, even if tomorrow was Saturday. I was missing those perks of power more with each passing minute.

"May I ask why you're conducting this search?" Todd asked. "For medical reasons?"

I shook my head. "Not really. I think that if there were to be any medical problems, they'd have surfaced in the past eighty-two years, don't you? I just want to know where we come from."

"Three generations is pretty far back to try to trace."

I bristled at yet another person's implied criticism. "My grandparents raised my brother and me. So three generations doesn't feel that far removed to me."

He nodded, his hands folded on his desk like he was about to go to prayer. "I feel compelled to inform you that you may be wasting a lot of time and money on this project, Miss Bentley."

"Mr. Reasoner," I said, my index finger coming up to stab the air. "I feel compelled to inform you that I am not asking for your approval of my project. I am merely seeking your legal expertise." I gave him my imitation of Mrs. Smiley's gimlet eye. "Your friend Martin Somebody from the offices of Havens, Smith, and Associates recommended you."

Todd looked surprised. "Martin Stewart?"

I shrugged. "He seems to feel you are more than competent." I unfortunately made that fact sound somewhat questionable.

He clenched his fine jaw but only nodded. *"Res ipsa loquitor."*

"Yes," I said, rising. There was no way I was going to ask what in the world he'd just said. With my nose deplorably high in the air I asked, "Shall I make an appointment with Mrs. Smiley, or will you call when you are *finally* prepared?"

Suddenly one corner of his mouth twitched while he leveled his fine brown eyes at me. "May I inquire as to your profession, Miss Bentley?"

Nonplused by the quick change of subject, I said, "I'm a writer."

"Ah," he said, nodding. "Of course. A wordsmith." He raised an eyebrow. "And you use them so well."

"Res ipsa loquitor," I said, hoping I wasn't saying that the judge would be back in a minute.

FOUR

S aturday morning I sat on my bed at the Horse-and-
Buggy, pillows plumped against the headboard behind
me, Lancaster area phone book in my lap. I turned to
the Bs and looked up Biemsderfer. There were eleven names
listed. I took a deep breath and reached for the phone.

I hated to admit it, but I'd been disappointed in my meeting
with Todd Reasoner yesterday. I'd expected him to be clever
enough to tell me just how I could get the information about
Pop's family in spite of the general consensus about the difficulties, no, the impossibilities involved.

"Go here and ask this question of that person," my fine new
attorney would tell me. Talk about naïve, but that's what I'd
hoped for, expected, wanted so badly I believed sheer wanting
would make it happen.

Instead he hadn't even offered me hope.

*"Pennsylvania guards its adoption records very carefully. In fact
they are locked in a safe for protection. It would be very difficult for
a person to gain access to her own adoption records. To gain access
to someone else's is virtually impossible."*

It was disappointing to realize that he probably was right.
Probably? He was right. He was, after all, the lawyer. He knew
the law. And what he didn't know, he was researching. We had
an appointment for Wednesday at three, a fact that had given
Mrs. Smiley no great joy. Then he would tell me all he had
learned.

"You've made yourself this sweet, cozy little world, Cara," Ward

had told me the night we discussed my plans to search. *"Only good things happen there. True love always wins there. And if something goes wrong, well, you just rewrite it."*

It was embarrassing to admit even to myself, but I had come hoping to rewrite what usually happened in adoption searches. For me, doors would open. For me, answers would appear. I, in true Bentley fashion, would be in control of the situation. Wasn't that what Marnie had said? I liked to be in control? Just like Pop and Ward?

"You can control your writing," she had said. *"The trouble is, you can't control life, especially in a quest like the one you're setting for yourself."*

I might as well face it; I wasn't going to walk into the Lancaster County Courthouse and be given the information I sought. Neither was Todd. If it was out there somewhere, I was going to have to search it out in unorthodox ways.

Not, I thought, smiling softly to myself, that Todd Reasoner was a total washout. Far from it. I remembered his broad shoulders, his chiseled jaw, his bottomless brown eyes. I closed my eyes and actually heard myself sigh.

I froze, appalled. I sounded just like one of my heroines! I glanced guiltily at Rainbow to see if she'd heard me. She slept curled on the pillow of the other bed, deaf to my indiscretion. I sagged in relief, then straightened my spine to take control of things once again.

Besides, how did I know his eyes were bottomless? I hadn't even been that close to him.

But I knew they were.

Taking a deep breath, I forced my gaze to the phone book and the page I'd settled on in the Bs. A snippet of a psalm came to mind: "God sets the lonely in families."

Father God, I ask that you'll set me in my family. Help me know where and how to go about this search.

I put my finger under the first Biemsderfer, an Alan with one L and no Es, and dialed.

As the phone rang, I muttered, *"Res ipsa loquitor,"* using Todd's ridiculous Latin quote as a good luck talisman, sort of like, "You go, girl."

"Yeah?" demanded a teenage girl with no telephone finesse whatsoever.

"May I speak to Alan Biemsderfer, please?" I asked nicely, just to show her how it was done in polite company.

"Sure," she mumbled around a couple of cracks of her chewing gum. "Hey, Dad," she screamed, the phone mere inches from her mouth. "It's some lady for you."

I shook my head to still the roar careening about my skull. If I were related to this particular set of Biemsderfers, phone etiquette would be among my first efforts at communication.

In a short time Alan Biemsderfer picked up an extension and asked in a decibel level much more conducive to conversation, "Yes?"

My stomach flip-flopped and my palms became so sweaty I had to grip the phone extra tightly lest it slip from my grip. Once again foolish hope ballooned inside, pressing the air from my lungs. Maybe he was a long lost cousin!

I took a deep breath and launched into my spiel. I was pleased and amazed at how normal my voice sounded. "Mr. Biemsderfer, my name is Cara Bentley, and I'm doing some genealogical research. My grandfather was born Lehman Biemsderfer here in Lancaster, and I'm trying to trace his family. That's L-e-h-m-a-n."

"What is this?" Alan asked. "One of those things where you're supposed to buy your family tree and crest or something?" His voice bore the suspicions of one barraged by telemarketers.

"No," I said earnestly. "I'm trying to trace my grandfather's origins. Seriously."

"Mmm." There was a small silence. "Well, maybe you are legitimate, maybe you're not, but either way I can't help. I never heard of anyone in our family with the first name Lehman."

The way he emphasized *first name* ever so slightly made me sit up straight. "How about middle name?" I asked, trying to keep my voice calm. Wouldn't it be a miracle, a true God-thing, if he actually knew someone who had both Lehman and Biemsderfer in his name, even if Lehman wasn't a first name?

"Nope," he said. "I've only heard of Lehman as a last name. There are lots of Lehmans in this area. Maybe you could try them. Now, I've got to go."

I thanked Alan and hung up. I felt disappointed and was mad at myself for it. When would I become realistic about this stuff? I grinned wryly. Not today, I didn't think. I quickly dialed Biemsderfer, Beatrice.

"I don't answer questions on the telephone," a testy voice stated.

"But—" And just that quickly I found myself talking to dead air.

Next was Biemsderfer, Edward.

Mrs. Edward answered. "Sorry, Ed's not here. Can I take a message?"

I explained about tracing Lehman Biemsderfer.

"Gee, I don't know much about the family history. Ed and I've only been married a couple of years, and I'm still learning all the ins and outs, you know? But if you want someone who can help, you ought to talk to Great Aunt Lizzie. She's your woman."

I scanned the phone book. "I don't see an Elizabeth in the

listings. Or should I be looking for a Mrs. Someone?"

"No, she's not in the book," Mrs. Edward said. "She's in a nursing home someplace. I've never even met her. I just hear them talking about her. Her last name's not Biemsderfer. I think it's Yost or Yoder or something. Her mother was a Biemsderfer. You could call Ed another time and ask about it if you want."

I thanked her and we disconnected.

Biemsderfer, Gerhard and Biemsderfer, K. M. were not home. Biemsderfer, Marlin, Jr. said, as soon as I mentioned genealogy, "Great Aunt Lizzie. She knows it all."

"Where do I find her?"

There was a silence. Then, "I don't think I should tell you. No offense, but I don't think I should." And he quietly hung up.

I tried Biemsderfer, Marlin, Sr., and an elderly woman answered.

"I'm trying to trace my family," I said.

"Isn't that lovely, dear," she said, her voice sweet and slightly breathless. "I hope you can. I wouldn't want to be alone. I don't know what I'd do without my boys."

"I'm looking for someone who may be able to give me information about my grandfather, Lehman Biemsderfer."

"I'm afraid I don't know anyone in the family with the first name Lehman," she said. She sounded truly sorry for her lack of information. Again I heard that slight emphasis on *first name*.

"Maybe you know someone where Lehman is the middle name?"

"No, dear. I'm sorry. I only know people with Lehman as the last name. There are lots of Lehmans in this area, you know."

I sighed. The nice thing about Biemsderfer was that it was fairly uncommon, unlike Lehman. The process of elimination wouldn't be so lengthy. "The man I'm trying to trace was born a long time ago," I said. "Lehman was born in 1917 and adopted in 1918."

"1917? Why, that's almost as old as me. I wish there was someone left around here who was as old as I am. It gets lonely. Everybody keeps dying or going into those awful nursing homes. Retirement homes, they call them nowadays, but they're just death traps, whatever their name. I made the boys promise me never, never! I've been a widow for almost ten years, you know. Too long. And they made me move to a smaller house. But that's okay because it wasn't a retirement home. I always say, I'm not homesick. I'm dog sick. They wouldn't let me bring Bingo with me. We called him Bingo after that song the grandchildren liked to sing." And she began to quaver, "B-I-N-G-O, and Bingo was his name-o."

I stared at the list of Biemsderfers remaining uncalled, and wondered how to get away from this lonely, slightly fey woman without being rude. Then an idea struck.

"Say, Mrs. Biemsderfer, how many sons do you have?"

"Five."

"And do they live locally?"

"Three do. And so do five grandsons."

"Can you give me their names?"

"Alan, Gerhard, Marlin, Link, Edward, Dwayne, Wesley, and Peter."

I glanced down the list of names again. Alan, Edward, Gerhard, Peter, and Wesley were all there. Dwayne and Link were not. They were probably younger grandsons who still lived with their parents and didn't have their own phones.

"Thanks. You've saved me from making some phone calls, I think."

"You know," she said, sounding suddenly very alert and

authoritative. "The boys never had any interest in genealogy. They said it was boring. But that Alma is a different story. She's close to obsessed. At least I tease her that she is."

"Alma?"

"My daughter. She's taken courses on genealogy and everything. She's done all types of family studies and has this very complicated family tree she's compiled."

My mouth began watering for a view of that tree.

"I think she got it from Lizzie," Mrs. Marlin said. "The interest, I mean. And undoubtedly much of the information, come to think of it."

"Tell me about Lizzie," I said, fascinated that I was hearing this name again.

But before the next breath was drawn and sentence was spoken, the clouds of mental fog rolled in again, blocking the sweet sun of sanity from Mrs. Marlin. Even the sound of her voice became different, slow and tremulous, breathy.

"When Lizzie was a little girl, our families were good friends, and she and I used to play together a lot. We'd sneak away and play down by the river on the farm. That's the Conestoga River, you know. We always got in trouble because the adults thought we would fall in and drown. But they didn't tell us that was their reason. They always said, 'You'll get yourselves too muddy down there.' I guess they didn't want to scare us."

Her voice was fuzzy with reminiscence. "Once Lizzie did fall in, but I pulled her out. Then we had to take off her dress and wash it in the river so that she wouldn't go back to the house with a muddy dress. We never thought about the fact that a soaking wet dress might give us away." She laughed like a child, high and giggly.

Feeling like Alice down the rabbit hole, I said desperately,

"But you know of no Lehman Biemsderfer?"

"No, dear."

"And no one in your family gave up a baby for adoption?"

"My grandniece did about two years ago. I was so sad when she got pregnant, but kids today don't seem to mind, do they? It's not like it used to be, believe me. I didn't even know that men and women did such things when I got married. I thought it was only animals. I'm a farm girl, you know. I don't know where I thought babies came from, maybe kissing. Nice girls never knew in my day." She sighed. "But," and I could hear a smile come into her voice, "Marlin taught me everything I needed to know. He was a very good teacher."

I thought she and Marlin must have enjoyed their marriage quite a bit. Five sons and a daughter were some indication.

"Did you know he's been dead almost ten years now? The boys are so good to me. They made me move, but they didn't make me go to a retirement home. I don't get homesick, I always say. I get dog sick. They wouldn't let me bring him with me, you know. His name was Bingo, after that children's song."

I knew she was going to sing to me any second, so I cut in desperately. "Mrs. Biemsderfer, how can I get in touch with Lizzie? Or Alma?"

"Lizzie lives in one of those retirement homes, poor thing."

"Where's that?"

Mrs. Biemsderfer didn't answer me. Instead she said, "Call Alma. She can help you. Sometimes my mind wanders, I think. But Alma can help."

I scanned the phone book, but I already knew there was no Alma Biemsderfer. I took a minute to mourn all the Biemsderfer women who were no longer known by this name and therefore impossible for me to find easily.

"Alma Stoltzfus," Mrs. Marlin, Sr. said.

Stoltzfus. What a unique name.

I flipped to the Ss and stared in horror. Apparently it wasn't so unique after all.

"What's her husband's name?" I asked.

"Art. They live in Camp Hill."

"Camp Hill?"

"Yes. It's near Harrisburg, just across the river a bit. That's the Susquehanna, dear, not the Conestoga."

"Do you have her phone number?"

"Of course," she said. "It's here somewhere."

I heard her put down the phone and pictured her wandering about her room, looking for her address book. When the wandering went on for several minutes, I realized that Mrs. Biemsderfer wasn't going to give me Alma's number. She had, in fact, forgotten about me.

Just then the phone was picked up, and I thought for a brief flicker of time that I had misread the woman. A quick click of the receiver as she hung up her phone disabused me of that idea.

I smiled sadly at the buzzing dial tone and was thankful neither Mom nor Pop had gotten so mentally confused. The physical deterioration had been bad enough to watch. I couldn't imagine witnessing a mental decline that took away a person you had loved for so many years.

I stared at the phone for a few minutes. Should I call Alma Stoltzfus, or was that name and its potential help just the imagining of a confused mind? But the old lady had seemed very aware during that brief part of our conversation. I shrugged. Why not call? I had spent the morning talking to a bunch of strangers. Why not one more?

I dialed information and asked for the number of an Art Stoltzfus in Camp Hill. I hoped the name wasn't as common over there in Dauphin County as it was in Lancaster County.

In a short time I was connected with Alma Stoltzfus, nee Biemsderfer. Once again I explained what I was looking for.

"Lehman Biemsderfer?" she said. "Never heard of anyone named that. Lehman's usually a last name."

"Yes, so I understand." I found I was gripping the phone again like it was my lifeline and I was a drowning person. I forced my hand to relax, and it actually did for about five seconds. "Your mother told me you had a family tree. I thought maybe it could give me some help. You know, all the branches of Biemsderfers."

I held my breath. Was this where she told me she couldn't exchange family information over the phone? After all, sensible middle-aged women were usually cautious.

"You know," she said warily, "I hate to give out private family information on the phone."

I sighed. What a surprise. And I couldn't blame her.

"After all," she said, "how do I know you're trustworthy? How do I know you aren't trying to pull some scam?" There was no animosity in her voice, just a reasonable understanding that the world is full of con artists.

"I sympathize with your concern. I know I'm reputable, but how can I convince you?" I thought for a minute. Too bad I couldn't tell her I was a Bentley of Bentley Marts, but come to think of it, why should she believe that? "You could contact my attorney."

"Mmm," she said. "That's a possibility. And who might that be?"

I gave her not only Todd's name and number, but I fished Mr. Havens's business card out of my purse and gave her that name, too.

"A lawyer in both Pennsylvania and New Jersey?" she said.

"I live in New Jersey. I'm here seeking this information, and I needed to know Pennsylvania law about adoption and adoption searches."

"This is an adoption thing?" Alma asked, her voice pricking with interest. "I didn't realize that." She was silent for a couple of beats. "Illegitimacy in 1917 was quite a stigma, especially in Lancaster County, steeped as it is in Amish and Mennonite culture."

"I know. I've thought a lot about that and how desperate Pop's mother must have been."

"Anyone who was a mother back then would be long dead," Alma said.

"Yes. Even if I knew her name, I couldn't speak with her. And adoption papers are guarded like the gold at Fort Knox. Getting to them is next to impossible. Otherwise I wouldn't be bothering you like this."

There was a moment of silence during which I could almost hear Alma thinking.

"Look," she finally said. "I'd like to help you if I can. I don't know that our family is who you're looking for, but who knows, maybe we are. I'm coming to Lancaster next Thursday to visit Mom. Why don't you and I meet then? I'll check your references, and I'll bring along the family tree and any other family documents I think might be pertinent."

"And I'll bring along Pop's adoption certificate and the papers I have."

We set noon as our meeting time and the Olive Garden by Park City Mall as our meeting place.

When I hung up, I was both restless and excited. Five days. I had to wait five whole days. I started to pace. It seemed such a long time, but it looked like I might be on the verge of getting some excellent information. I shivered with anticipation. But five days! I could hardly stand it.

I looked around at the tan walls, the brown plaid comforters with the orange accent stripes, the brown rug, and the cheap bureau with the portable TV bolted to its surface. I thought of the paper-thin towels hanging on the corroded rack in the dingy bathroom. They couldn't begin to cope with my hair when it was wet.

If I had to wait almost a week for my appointment with Alma, I knew I couldn't wait in this room. I'd go nuts. In fact, I couldn't stay in it for a minute longer. I grabbed my purse and went outside into the humid June day. The sun was high, the sky a misty blue wash, and the highway bursting with traffic.

I looked at all the cars, vans, and tour buses with disfavor, climbed into my car, and joined the flow going west toward Lancaster. I stopped in a little restaurant called T. Burk and Co. and read an inspirational romance by one of my competitors as I ate. I had to admit the book wasn't half bad, but I also had to admit that I thought I did it better. Feeling somewhat smug, I returned to the Horse-and-Buggy.

I spent a relaxing afternoon at the pool in the front yard of the motel. Granted, in one way it was hard to relax under the scrutiny of all the traffic streaming by just a few feet from the fenced area in which I sat on a plastic recliner; but in another way, the sheer number of cars made the people in them meaningless.

When I dragged myself back to my room, I was sleepy with sun.

"Just a quick minute," I said to Rainbow as I lay down on my bed. "Just a quick minute."

I woke two hours later, rested and restless. I took a shower, pulled my still wet hair back in a tan scrunchie, threw on my new tan jeans and a beige T-shirt, and went looking for somewhere to eat dinner. This time I turned east and found the Bird-in-Hand Restaurant. The parking lot was full, a good sign. I went in and found a lobby full of people waiting for tables. Since I had nothing better to do, I decided I might as well turn my name in and wait. I could people-watch or read the next book on my list. I never went anywhere without a book. When I packed for vacation, I packed my books first and my clothes second.

On my way to give the hostess my name, I noticed a circular rack of books and stopped dead in my tracks. Staring at me were several copies of *As the Deer*. My book! Here in the lobby of a restaurant! For anybody to buy! I glanced at the top of the rack and read Choice Books. I looked at the other titles and realized every book was from one Christian publishing house or another. Some titles were fiction, some nonfiction, some were by friends, some by people I'd never heard of. As I circled the rack, I came to *So My Soul*.

Yes, I thought, mentally waving my fist triumphantly in the air. I hated it when I found *As the Deer* without *So My Soul*, since they were written to be a pair. *As the Deer* followed the heroine, one Marci Lerner, to the point of her conversion to Jesus Christ. *So My Soul* examined the ramifications of this decision on her life and the lives of the others with whom she was involved. Through both books I developed her romance with Scott Henderson.

By the time the books were finished, I wanted to meet my own Scott Henderson. Not only was he tall and handsome, intelligent, and had a heart for God, but he also knew how to make a woman happy. He was always there to support Marci through all her trials. He held her hand when she was hurt and offered a strong shoulder to cry on. He prayed for her and loved her unreservedly. He accepted her just as she was, encouraging her in the process of becoming God's woman.

Sometimes I was afraid that Scott existed only in fiction. I certainly never met guys like him. Then I'd think of Mom and Pop and Ward and Marnie. They'd found true love, real love. And I'd pray almost desperately that God would let me find the same.

I rubbed a finger softly over the cover of *So My Soul*. Other authors wrote trilogies. I wrote series of two. Duologies? Maybe some day I'd think up enough stuff to warrant a trilogy, but for now, two did it. And these two were doing it exceedingly well.

I was standing there grinning to myself when someone bumped my arm. I turned to say I was sorry and found myself face-to-face with the handsomest lawyer in Lancaster County.

"Hey," I said cleverly as I tried not to stare at that magnificent jawline.

"Well, hi," he said, slightly more articulate.

"Here for dinner?" I asked.

He nodded. "I find restaurants good places to come for dinner, don't you?"

I grinned. It was either that or blush a zillion shades of red for my inane remark. "Chitchat's not my strong suit," I said. "Whatever comes to mind comes out, idiotic or not."

He grinned back politely.

"Guess what I did today?" I said.

Of course he hadn't the vaguest idea.

"I called all the Biemsderfers in the phone book."

He nodded as though he was actually interested. "Any of them confess to being long lost relatives?"

I shook my head.

"I'm glad," he said. "I'd hate to lose a billing before I had a chance to reap all the profits possible."

"Ah. *Res ipsa loquitor.*"

He shook his head. *"Carpe diem."*

"I know that one," I said. "Seize the day. I also know *et al, ipso facto,* and *et cetera.*"

"I'm impressed. I've always appreciated multilingual people."

I think this time I actually did blush at his faux compliment, but I'm not certain. It could have been the heat from my afternoon's sunburn.

A woman's voice said, "Two?" and I realized we were standing before the hostess. She looked at Todd, obviously anticipating a yes.

I definitely flushed now, expecting him to say, "Oh, no, I'm not here with her. I'm just making pleasant conversation because she's a client. I'm really here with that beautiful woman over there."

Instead he looked at me and raised an eyebrow in invitation. Surprised and pleased, I gave a small nod.

"Yes, two. Reasoner," he said. Then, in an aside to me, he said, "Thanks for being here. Now I can claim the meal as a business deduction."

Startled, I looked at him and caught a gleam of humor in those brown eyes, those bottomless brown eyes. I'd been right.

"Thirty to forty minutes," the hostess said.

We nodded and moved away. Just then a couple got up from a bench along the wall, and we took the deserted seats.

"Tell me about your phone calls," Todd asked. And I did. He listened attentively, asking questions every so often, laughing at Mrs. Marlin, Sr. hanging up on me.

"So I'm going to have lunch with Alma next Thursday when she comes to take her mother to her home. She's bringing the family tree with her."

When I finished, he just looked at me, a smile on his face.

"And you're not the least bit excited about this meeting, are you?"

"It shows?"

"Cara, you're positively vibrating with excitement."

I stared at him. "Me? Vibrating? I never vibrate. I'm low key. I'm quiet and laid back."

He looked at me skeptically.

"Truly," I said. "I'm a writer. I lead a quiet life. My brother and sister-in-law say I only live through my characters. Pop kept at me all the time to get a life."

He shook his head. "I don't know about then, but this is now, and now you're having a hard time sitting still."

I grinned. "I am fidgeting a bit, aren't I? But isn't it exciting? I may be meeting my family!"

"Reasoner, party of two," a metallic voice called over a PA system. "Reasoner, party of two."

We followed a young woman in a head covering to a booth along the outside wall of the restaurant. She left us studying two large menus with amazingly inexpensive meals.

"Is she Amish?" I asked Todd.

He followed my eyes after the hostess and shook his head. "No, she's Mennonite."

"What's the difference? They both wear those prayer cap things."

"They come from the same Anabaptist heritage, but they've diverged through the years."

"How?"

"While the Amish have stayed as separate from the general culture as they can, the Mennonites have accepted change and have integrated it into their religious lives. They share the Anabaptist heritage of nonresistance and adult baptism, but they're thoroughly modern."

I laid my menu on the table. "I know Southern Baptist and General Baptist and Regular Baptist and lots of other Baptists. What's Anabaptist?"

He leaned back in his seat and rested a hand on the edge of the table. He lowered his menu so he could see me more easily. "Back in the Protestant Reformation, a group of dissidents decided they didn't agree with the Roman Catholic practice of infant baptism. They argued that a person shouldn't be baptized until he is old enough to understand what faith in Christ is all about. So these dissidents rebaptized themselves in the early 1500s. That's what Anabaptist means. Rebaptized or baptized again. One group of the Anabaptists followed a man named Menno Simons and became known as Mennonites. More than a century later, another group broke from the Mennonites and followed a fiery preacher named Jakob Ammonn. They became known as Amish."

"How did the two groups both end up in this area?"

"Religious persecution."

"Pacifists were persecuted? But weren't they gentle people?"

"Yes, in that they wouldn't retaliate. No, in that they stood against the institution of the state church and were considered very dangerous to the political and social order of the day."

"So they got kicked around?"

"Kicked around nothing. They got drowned and burned and murdered in great numbers. They came here to escape, and they ended up in one of the most fertile areas in the world."

Our waitress came for our order. I decided on stuffed chicken breast, baked potato, and a salad. Todd had pork and sauerkraut, mashed potatoes, and cottage cheese with apple butter. We both ordered sweetened iced tea.

She returned in record time with our drinks, my salad, and

Todd's cottage cheese, topped with a dark brown substance the consistency of burnt applesauce.

"What's that?" I asked suspiciously.

"Apple butter."

"It's brown."

"Umm."

"You actually eat brown food?" I stared at his dish.

"With great relish," he said, taking a forkful. "And you eat brown food, too. Meat's brown."

"Meat doesn't count. It sort of matches your eyes," I said, pointing at the apple butter.

He made a choking sound. "What?"

"Well, it does."

"If you say. No one's ever made that comparison before. Want to try some?" He offered me his dish.

I looked at it dubiously.

"Come on," he said. "When in Rome…"

"Res ipsa loquitor," I said.

"Precisely," he said.

I stuck my fork in his dish just enough to get the tines damp.

"Coward," he said.

"Precisely," I said, and with great trepidation stuck my fork in my mouth. I was very pleasantly surprised. "It's sweet."

He laughed. "What did you expect?"

"Brown food? Meat. Gravy. They're not sweet." I took a real forkful this time, making certain to get some of the cottage cheese, too. "I like it."

"Uh-oh," he said and pulled his dish back to the safety of his own place mat. I politely ate my own salad.

"Tell me about your family," I said as we started our main course.

70

He shrugged. "Not much to tell. I'm an only child of elderly parents. My mother died when I was five, and my father tried his best, but it was hard."

I could tell by the expression on his face that it was still hard, or at least the memories were.

"How old is elderly?"

"My father was fifty-five when I was born, my mother forty-three. They had long since given up on the idea of a child."

"So your mother was only forty-eight when she died?"

He nodded.

"Mine was twenty-nine," I said. "I was two."

We looked at each other with sympathy.

"So your father raised you, too?" Todd asked.

I shook my head. "Trey died with Caroline. Drunk driver."

"Ovarian cancer," he said.

We were quiet a minute, chewing, contemplating.

"So who raised you?" he asked.

I spent most of the main course telling him about Mom and Pop, laughing, filled with warm memories.

Todd listened, a sad kind of envy just below the surface. "You had a wonderful childhood, didn't you? Just like in books."

I nodded. "Lots of love, lots of laughter, and a real, practical faith modeled rigorously."

Todd sighed. "Well, I had the faith part anyway, and I truly am appreciative of that. My father loved the Lord and saw to it that I had opportunity for a real faith, too. Church and Bible school every Sunday morning and youth group every Sunday night. Vacation Bible school. Church camp. But the love and laughter part weren't there." He put his knife and fork onto his empty plate and leaned back against his seat, trying to keep his face impassive but not quite succeeding.

"My father is a nice enough man, I guess," he said. "He has a Ph.D. in English lit. and taught at Millersville University for years and years. He was there when it was a state teachers college, then a state college, and finally a state university. He was very scholarly, highly respected in academic circles, and very introverted. His life was medieval literature and culture. Samuel Pepys' diary and John Milton were much more important to him than I ever was."

I thought of Pop and his great lust for life. I imagined a little Todd being read a bedtime story from Dante's *Inferno*. I shivered. Certainly one of the rings of hell.

Todd reached for his iced tea and turned the glass in circles on the table. He stared at the water marks as he talked. "I learned as a little kid that my father was happy when I was quiet and invisible, so I became quiet and invisible. He almost smiled when I got good grades, so I got good grades, always hoping. He was almost impressed if I excelled in whatever academic pursuit I followed, from academic teams to science fairs. I tried everything I could think of to please him, but I don't think I ever got a compliment."

I leaned my elbow on the table and looked at the handsome, competent, well-educated man across the table from me. I concentrated on his words, trying to see the deeper truths behind them, marveling that he was telling me all this information. I was willing to bet he rarely talked about his father and certainly didn't talk about their painful relationship. I felt complimented beyond reason. He looked up suddenly and saw my intense, almost worried look.

He smiled wryly and shook his head. "Sorry. I didn't mean to whine."

"Hey," I said, reaching across the table and putting my hand on his arm. "I didn't hear whining. I heard part of a life story. I was just imagining that little boy sitting in an overstuffed chair too big for him, his legs sticking straight out in front of him as he studied the encyclopedia so he could converse with his father."

He nodded thoughtfully. "But it was the sofa with a brown print that was ugly as sin, and it was *Paradise Lost.*"

I didn't know whether to laugh or cry as I put my hand back in my lap. "We, on the other hand, saw all the Star Wars and Indiana Jones movies."

"Sounds good to me. Now what do you want for dessert?" This last was asked as our waitress began clearing the table. He smiled and rubbed his hands, apparently glad for the opportunity to dissipate the emotional tension of our conversation. "How about some shoofly pie?"

"What is shoofly pie? It sounds awful."

"It's a molasses pie," answered the waitress, obviously used to the question.

"A molasses pie?" It still sounded awful. "Filled with flies?"

"It's delicious," Todd assured me.

"I'll take coconut custard," I said emphatically.

"Warm shoofly with whipped cream," Todd said. After the waitress walked away, he looked at me. "You should have trusted me on the pie. You'll be sorry."

When the desserts came, I looked at his. "It's brown! What is it with you Pennsylvania Dutch people and brown food?"

"I'm not Pennsylvania Dutch," Todd said. "And what is it with you tourists that you won't try new stuff?"

"Speaking of being a tourist," I said, enjoying my nice, creamy, familiar coconut custard, "I'd like to find some place to live besides a motel. Do you know of a boarding house or an apartment or something that might be available but won't demand a year's lease?"

He thought for a minute. "You know, I just might."

I looked at him hopefully.

"What would you think about living on an Amish farm?"

I stared at him. "You're kidding."

"I've a friend who used to be Amish before his *rumsch-pringes.*"

"His what?"

"His wild oat sowing. His teenage rebellion."

"Ah."

"Anyway, Jake was in a motorcycle accident and is now a paraplegic. His parents, who are still Old Order Amish, brought him home to the annex on the house and brought in electricity and a phone for him because they realize he'll never be Amish again. Anyway, he rents the rooms on the second floor of the annex so he can have some income. I happen to know the rooms are recently available because the woman who used to rent them just got married."

"An Amish farm? Cows and horses and buggies?"

Todd nodded. "And smelly barns. And some of the nicest people you'll ever meet. And Jake put in a bathroom on the second floor after Kristie moved out."

I looked at him, startled. "What did Kristie have to use? An outhouse?"

Todd laughed. "Don't worry. She had indoor plumbing. She just had to share the family's bathroom on the first floor. You won't have to do that, but you can eat dinner with them whenever you want. And you'll want to often, believe me. Mary's a great cook."

I stared at my cup of coffee, its steam rising into the artificially cooled air. An Amish farm. I bet even Pop would consider that getting a life. "If I can have a lease for, say, three months, I'll do it."

FIVE

et me go call Jake," Todd said. "I'll see if he's got a rental lined up already or whether the place is still free."

"You're going to call right now?"

"Sure," he said, sliding out of the booth. "It'll only take a minute. Just don't eat my pie while I'm gone."

"Fat chance of that." I eyed the repulsive brown thing.

I took a sip of coffee as I watched Todd walk across the dining room to a bank of phones in the lobby. I noticed a table of women watch him, too. I felt a sudden delight that he was eating with me.

I looked at the shoofly pie again. I had seen three pieces of it sitting on the table of the four women who had eyed Todd with such interest. I watched as our waitress put two pieces on the table across the aisle from me.

Surely if all these people were eating the disgusting thing, it couldn't be all that bad. I glanced toward the phones and saw that Todd was thoroughly occupied. I looked at the pie again. I looked at the people across the aisle enthusiastically enjoying their dessert.

One tiny taste, I thought. Then I'll know what all the fuss is about, and he'll never even notice. Besides, I like whipped cream.

I licked all the coconut custard off my fork and reached across the table. I took a smidgen of crumbs and custard. I sniffed it with distrust. I reached back for a bit of whipped cream and stuffed the mess in my mouth. I blinked in surprise.

"Told you you'd like it," Todd said as he slid into his seat. Then he scowled. "But I also told you not to take any."

"What makes you think I took any?" I said as I reached across the table for a decent-sized bite. It was either that or be embarrassed out of my mind.

"Do you steal the food off the plates of all your dates?" he asked.

I blinked again. This was a date? "Only the ones I like," I said placidly.

He pushed the pie to the center of the table and we took turns taking bites.

"Jake says the rooms are still available and that if we come out tomorrow afternoon, you can look them over. He says tomorrow is a good day because it's an off Sunday and the family's going to visit Ruth and Isaiah."

I savored the last bite of pie and asked, "What's an off Sunday and who are Ruth and Isaiah?"

"The Old Order Amish have church every other Sunday at each other's homes. When there's no church, it's an off Sunday, and they often go visiting. Ruth and Isaiah are the Zooks's daughter and son-in-law."

"They only go to church every other Sunday?" That surprised me for such a religious people.

Todd nodded. "So are you free tomorrow afternoon to go out to the farm? I'll take you if you are."

"Sure. Sounds good." It sounded more than good, but I wasn't going to tell him. "By the way, can you recommend a good church? I'd like to go tomorrow."

"Sure," he said. "My church. Why don't I pick you up for the service, then we can grab a bite to eat afterwards and go to the farm."

I shrugged nonchalantly, thinking that I should have come

to Bird-in-Hand a lot sooner. Haddonfield was never like this. "Sounds like a good plan."

We split the bill in half and left the restaurant.

"But you should have paid more," Todd said as we walked across the parking lot. "After all, you ate half of my dinner."

"Only the brown stuff," I said as I looked into his bottomless brown eyes.

We came to my beige Saturn, but instead of saying goodbye, Todd leaned against the fender and asked, "So are you enjoying your time here?"

"I am. Last night I went for a drive all over the place. No matter where I looked, the view was beautiful. I think it's the size of the farms, so compact, the fields all bursting with crops, and the barns and houses so picturesque."

"Is it picturesque?" Todd asked, looking around. "I have never gotten as caught up in the whole Amish thing as lots of people do. Maybe living in the area all my life has made it too common."

I stared at him. "You mean you don't see the beauty of these farms and the fascination of this unique culture?"

He grinned with one corner of his mouth. "I know. I've no depth of soul or appreciation for the finer things. I'm shallow and insensitive. I see the glass half empty instead of half full. But honestly, instead of a sociological paradise, I see a culture that, in order to survive, is fraught with inconsistencies. In fact, there goes one now." And he pointed to the street.

I looked and saw a van full of Amish people driving by.

"An Amish taxi," Todd said. "There are lots of retired men who have a nice second career as drivers for Amish folks. The Amish take the taxis places they either want or need to go quickly. Why, I ask you, is it all right to ride in a car but not drive one? Or take the bus for that matter."

"The Amish use buses?"

Todd nodded. "I used to think they were almost fraudulent in these inconsistencies, but I've changed my mind since I've come to know the Zooks. I've decided that they're just trying to keep their culture alive. My question, I guess, is whether it's worth keeping alive."

"Sure it is," I said, slightly scandalized at his question.

"Yeah? Why?"

"I don't know. I don't know enough about them to know. But it must be."

I watched a pair of Amish boys in straw hats push their way along the road on scooters, thinking how sad it would be to lose something so singular.

"Bikes would be faster," I said.

"But bikes aren't allowed. Too far too fast."

I looked at him. "I don't understand."

"As far as I can figure out, anything that pushes the parameters of the culture beyond their concept of what family and church should be is bad. Farms are small and picturesque because they are the size an individual family can handle without the use of modern farming equipment in the fields. Bikes and cars are forbidden because they would take individuals beyond the boundaries of the group. Electricity off utility poles would bring in the questionable world of TV, radio, and computers as well as the benefits of electric lights. So they stick with lanterns for the sake of guarding their beliefs and use twelve-volt batteries for power. Lanterns, dress, and buggies are the outward signs of a very exclusive community."

"Do they proselytize?" I asked, trying to imagine an Amishman on a street corner handing out tracts or standing on a soapbox pleading with a crowd.

He shook his head. "They don't seek converts like most religions do, but they are willing to accept them if folks from outside want to join. Not many who seek actually stay. The divide between Plain and fancy is too wide."

I watched a buggy roll slowly by, a line of cars stacked up behind it.

"Have you ever ridden in a buggy?"

Todd looked at me as though I'd gone crazy. "Of course not."

"Haven't you ever wondered what it feels like to sit in one of those things, especially when a tour bus zooms past?"

He stuffed his hands in his jeans pockets and shook his head. "I can honestly say I've never pondered that for any length of time."

"Never?"

"Never." It was obvious from his tone of voice that he thought the topic ridiculous.

"Then let's go for a buggy ride and find out what it's like."

He stared at me, horrified.

"Oh, come on," I said. "Where's your spirit of adventure?"

"Cara, a buggy ride? That's crazy. Besides, it's too touristy."

I shrugged. "So what? I'm a tourist."

"Well, I'm not." I watched as he hunkered down, all but attaching himself to my car, a limpet clinging to his rock.

"Todd," I said, smiling as sweetly as I could. "Where's your sense of adventure?"

"I don't have one, and I don't want to develop one in an Amish buggy." And he clenched his marvelous jaw, clearly convinced he'd made his definitive statement on the issue.

I leaned toward him and narrowed my eyes to slits as I stared directly into his marvelous brown eyes.

He blinked and backed up instinctively. "What?" he said.

"Todd," and I pointed my index finger at his chest, "when you grow up, do you want to be like your father or like Pop?"

He blinked. Then he clamped his jaw and glared at me through eyes as narrowed as mine. The muscle in his cheek jumped as he clenched and unclenched his teeth.

Finally he spoke, his words clipped and hard. "That is a very nervy question. Do you always play hardball like that?"

My voice was a hoarse whisper as I forced my answer around the lump in my throat. "Only when the outcome matters."

He blinked again. We both knew I wasn't talking about any buggy ride. We stood frozen, staring at each other, as all around us life flowed on.

My heart pounded to the point of pain, and ribbons of dread unfurled in my chest. What if he wanted to be his father? Or what if he couldn't help being his father? I felt like my whole future was on the line even as I recognized the folly of such a thought. I'd only met the man yesterday. But somehow I knew it was true.

Dear God, it's the brown eyes, isn't it? And the beautiful curls and that jaw. And he shared his shoofly pie with me. And he found a place for me to live. And he's taking me to church! *Oh, Lord, please let him be able to have fun.*

Finally Todd broke the tension. He took a deep breath, twitched his shoulders a bit, nodded, and said mildly, "I guess we'd better take a buggy ride, hadn't we?"

My breath rushed from my lungs, and I realized for the first time that I'd been holding it. Almost giddy with relief I said, "Abe's Buggy Rides is just down the street."

He looked slightly pained. "I know Abe's Buggy Rides." He peeled himself off my fender and sighed. "Give me your car keys and let's get this over with."

"You're driving my car?"

"Why not? We're standing right beside it."

"But it's my car. I should drive."

"Don't push it, Cara. Let me have some semblance of control."

I gave him the keys and climbed in the passenger side. He backed out of the parking space and pulled onto 340, turning left. In a short time we were at Abe's Buggy Rides. We parked and climbed out. When we met at the back of the car, Todd looked at me with a pained expression.

"I've driven past this place for years, always with a great feeling of superiority toward the people who took the rides." He shuddered so intensely that his curls shook. "Now I'm about to become one of them."

I patted his arm. "I don't know whether it helps or not, but I think you're brave and wonderful."

He snorted. "Don't think I don't recognize sarcasm when I hear it."

I grinned and started for the sidewalk where the buggies stood waiting.

He trailed me, still busy carping. "You eat my food, you don't pay your fair share, you complain when I want to drive your car, and you make me go on a buggy ride." The horror in his voice was comical. "I've never met anyone like you before." I turned to him, startled, and he added quickly, "And that's not a compliment."

Glad for a lifetime of dealing with Pop and Ward, I scowled at him. "'Fraidy cat."

"What?"

"You heard me. You're afraid to have fun."

"I am not."

"Hah!"

"Hi," said a happy teenage voice behind us. "My name's Angie, and I'll be your driver for the buggy tour."

We spun to find a grinning Angie in jeans with the knee missing and a rose T-shirt.

"Hi, Angie," I said. "I'm Cara. And this scowling hulk is—"

"Yeah, I know who he is. We go to the same church. What are you doing going on a buggy ride, Todd?"

"Don't ask," he said, but I noticed the scowl was gone. He looked pointedly at me. "I got conned."

Angie laughed and led the way to a gray buggy with black trim waiting at the edge of the road. She reached in and pulled the front seat aside to give access to the back. Todd stood aside and let me get in first. I put my foot on the round metal step on the side of the buggy and stepped up and in. I sat on a seat covered with burgundy crushed velvet.

Angie pulled the front seat into place and Todd climbed in. He sat on the right of the seat while Angie sat on the left. She took the reins and slapped them gently on the rump of our horse who knew from frequent practice just what to do. He began ambling slowly along the shoulder of 340.

We turned right off of 340 and drove down a country road. It pleased me how quickly the bustle of the major tourist thoroughfare was left behind. Angie kept up a steady patter of information which Todd ignored but I found fascinating. We passed several farms and an Amish school. I was appalled when I learned that Amish children only went to school until eighth grade.

"Education takes you from the culture," Todd commented, his arm resting on the open window frame. "It makes you independent, and the Amish prize a cooperative, group mentality."

With the open door and side window and the open front and back windows, there was a soft breeze through the buggy in spite of the warm temperature. I was enjoying my ride and so, I thought, was Todd, looking all relaxed and handsome.

At least he was enjoying it until the horse did what comes

naturally. He raised his tail, and Todd reacted.

"Ah, geez!" he muttered and leaned as far back into the buggy as he could.

Angie and I both laughed at him as the manure fell harmlessly onto the road.

"No one would ever take you for a farmer," Angie said.

When we arrived at our starting place after tracing a two-mile square, we climbed out of the buggy, thanked Angie, and walked to the car. Todd went automatically to the driver's side again. I shook my head, amused at his presumption, and climbed into the passenger side.

"So?" I said.

"So what?"

"Did you have fun?"

He snorted and gave me a look of imperious scorn. I started laughing.

"You're a phony," I said.

"You're bossy."

"Quid pro quo," I said.

"Exactly."

We rode in companionable silence to and past the restaurant.

"Hey, where are we going?" I said, spinning to look back over my shoulder. "Don't you have to get your car? Or do you like mine better and you plan to keep it?"

"My car's not there. I walked."

We turned off 340 and drove for a bit, made another turn, and pulled into a drive before a brick Cape Cod with white clapboard dormers, a red door, and white shutters. A split-rail fence separated a yard about an acre in size from the press of cornfields on three sides.

"You live here?"

He nodded. "This is my house."

"I thought you didn't like farms. There's nothing around you but farms."

"I don't like manure, and I'll admit that February and March were a bit fragrant when my neighbors were putting down their homemade fertilizer. But I love the privacy and peace. For that I'll overlook the other."

"Compromise," I said, smiling. "The Amish aren't the only ones."

We sat in the car with the windows down, enjoying the warm magic of dusk. Neither of us seemed to want to move. We listened to the crickets' symphony and watched the lightning bugs flash in the shrubs as sunset faded from lavender and peach to pearl gray velvet to deep night lit by a full moon.

"Smell the honeysuckle?" I asked, thinking that nothing meant peace and summer like that scent.

"Come with me," Todd said.

He got out of the car and walked to the edge of the lawn where a vine grew up a fence post. I followed willingly. He broke off a sprig from the vine and handed it to me. I held it to my nose and inhaled deeply. Sweet, sweet honeysuckle.

"Ever draw the nectar from the flower?" he asked, pulling a blossom free.

"Sure," I said. "We Jersey girls love honeysuckle."

I watched as he pinched the base of the flower and slowly pulled the long stamen free. He put it in his mouth and, closing his lips over it, slowly withdrew it, savoring the sweetness.

"That's one way to do it," I said.

"You've got a better way, I suppose."

"Sure." I plucked a blossom and putting the end in my mouth, bit it off. Then I inhaled the sweet trace of nectar. "Simple, easy, and quick."

We pulled every flower off the sprig and several off the vine on the post, Todd carefully pulling the stamen free, me biting the tip and pulling in the nectar.

Finally we wandered back to my car, and Todd handed me my keys.

"I'll see you tomorrow morning," he said. "How about if I bring us some breakfast? Egg McMuffins?"

"With orange juice and a large coffee. We can eat out by the pool."

I climbed in and Todd shut my door. He leaned in the open window.

"I'm glad we met this evening." He grinned. "I had a good time."

I grinned back. "And I'm supposed to believe that?"

He stood up. "Yep. It's the truth."

As I backed out of the driveway, I couldn't wait for tomorrow morning.

"Cara, I'd like you to meet some friends," Todd said after the service Sunday morning. We were standing in the parking lot. "This is Clarke and Kristie Griffin."

I smiled at the couple, he tall with very dark brows under sandy colored hair, she slim and somehow lovely despite being dressed in swirls of ruby, emerald, and sapphire with shiny gold dots over them.

"This is Cara Bentley, a client of mine," Todd said. "I'm taking her out to the Zooks' to see about renting your old rooms, Kristie."

Kristie's eyes lit up. "Oh, Cara, you'll love it there. I had the most wonderful year."

"Sure you did," Clarke said, putting a hand on her shoulder. "You met me."

Kristie smiled broadly and leaned into his side. I remembered

Todd saying that the woman who had rented the rooms before me had just gotten married. It showed in the way she looked at Clarke and the way he smiled happily back.

"You'll love the Zooks," Kristie assured me when she pulled her gaze reluctantly from her husband. "Mary and John are so pleasant and nice and hospitable."

"And Mary is a great cook," Clarke said. "Don't overlook that very important fact."

"Jake is a bit touchy at times," Kristie said, "but he's getting better. I think anybody'd be grouchy and morose if he suddenly became a paraplegic."

"Jake's really a nice guy," Clarke said. "He and I've been friends for a long time. And getting approval to take those classes at Millersville University has been great for him."

"First class tomorrow," Todd said.

"That's all your doing, Todd," Clarke said. "If it weren't for your pushing, I don't think he'd have gotten that high school equivalency degree."

Todd shook his head dismissively. "I'm just concerned that he do well in these college classes. He has to if he wants to gain full admission."

When Clarke and Kristie said good-bye, I watched them walk to their car hand in hand. I turned to Todd to make some snide remark about their obvious affection and was surprised by an expression of deep longing on his face.

An unexpected and intense shaft of pain shot through me. I swallowed hard to tamp down the hurt.

"She's very pretty," I said, my eyes again following her. I tried to keep my voice neutral, though I wasn't completely successful. A faint misting of melancholy hung over the words.

He looked at me with one eyebrow raised and said carefully, "Yes, she is."

"Colorful," I said.

He nodded. "Very."

I felt the beginnings of a headache, the special one reserved for sufferers of vain imaginings. It didn't matter that I knew I was foolish; the pain still attacked behind my left eye.

"But then beige is nice too," he added politely, looking me up and down. "Restful."

It was the third day I'd known him and the third beige outfit. Who cared that it was a pricey raw silk sheath? It was beige! Suddenly I felt as boring as white bread.

"You used to go with her, didn't you?" I asked, my eyes still on the lovely Kristie. I already knew the answer by some inner radar.

He nodded. "For a couple of years."

"What happened?"

"We broke up."

"Your idea or hers?" I wanted it to be his, but I knew it was hers.

"Hers. She told me I wanted to remake her and she didn't want to be remade."

I thought about that for a few minutes. "Did you?"

"Want to remake her? Probably. All her quirks that Clarke thinks are enchanting I thought were idiotic."

"Not a good sign for a relationship."

He nodded agreeably.

"Do you miss her?"

He looked at me with a funny half smile. "Do you pick at scabs often?"

I sighed. I was so obvious, poking where I had no business poking, even when it hurt me. "Only when the—"

"I know. Only when the outcome matters." He continued to stare at me. "And it matters in this case?"

I blushed and looked at my shoes. They were bone-colored

flats. Boring. "I think I'd like a piece of shoofly pie for dessert, wouldn't you?" I said too brightly to his shirt button. I couldn't bring myself to meet his gaze. "Where do you think we should eat?"

He put a finger under my chin and lifted, forcing my eyes to his. "I'm over her, Cara," he said softly. "I've been over her for some time. Her analysis was right. I liked what I wanted her to be, not what she was."

I refused to be comforted. "Yeah, but you didn't see your face."

"My face?"

"Watching her walk away."

He shook his head, confused. "I'm sorry. I'm not following you."

"You looked like you were dying inside."

He pulled back. "Unh-uh. I don't know what you think you saw, but it wasn't that."

"Deep longing," I said stubbornly. He was right. I did like to pick scabs.

"Not for her," Todd said. Perplexed, he ran his hands through his hair, disturbing his curls. One fell over his forehead and I itched to push it back. I watched him try to figure out what I was talking about and thought he was treating my paranoia more kindly than I deserved.

"Let's forget I said anything," I said, turning toward the car. "What you felt or feel for her is none of my business, is it?"

Todd put a restraining hand on my arm. "Stay here. We need to figure this out." And he stared off into space.

"No, we don't," I said. But I stayed.

Finally he looked at me. "When I think of Clarke and Kristie, mostly I think of how suited they are for each other and how great it was that the Lord brought them together. The only other thing I think is that someday I hope I have whatever it is they've found. I haven't seen it all that much in my life, but it's what I want and pray I'll find."

I stared at him, overwhelmed and terrified. He yearned to find true love? I couldn't think of a single thing to say except hallelujah, and I didn't think that was appropriate.

Dear God, it's too good to be true. He's too good to be true. But I'm going to enjoy every moment I get before he disappears.

"Come on," he said, ignoring the sudden onset of my dumbness or perhaps enjoying it. He guided me toward the car, his hand on the small of my back. "Let's eat so I can get you to the farm."

I moved into my rooms at the Zook farm that afternoon. Not that it took long when all I had with me were my suitcase, laptop, Rainbow, and her litter box.

When Todd drove me back to the Horse-and-Buggy after I met Jake and saw the farm, I thanked him prettily for telling me about Jake's rooms.

"It will be so wonderful living there," I said as we pulled up in front of my motel room.

Todd looked at me and grinned. "You're vibrating again."

"I am not."

"Vibrating," he said, nodding his head.

"I do not vibrate. I'm quiet and reserved."

"You don't know yourself very well, do you?"

"I do not vibrate."

"Just like you don't ask impertinent questions?"

"Oh, I do that. It's a Bentley curse. I just don't vibrate."

I climbed out of the car with great dignity. I took my key from my purse with ladylike grace. I lifted my hand in a slow-motion farewell.

"Phony," Todd called.

"Critic," I responded.

He threw his car in reverse, and as he looked over his shoulder to back out, I gave in to my excitement about the farm and bounced a couple of times on my toes.

"I saw that," Todd said as he straightened his car out. "Definitely vibrating."

I was grinning when I went to collect my things, and I was downright giddy when I turned in my key and left the Horse-and-Buggy.

"Wait till you see it, Rainbow," I told the unhappy animal as she lay in her travel cage. "You'll love it! Lots of yard to run in and lots of barn cats to give you a run for your money. In fact, you almost soured the deal, my friend. These farm folk aren't used to house cats. I had to promise that you'd be the best cat in the world, that you'd stay in our rooms, and that you'd use the litter box with never an accident."

"Elp!" yelled Rainbow.

"Yeah," I agreed. "Help is right, given your feeling about a litter box. Just do your best, okay?"

I loved the farmhouse. It was white with green trim and had a great front porch with a blooming wisteria climbing one end and dripping fragrant lavender orbs among the gray green leaves. A great maple tree shaded much of the front yard, and the side yard was filled with a large vegetable garden edged with cyclamen petunias.

"Their smell helps keep the rabbits out," Jake explained.

My rooms were on the second floor, and I had to walk through the Zook family's living room to get to my stairs. Jake shared the ability to get to his rooms via the living room, but he also had a separate entrance to his apartment with a ramp for his wheelchair.

My rooms weren't large, but they were airy and open. The living room had a motley collection of secondhand furniture that somehow looked just right. A large blond desk like my schoolteachers used to have sat by a window. I put my laptop on it and knew I'd enjoy sitting there to write, provided I didn't keep staring at the pastoral scene before me.

Fields of tilled brown and verdant green swept to the horizon over gentle swells of land. A white farmhouse, barn, and silo lay in the humid, hazy distance to my right, and to my left was a farm pond fed by a stream that flowed briskly from a small, dense wood. Around the pond stood several black-and-white speckled cows, but I liked best the one that stood mooing knee-deep in the water. The vegetable garden was directly below me, beans and peas scaling stakes, lettuce waving leafy fronds, carrots fluttering delicate and ferny foliation.

My bedroom had an ancient sleigh bed with a great curved head and foot and wore a beautiful handmade quilt in calico prints of royal blue, cream, and crimson. A handmade braided rug covered the floor by the bed. There was no closet in the room but rather wall pegs for my clothes. I hung my beige silk sheath on a peg beside the door to the new bathroom, which was small but complete, every surface in it a blinding white. I put Rainbow's litter box in the space between the pedestal sink and the toilet. I put her in the box several times as I unpacked my meager belongings.

"You got the idea?" I asked her as I held her in the litter, petting her and telling her how wonderful she was. She murped and jumped out, shaking her feet fastidiously to get rid of any granules caught in her pads. She stalked to the bedroom window and in that marvelous liquid motion cats have, leapt to the windowsill. She settled down to chatter through the screen at the barn swallows that dipped and soared after the late afternoon insects.

"I'm going to Haddonfield tomorrow to collect some more clothes," I told Rainbow. "Will you be all right here alone?"

She didn't deign to answer.

I thought of pictures and plants and personal things I'd bring back with me to make these rooms my own. I wondered if the Zooks would mind if I hung some curtains. I'd noticed that they didn't have any in their house. Maybe they thought curtains were worldly or something.

"Would they mind?" I asked Jake when I found him out by his van in the drive. "I'll use spring-tension rods so I don't make holes in the frames."

"What you do to your rooms is up to you," he hastened to tell me. "The family understands that my tenants will be English, and that means things like curtains and TV."

"I'm not English," I said, though come to think of it, how did I know what nationality I was?

"You're English in that you're not Pennsylvania Dutch," Jake explained. "It's a colloquialism."

"Ah. Interesting."

Jake smiled and said, "You'll learn a lot more unusual stuff—at least it'll seem unusual to you—before you're finished. I'm going to go get a hoagie for dinner. Want me to pick up one for you?"

I nodded. I wasn't all that hungry yet, but I knew I would be before the evening was over.

"Oil or mayonnaise?" he asked.

"What?"

"Oil or mayonnaise on your hoagie?"

"You can't put mayonnaise on a hoagie," I said, scandalized at the very idea.

Jake shrugged. "I do."

"Then it's not a hoagie. It's a sandwich on a long roll."

"You sound like Todd. He's an oil man, too."

Forty-five minutes later Jake and I sat at his mother's kitchen table and ate our hoagies. Jake was a dark man with heavy shoulders and a strong upper body, and an anger that radiated from him. He had a powered wheelchair that he handled with great ease.

"I met Kristie this morning," I said. "She told me how much she loved it here."

Jake nodded. "She did. She liked painting things around here."

"She's a painter? Is she any good?"

"I think so. She did a watercolor of our barn." And he pointed through the window.

I looked at the swaybacked building and frowned in thought. "Todd!" I said suddenly. "He has that picture hanging in his office."

"I wouldn't be surprised," Jake said. "Even though he used to think her painting was foolish, he came around when he saw how well she was starting to sell and when he saw how much Clarke encouraged her."

I grew thoughtful. "I wonder if he thinks writing romances is foolish."

"Is that what you do?" He looked at me as though he thought it was foolish.

I nodded. "It's great fun. I just love it."

"Have you been published?"

Since the answer was yes, I loved answering that frequently asked question. "Seven books."

"And you can make a living at it?"

"I've been blessed that I can. Most people can't."

He looked at me with an expression that said he couldn't

quite believe writing romances was an honorable way to earn a living. He wasn't alone.

"Romances are about people and relationships, love and marriage and family," I said, wanting to convince him how wonderful they could be when they weren't obsessed with the physical side of love. "They're also very big business, and inspirational romances have a strong market niche of their own. Lots of women enjoy reading them, and you can say some pretty important things in fiction."

He didn't look convinced, but he didn't pick a fight, either. Instead he asked, "Why did you decide to move to Bird-in-Hand?"

"I'm looking for my grandfather's family. He was given up for adoption a long time ago, and I want to find out where he—and the rest of us—came from."

Jake nodded as he wiped a glob of mayonnaise from the corner of his mouth. I refrained from telling him that if he used oil like he was supposed to, he wouldn't have to worry about neatness. Unless, of course, there was too much oil and the hoagie dripped.

"I see adopted people on TV who are looking for parents," he said, "and they all sound like such unhappy folks, like there's a big hole or something in their lives. Is that how you feel?"

I shook my head. "No. At least I don't think I do. If I were adopted myself, maybe I'd feel that. I don't know. I'm just curious to know about Pop. If he wasn't a Bentley, then who was he? Who are we? Do I have family out here? Pop was an only child and so was Trey, so family would be nice."

"Trey?"

"My father. And Caroline's family—that's my mother—they live so far away, they might as well not exist. Maybe there are some people my brother and I can belong to."

"So belonging's why you're doing this?"

"Part of it. There's also tracing blood ties and all that implies."

"DNA, genetics, inherited traits?"

I nodded. "That's what makes family."

Jake looked thoughtfully at his empty hoagie wrapper, then balled it and one-handed it into the trash basket beside the propane refrigerator. "I don't know about that. Take my family. There are six of us kids. Sarah's the oldest and she's Plain. Andy's next and he's not. He left over the issue of works versus grace, saying he believed in salvation by grace, not by keeping the *Ordnung*."

"What's the *Ordnung*?"

"It's the unwritten laws that govern the Amish."

"If they're unwritten, how does everyone know them?"

"You're taught them your whole life. But some, like Zeke and me, just don't want all those rules. There was nothing religious about our choice to leave the church. We chose not to remain Plain because we wanted freedom and fun and speed."

He bounced his hand on the arm of his chair. "Not that speed did me any good."

We were silent a minute. Then he continued.

"Elam and Ruth, the youngest two, have chosen to remain Amish. Now why this diversity of opinion among us when we were all taught with the same intensity and commitment from our parents? Wouldn't DNA and traits and all that tend to make us more similar rather than less, which it seems we are? How come Andy and Zeke and I got independent thinking genes and Sarah, Ruth, and Elam got cooperative ones?"

"Genetics doesn't make you completely the same. It just guarantees certain similarities."

"Yeah, but what makes family is stuff like Mom and Father taking me in and willingly dealing with all that that entails even though they don't agree with my choices. It's more love, isn't it? Like you write about in your books?"

At this point we were interrupted by the arrival of a horse and buggy in the drive. We both looked out the window as a slim woman in a royal blue dress and black apron climbed out. She wore her hair pulled straight back in a knot and had her head covered with a white *kapp*. She stopped and said something to the bearded man holding the reins. He laughed and drove to the barn.

"Mom and Father," Jake said unnecessarily. "No Elam. He's probably gone to a sing somewhere."

So I met John and Mary, and they were every bit as welcoming and delightful as Kristie had said they'd be. But I went to bed thinking about what Jake had said. *It's more love, isn't it? Like you write about in your books?*

He sounded like Ward. Certainly love was part of family; no one would argue that. But I kept coming back to Psalm 78. It was generation to generation. It was DNA and genes and bone and sinew. It was.

SIX

When I woke up Monday morning, I lay in my sleigh bed and stretched contentedly. If change could bring such wondrous things as Amish farms and families and handsome lawyers into my life, I might have to reassess my lifelong aversion to it. I felt myself tense as I thought of actually becoming flexible, but when I remembered I didn't need to achieve that goal today, my shoulders fell to their normal position.

I pushed aside the crispy white sheets that smelled of sunshine from their drying on a line and went into my new little bathroom. I decided that I'd bring some towels from home to add a little color to the utilitarian white, but it was a delight to be the first to shower in the new-smelling stall and the first to steam up the mirror and the first to drape a damp towel over the rack.

I put on tan shorts and a white T-shirt and brown sandals. I braided my hair loosely so that it might actually dry before I went to bed this evening and tied off the braid with a rubber band. It flopped back to fall below my shoulder blades. Then I went to my laptop on my desk.

I sat down, intending to pull up my Bible program and have my devotions, writing my thoughts in my electronic journal. Instead, I became mesmerized by the glorious June day outside my window. Muzzy pale sky indicated heat and humidity ahead, but the faint morning coolness made that threat toothless at the moment. I stared at the fields of tender corn plants, golden winter wheat, and tomato shoots and sniffed greedily the rich scent of dew-moistened earth.

God, you are so good to me! I typed. *Thank you, thank you!*

I opened to Psalm 78 and read it again as I hummed "Generation to Generation" under my breath.

> *He decreed statutes for Jacob*
> > *and established the law in Israel,*
> *which he commanded our forefathers*
> > *to teach their children,*
> *so the next generation would know them,*
> > *even the children yet to be born,*
> > *and they in turn would tell their children.*
> *Then they would put their trust in God*
> > *and would not forget his deeds*
> > *but would keep his commands.*

I turned to my journal again.

I want to know the missing generations in our family. I want to meet them, to find out things that I don't know, to learn family stories that are missing from our heritage. And Lord, I want to make certain the generations still living know about you.

When I finally came down for breakfast at eight o'clock, Mary insisted on cooking for me, though I knew the family had eaten hours ago. She left a huge pile of cut strawberries sitting on the counter, and in no time two eggs and toast made from her own whole wheat bread sat before me.

"Are you making strawberry jam?" I asked when she came upstairs from a trip to the basement with her arms full of small Mason jars.

She nodded, smiling. "I love this job. When I'm done, I

have this wonderful feeling that I've done something worth-while. And next winter when John and Elam enjoy the jam on their potato rusk or oatmeal bread, I'll feel pleased all over again."

I thought about my ignorance of tasks like making jam and decided that though I thought Mary was clever and conscientious, I had no desire to learn this particular art. I'd rather just eat Mary's or Smucker's.

Mary put her hand to her mouth, looking distressed. "I hope I didn't sound proud just then. I only meant that I like making jam—though I forget that sometimes in the middle of the job when I'm hot and tired."

"You didn't sound proud," I said, thinking she should meet some writers I knew if she wanted to hear proud. "You sounded like a woman who is fortunate enough to do something that gives her satisfaction."

"You don't do things you like?" she asked, looking at me carefully.

"Oh, but I do," I assured her. "I love what I do. But lots of women don't."

"A lot of women don't?" Mary was surprised by this statement. "Everyone I know is content with what they do." And she went back down to the basement at a rapid pace.

I thought about Mary's comment. I couldn't say the same thing about many of my friends, even the successful ones. And my friends were the women with a wide range of life choices, especially compared to Mary's friends. Interesting.

I rose, washed and dried my breakfast dishes, and thought about how much I was going to miss a dishwasher during my stay with the Zooks. Some modern conveniences were required for quality of life, weren't they?

I was looking out the window above the sink when Mary

reappeared with another armful of jelly jars.

"There goes Jake," I said. "First day at college. You must be proud of him."

I looked at Mary and found her watching Jake back the van from the drive. Her face reflected great misgivings and no little sorrow. She felt my glance, gave a small smile, and turned back to sorting her jars.

Mary started to speak at the same time I realized how inappropriate my comment had been, given the family's culture. Eighth grade education, I remembered. College must seem strange and frightening.

"I'm sorry," I said, but she waved me off.

"I guess I'm happy for him in one way," she finally said, filling a large pot with water and putting it on the stove to boil. "I'm glad he's making a life for himself in spite of his injury, but—" She paused and blinked rapidly. "Watching him go off to college is hard. It's just another proof that he'll never choose to come back."

I knew she meant back to the Amish community, and while my heart ached for her pain, I knew she was right.

"It's funny," she said. "John and I tried so hard to teach them right. I've never been able to figure out what we did wrong."

"Maybe you did nothing wrong," I said as I opened cupboards, looking for a place for my washed dishes. "Children all make their own choices."

"I keep telling myself that," Mary said. "But it hurts. And I know some of the people in our district sit in judgment on us. Lots of families have maybe one child who turns from the faith, but we have three." She turned and faced me. "Did you know that most Amish children are baptized and remain in the community? The world doesn't realize that, I don't think. They can't understand why a young person would choose to remain, but I can't understand why anyone would want to leave. Yet half of my children did."

I slipped my silverware into the drawer. "Jake says it's because he's too independent and so are his brothers."

"But how did they get that way?" Mary asked as she scalded the jelly jars with the now boiling water. "We taught them the virtues of obedience and submission. We told them over and over that it wasn't being an individual but being part of the community that's important."

"Have they ever told you why they left?" I leaned against the counter, taking care to be far from the strawberry juice leaking in a glorious shade of red from the pile of cut berries.

"Andy did. He was the first to leave. He became good friends with Clarke Griffin when he lived with his aunt and uncle down the street during high school. Clarke told him all about what Andy calls grace, and Andy listened. He wouldn't join the church because he said we were too 'works oriented,' whatever that means. He used to quote things to John from Martin Luther."

I thought for a minute, surprised she knew of Martin Luther. "You mean like *sola fide* or *sola scriptura?*"

"Maybe. I think. What do they mean?"

"Only faith and *only the Scriptures."*

"Not the *Ordnung,*" Mary said sadly.

"Not the *Ordnung,*" I agreed.

Mary was silent for a while, the only sounds the rapid chopping of more strawberries as she cut them in pieces so small they were almost pulp.

"But at least he believes something!" she burst out in what I later realized was a rare display of emotion. "Zeke and Jake don't believe anything. They just got rebellious. It's like they never got over their *rumschpringes,* ain't?"

101

"I guess it is," I said.

She nodded. "And Jake's so bitter most of the time. You won't believe it, but he was a happy little boy. He loved to giggle and play jokes on the rest of us. Always a smile." She mixed pectin and sugar and put them to cook, and slowly added the strawberry pieces. "Now I'd give anything for some of that joy."

I was thoughtful as I left for Haddonfield, my heart aching for Mary but understanding Jake and his brothers' need for more room to stretch. But the lovely day and the feeling of adventure about my move to Bird-in-Hand soon dispelled any pensiveness. I listened to tapes and sang along at the top of my voice, something I did only in the privacy of my car or shower.

When I got home, it didn't take me long to collect all the clothes and items I wanted to take back with me. I carefully packed the car, buckling my printer/fax in the backseat and stacking files and correspondence I thought I might need over the summer in cardboard boxes. I put my dictionary and thesaurus in a box with my printer paper and spare toner cartridge. For some reason I never quite trusted the thesaurus and dictionary in my word processing package. I think it had to do with my phobia about change, though I was all too glad I lived in an age that allowed me to change from a typewriter to a computer. Selective change?

I commandeered the small TV Pop had put in his room so he could face the nights alone after Mom died. I stuffed three sets of towels and two sets of patterned sheets in a duffel. I noticed as I put my shirts, shorts, and slacks in a suitcase that I had an inordinate amount of beige, tan, and ivory. And the dresses that I draped on top of everything were beige, too. Why could I buy colorful linens but not clothes?

You're in a rut, Cara. You need color! After all, if you vibrate—

which of course you don't—you need color. Even a yellow would be wild for you!

Just before I left, I called Marnie to tell her all about my new life.

"Cara! I don't believe you!" She was clearly shocked and delighted.

"Come and visit me," I said. "See where I live. Meet the Zooks. Meet Todd."

"Try to keep us away," she said. "We'll be there in time for dinner Friday."

"Hadn't you better check with Ward? He might be busy."

"If he is, he'll cancel. He'll be so concerned about his big sister and this lawyer who's obviously out for your money that he'll have a hard time waiting until Friday."

"Todd doesn't even know I have money. Does Ward complain about me much?"

"Only in the mornings and the evenings." Her tone of voice was both wry and affectionate.

I laughed. "Poor Marnie. I'll make dinner reservations for four and ask Todd along." If I got the nerve to give such an invitation. The thought of it made me sweat with tension and hyperventilate with possibilities all at the same time.

I got back to the farm just before dinner. Todd arrived about five minutes after I did, and he'd obviously come straight from the office. His suit jacket lay on the backseat, a light loden slash against the gray of the upholstery. His tie, a darker loden with the tiniest gold medallions I'd ever seen, hung open against his white shirt. His cordovan loafers shone beneath his cuffed slacks.

"Just checking to see how Jake's first day went," he explained, but I noticed he smiled at me as he said it. He also helped me lug everything up to my rooms.

As he set my printer on the big desk next to my laptop, he said, "You take your writing seriously, don't you?" There was a mix of surprise and uneasiness in his voice.

"It's how I make my living," I said. "I have to take it seriously."

"Romances?" He looked dubious.

"Romances. Want to read one or two?"

He looked nonplused. To give him time to deal with the idea of reading a romance, I fished in one of my boxes and pulled out copies of *As the Deer* and *So My Soul*.

"You don't have to tell anyone," I said as I held them out.

He took them somewhat reluctantly, which did little for my ego. Then he redeemed himself by suddenly asking, "You'll sign them, won't you?"

I took the books and penned a nice, generic sentiment and signature. He took the books back with a fair amount of aplomb, and I thought there was a chance he might actually read them. I knew, though, that I'd never ask if he did. I didn't want the hurt of finding out he hadn't.

We went downstairs and Mary asked Todd to stay for dinner.

"I was afraid you'd never ask," he said and took a seat next to me.

Most of dinner was a discussion of the crops and weather and people I'd never heard of. Near the end things turned to Jake's day.

"You know," he said, eyes sparkling. "I loved it. I was afraid I wouldn't be able to follow the lecture, or that I wouldn't know what they were talking about, but I did. But you won't believe the amount of reading I have to do for tomorrow! I've got to get started right after dinner."

I grinned at both his enthusiasm and his naivete. Next thing we knew, he'd actually be smiling.

John looked at his son uncertainly. "They aren't working

you too hard, are they, boy? *Himmel,* you don't want to get run down or nothing."

Jake smiled, at least with his lips. "Don't worry, Father. I'm fine."

Mary served us apple dumplings with real cream for dessert.

"Mom," Jake said. "My favorite. Thanks."

I smiled at Mary. It was obvious that while she and John didn't understand their son, they loved him. Apple dumplings were a fine, nonprideful way to show it.

Todd helped Mary and me deal with the dirty dishes, something both John and Jake thought amusing. I thought it was wonderful.

"Want to take a walk?" Todd asked after the last dish was dried.

I nodded, aware of a lightness that came over me at the invitation. I could have walked from here to Haddonfield and back.

We turned left at the end of the drive and walked along the edge of the road, the westering sun warming our backs. We didn't speak, just enjoyed the somnolent tranquillity. We watched adult purple martens flying in and out of their nests in the multistoried, apartment style purple marten house, still feeding their fast maturing birdlings. A pair of fat rabbits raced across the road ahead of us, disappearing in a patch of orange day lilies, and a crimson streak of cardinal flashed overhead. On a fence post, a mockingbird sang his patchwork melodies, one moment mewing harshly like a herring gull, the next warbling sweetly like a song sparrow or a wood thrush.

We came to the clump of woods I could see from my bedroom window and by unspoken accord turned into it. We walked through the light underbrush until we came to the stream. It burbled breathlessly over mossy rocks, forming a small, serene pool. We sat on a pair of large rocks beside the brook and watched a long-legged water bug walk on water, surface tension holding him successfully aloft.

"I think I'll drive up to Harrisburg tomorrow to visit the Bureau of Vital Statistics," I said apropos to nothing. "I'll ask for a copy of Pop's birth certificate."

"You won't get it, not even in his Bentley name," Todd said emphatically. "And they'd never give you a certificate in his birth name. Privileged information. I had to deal with the state once about a birth certificate for an adopted person who needed one for a passport. He was an older man who was adopted long before the state automatically issued new certificates in the adoptive name. We wrote letters, went to Harrisburg, practically got down on our hands and knees and begged before they would grant him the proper certificate, *cera impressa*. And that was for a certificate in the person's adoptive name. And he had a sister who could swear to who he was."

"I can swear to who Pop was."

"But you're hardly a contemporary who can swear to his arrival, etc. We had the man's birth name, the date of birth, even the name of the delivering doctor, though the doctor was dead by the time the man sought the papers. It still took us forever."

I frowned. I hated roadblocks in my plans.

"Besides—"

I could tell this was Todd's culminating argument by the way he leaned into his comment. I imagined him leaning into a jury just this way.

"Besides, why would they give you a birth certificate for a dead man?"

I grimaced. He was making a very good point.

"I won't tell them he's dead."

Todd grinned at me and shook his head. "And when they ask why you're there instead of him?"

"Maybe they won't ask."

He leaned back, resting his weight on his outstretched arms. "I wish I could say you had a good plan here, Cara, but you don't. My advice as your attorney is don't waste your time and gas."

I stared at the pool, brooding, my arms around my drawn-up knees, my braid hanging forward over my shoulder.

"Don't look so discouraged," Todd said. "You've got your meeting Thursday with Alma Stoltzfus."

I nodded. I was looking forward to that meeting, but I still hated being foiled in what had seemed a good plan.

"Now I've got a nonbusiness question for you." He leaned forward until his head was even with mine.

I turned and looked at him expectantly.

"How'd you like to go to a formal garden party Saturday evening?"

I stared. "With you?"

"Of course with me. Do you think I'm into setting you up with other men?"

I grinned sheepishly. "Sorry. I'm just not used to invitations to formal garden parties from my attorney, I guess. If you knew Mr. Havens, you'd understand."

"I usually don't enjoy going to these things because I'm not a great chitchat person, but if you'll go with me, it might actually be fun."

Be still my beating heart. "What's the occasion?"

"Each year the president of the Lancaster County Bar has a bench/bar reception, and this year it's at The Paddock with outdoor dining and lots of schmoozing."

"And it's formal? Truly formal?"

Todd nodded. "I'll be pulling my tux out of mothballs. And The Paddock is a beautiful home. I think you'll enjoy the evening."

I had no doubt whatsoever. "I promise not to wear beige."

He laughed. "I don't mind, honest. Like I said, it's restful."

Boring, I thought. I took a deep, empowering breath. "Now I've got an opportunity for you. My brother and sister-in-law are coming up Friday evening to see my new surroundings. Would you like to go to dinner with us?"

He looked startled but pleased at the invitation. "Sure. Sounds nice."

We wandered slowly out of the woods and back down the road. The sun was now hiding behind some clouds low on the horizon, and prisms of refracted light turned the sky fuchsia and orange and fierce purple. I loved the deep, rich silence and the fact that Todd seemed as easy with it as I.

It was a rude jolt to hear a car speeding down the road behind us, followed by the short burst of a siren as it neared us. We stepped to the side of the road as an ambulance rushed past. As always, I wondered where it was going and who the needy person might be at the end of its journey. I breathed a quick prayer.

I was floored when the ambulance slowed and turned into the Zook drive. Todd and I looked at each other, fear and uncertainty on both our faces.

"Jake!" Todd said, and we began to run.

But it wasn't Jake. It was Mary. She had taken the basement stairs too quickly in the fading light, jars of cooled jelly in her arms, and she'd tumbled to the bottom.

When we reached the house, the emergency medical technicians were already inside checking her as she lay half on the floor, half on the stairs, her right leg twisted around the upright that supported the railing. There was blood all over the place.

"She cut herself on broken glass," Jake said when he heard my gasp.

He sat in his chair at the top of the basement stairs, staring down, and John and Elam stood at the foot of the stairs watching, their faces pale and frightened.

Mary herself was in severe pain and trying not to show it too much. She did fairly well, probably much better than I ever would have done, as they worked on her.

"Breathing's okay," said a curly-haired young woman with glasses. "Her lungs are clear. Blood pressure's okay, too. There's no bleeding in the ear. The bleeding is external."

"Her pupils are equal," said the second EMT, a short, stocky man, busy applying pressure to a large gash in Mary's right thigh. "Hand me some pads and a couple of cling bandages."

"I missed my step," Mary whispered. "I was almost to the bottom, but I missed."

The girl nodded. "And your arms were full, so you couldn't protect yourself."

"I fell on the jars. That's why the bleeding."

Quickly the EMTs stanched the hemorrhaging.

"I don't think we need advanced life support," said the girl. "Certainly not the medevac helicopter."

"Let's just immobilize the leg," said her partner, "and get a KED around her back."

Working with speed and care, the EMTs padded Mary's broken leg with blanket rolls and wrapped it to hold the rolls securely.

"We want to protect this leg, Mary," said the girl. "But we don't want to try to straighten it. That's what this wrapping is all about. And we're going to put a KED splint on you to protect your back. A fall down the stairs is always a potentially dangerous thing."

"But I only fell three or four steps." Mary repeated in her weak voice.

"We can't take a risk here with spinal or cervical injury."

In a few minutes Mary was wrapped in a splint that went from her head to her hips, closed with Velcro straps all down the front. Then the EMTs transferred her to a rigid backboard.

The male EMT positioned himself at Mary's feet, the girl at her head.

"On three," she said. "One, two, three." And they lifted the backboard.

The girl began to ascend the stairs. Todd moved quickly to descend and grasp the board and help her with the weight. Elam stepped up to help at Mary's feet. I held the front door, and in no time, Mary was in the ambulance.

Jake had followed us outside by way of a detour into his apartment to use his ramp. His face was closed and dark, and when he turned to his father and brother and spoke, his voice was harsh.

"Come on. We'll follow her to the hospital."

John and Elam nodded and trailed him to his van, looking back at the ambulance as if they wanted to do something more for Mary. Jake kept his eyes straight ahead and his shoulders rigid. I thought he was struggling to hold himself together, and not just because his mother was badly hurt.

He hadn't been able to help. When it was time to carry her, he had to sit helplessly as others lifted her. He'd had to watch Todd, a friend, and me, a veritable stranger, assist his mother while he, her son, was forced to endure being useless. He'd had to turn away and roll into his rooms so he could use his ramp. He'd had to discover yet another searing limitation of his injury.

I think my heart ached for him more than for Mary.

As soon as Jake was out of sight, the young woman EMT approached me. She kept glancing over her shoulder after Jake.

"Excuse me," she said very softly. "Can you tell me his name? The guy in the wheelchair?"

"Jake Zook."

A secret smile swept across her face. She doubled her fist, pumped it discreetly, and said softly, "Yes!"

I watched her, intrigued. "Do you know him?"

"Yes," she said as she turned to the ambulance. "But not really."

Now there was a clear answer if I ever heard one.

The other EMT leaned out of the back door of the ambulance.

"Come on, Rose," he called impatiently. "You're holding us up!"

On Wednesday afternoon I went to Todd's office for my appointment. Mrs. Smiley was just as moved by my presence this time as she had been last week.

"Hello, Mrs. Smiley," I said with great gusto. "It's good to see you again, too. And I love your brown dress. It just matches your brown shoes. But aren't long sleeves a bit warm?"

I got no response beyond a look that would curdle milk, but then I didn't expect any, especially in the face of my phony jocularity.

"Miss Bentley, please have a seat." Her voice was cool and correct, and she gestured to the paisley chairs with a beautifully manicured hand. I noticed her nails were bright red today with the ring finger of each hand sporting a white diagonal stripe on the scarlet enamel. I didn't know who did her nails, but she clearly knew how to reach that hidden, repressed part of Mrs. Smiley that I could only guess at.

After ignoring me for a few minutes, Mrs. Smiley rose from her chair and nodded briefly at me. "This way, Miss Bentley. Mr. Reasoner will see you now."

How did she know he'd see me now, at this precise moment? I hadn't heard her call him. I hadn't heard him contact her. Maybe in her other, wild fingernail life, Mrs. Smiley was a spy, and the office was full of electronic gadgets that allowed her to snoop on Todd, clearly a man dangerous to the U.S. government if ever I'd seen one. I smiled at the receptionist, imagining her karate-kicking a villain from here to Paradise.

When I entered his office, Todd rose from behind his massive desk with alacrity, his hand extended in welcome. He showed me to the cozy alcove beneath Kristie's paintings and took a seat beside me on the sofa.

Mrs. Smiley signaled disapproval of me by a slight sniff as she closed the door.

"I don't think she likes me," I said.

He grinned. "She just likes playing mother hen and protecting me from predatory females."

"Ahh," I said and grinned back. I couldn't help grinning around him. He made me feel bubbly. Me, reserved, introverted Cara.

"So how's Mary?" he asked. "Is she still in as much pain?"

"She's still in the hospital, but she's going to be okay. I stopped in for a few minutes earlier today. She has that broken right leg and a couple of good gashes from broken jelly jars, especially one on her right hip and leg and one on her right forearm. But the break is clean. It will heal without complications, they say. She'll be home in a few days, and the home health nurse will come to deal with the cuts. They're pretty nasty, and one's gotten infected."

"How are they managing at the farm? Are you cooking?"

"On that wood stove? Are you kidding?"

He folded his hands across his stomach. "It is pretty intimidating, I imagine."

"Understatement." I shuddered at the thought of tackling it. "No, they've got a *maud.*"

"A *maud?*"

"A maid. A single woman from their church, Esther Yoder, has moved in for the duration. She's living in Ruth's old room. She's this cute little thing about nineteen years old with big dark eyes and rosy cheeks, and I notice that her eyes follow Elam more than casually."

"Watch it, romance writer. You're hatching a plot here."

I shook my head. "If I wanted to hatch a plot, I'd go after that EMT who knows but doesn't know Jake. Did you see how pleased she was when I told her his name? What do you think that was all about?"

"I'm supposed to know the answer to that?" Todd asked.

"Sure. I'm paying you to know all the answers, or at least to find them."

"Well," he said, settling back against his end of the sofa as if he'd finally found a topic of discussion he was comfortable with. "I've done some checking around and have come up with some suggestions for you on trying to find your grandfather's background."

I leaned forward eagerly. "So tell me."

"First, it'd be a good idea to go to the agency he was adopted through and ask them if they'll open his records. They'll probably say no, not without the assent of the Biemsderfers. They should then be willing to try to trace any family and ask on your behalf if they'll agree to opening the records."

I nodded. "I thought of that. I went to the library yesterday, and the research librarian and I spent some time trying to trace the Children's Home Society of the City of Lancaster: For the Relief of the Poor and the Care of Destitute Children."

The long title rolled off my tongue. It'd never make it in today's world of acronyms, but it sounded solid and slightly stuffy and very proper to me, very 1917, like men in neckties and vests and bowlers and ladies with gowns to the floor and gloves and large-brimmed hats.

"We found that the agency headquarters burned to the ground in 1926, and all records were lost. There's no hope of any information there."

"Oh." Todd looked slightly nonplused, though I wasn't certain if it was at my wealth of information or at the fact that I'd beaten him to the idea.

"When I learned there was no help to be had there," I continued, "I went to Harrisburg to the Bureau of Vital Statistics yesterday afternoon and talked to them."

"I told you that would be a useless trip." He was somewhat abrupt in his comment. "I told you not to waste your time."

I nodded. "You were absolutely right. But I had to try, you know."

"Why?" he asked. "My word wasn't good enough?"

"It's called double-checking."

"You think I don't double-check everything, Cara?"

"I'm sure you do," I said to soothe his ruffled feathers, though why they should be ruffled was beyond me.

He cleared his throat, trying to keep his pique controlled. "There's another very slim possibility, but you could check the papers for a birth announcement. I don't imagine there would be one, given that this is probably an illegitimate birth, but..." He shrugged.

"I thought of that, too," I said. "I went to the Lancaster Newspapers, Inc. offices today and spent some time with the researcher in the morgue. There's not a Biemsderfer mentioned in the paper from 1917 to 1919. In 1920 a Dwayne Biemsderfer married a Rebecca Crum. But I need a birth announcement, not a wedding announcement. And I need a female Biemsderfer, not a male."

Todd sat still, staring at me with unblinking eyes. I immediately had to blink like crazy. I looked away, my eyelids fluttering up and down like aspen leaves in the wind.

"Next I went to visit Orphan's Court to see if they could help me." I turned to him accusingly, blinking forgotten. "Did you know that Orphan's Court has nothing to do with orphans and adoptions? It has to do with probate issues and estates. Why in the world don't they just call it Probate Court or Estate Court? It would save innocent people lots of confusion. By the way, Lancaster has a very nice courthouse. I was impressed."

I smiled and sat primly, my bone sandals neatly side by side. Mrs. Smiley would have been proud had she seen me. I hoped Todd noticed that my cream pants outfit had a tiny coral flower pattern through it. Not all beige today, though certainly not full of pizzazz.

Todd's fingers, still folded over his stomach, were tapping, tapping. His face was carefully devoid of emotion. Completely gone was the pleasure he'd shown when I first arrived.

"May I ask you a question?" he said in a deadly quiet voice.

"Sure."

"Why did you bother to hire me?"

"For your legal advice."

"Which you've either ignored or not waited to hear."

"You're mad because I went to Harrisburg."

"I did not say that."

"You didn't need to. It shows."

"Hmph."

"You're really used to people doing exactly what you say, aren't you?"

"I did not say that, either."

It was my turn to say, "Hmph."

"Cara, if you're going to run off here, there, and everywhere all on your own, you don't need a lawyer."

"In other words, you don't want to be my lawyer anymore?"

"I did not say that."

"You aren't saying much of anything, are you?"

We stared at each other, eyes snapping, jaws set. While my eyes were a good match for his at snapping, my jaw was no match at setting.

"You really like to be in charge, don't you?" I said coolly.

"That's what I'm hired for," he said. "Because I'm the authority."

"So you say."

"If you want to talk about people who like control, you might just want to look at yourself," he suggested in an icy voice.

"I'm only doing what I do every time I write a book," I said. "I'm researching. We romance writers pride ourselves in our research skills."

He ran one hand through his hair, and the curls on the left side of his head leaped to disarrayed life. With his other hand he straightened his already straight tie. I could tell he was struggling for a calmness he didn't feel.

There was a gentle ping from his desk, and Todd spun toward it. "My next client is here," he said.

So that's how she did it. I rose. "Fine."

We walked stiffly to the door. He reached to open it for me.

"What time will you be picking me up Friday night for dinner with Ward and Marnie?" I asked, my voice neutral.

He started. "You still want me to come?"

I blinked. "Of course. Why not?"

"But we just had a fight."

I almost laughed. "You think that was a fight? That was just a good, old-fashioned clearing of the air."

"It was?"

"If you want to talk fight, you should have seen Mom and Pop when they had one of their rare disagreements. Those were real fights." I smiled at Todd. "We had a mere clashing of wills."

He looked at me thoughtfully. "Cultural divergence due to family background."

"Seems like it."

"A great gulf fixed? Or is there a sturdy bridge we can cross?"

I squeezed his hand, which somehow I found myself holding. "We'll find one."

He squeezed back. "Or build one."

We were staring at each other when Mrs. Smiley opened the door and snorted her disapproval.

SEVEN

I liked Alma Stoltzfus immediately. She was just the kind of woman I always wanted for an aunt. She laughed easily, talked readily, and seemed genuinely interested in helping me. If she didn't have the information I needed, she would do her best to help me find it.

Her brown eyes snapped and her expressive face showed a keen intelligence. She had legs to die for under a slightly plump, chesty body, and like Pop and Ward, she seemed unable to talk without using her hands. They sliced through the air in whorls and lines and circles, pointing, underlining, explaining. She was hard-pressed to get her spoon full of Tuscany potato soup to her mouth without waving it and losing its contents en route.

While we ate lunch, I told her about Pop and Mom, my family, and my writing. She told me about her husband, Art, and their children, Art, Jr. called Bub, Suzanne called Sissy, and the twins Theodore called Ned and Theodora called Dolly.

"I don't know why we named the kids one thing and called them another. I'm sure it says something about Art and me, but I haven't the vaguest idea what, and I frankly don't care. All I care is that Bub and Sissy have given me four of the cutest grandkids you ever saw, three from Bub and one so far from Sissy. When the twins finally get married, I expect several more, oh, lucky me. Believe me, Cara, there's nothing like grandkids." She pulled out a passel of pictures.

Nodding and looking, I felt a zip of pain that there was no

one I could ever give grandchildren to.

Finally I finished my pasta fagioli and salad and Alma her lunch, and we got down to the purpose of our visit. We pushed everything to one corner of the table and unrolled a large chart. Lines and brackets were laced with names and dates, beginning with a single name in 1821, Karl Biemsderfer, and getting progressively more dense and complex as the years passed.

"You can see this goes back several generations," she said, indicating the upper reaches of the chart. "But your point of interest begins with this generation—my grandfather's."

I looked where she pointed and read *Dwayne Biemsderfer m. Rebecca Crum.*

"I found their wedding announcement in the newspaper archives," I said. "I was looking for Biemsderfer birth announcements and found this instead."

"Old Dwayne was quite the looker," Alma said. "I've seen sepia photos of him and Rebecca. Even in those formal pictures, he looks very handsome. I can't say much about Rebecca though. The severe hairstyle of the day didn't do much for her."

"Maybe she had personality," I suggested.

"That's a kind thought," Alma said. She shrugged. "I don't remember Dwayne and Rebecca well enough to comment. They died when I was pretty young." She tapped another set of lines. "Now here's Dwayne's brother, Harold, who married Julia Miller and had five children, all my father's cousins. There are lots of people for you to trace in this branch of the family, but it will be more difficult and time-consuming because most of them have moved from Lancaster County. They're literally all over the world because several of them are missionaries."

I stared at Harold's name and the list of descendants that trailed from it. If I had to try and locate all those people, I'd be forever solving Pop's mystery. Of course, I could have the pleasure of traveling all over the world. Just think how much fun I have had since coming here, just an hour and a half from home!

"And here," Alma said, finger snapping against the chart, "is the baby of the family and the apple of everyone's eye, at least according to Grandfather Dwayne and my father. Here's Madeleine Biemsderfer who married Enos Lehman."

"What?" I stared at the paper, goose bumps on my arms. I reached out and put my finger on the name as though that would make it more real. "Enos Lehman? As in Lehman Biemsderfer?"

It couldn't be coincidence, could it? *Dear Lord, don't let it be just coincidence!*

Alma looked at me speculatively. "I knew you'd jump at that name, so I checked carefully. They married in 1920, well after Lehman Biemsderfer was born. And their children are listed here. Elizabeth who married Harlan Yost and Joshua who married Kay Proust."

"Of course Pop wouldn't be listed even if he were Madeleine's son." I put my hand to my chest over my rapidly palpitating heart, patting my fingers against my upper rib cage, trying to tamp down my excitement. "Children born on the wrong side of the blanket don't make family trees."

"True," Alma granted, her fingers rubbing over Madeleine's name, freeing the paper of nonexistent wrinkles.

"I need to know more about Madeleine," I said as much to myself as to Alma. "I need to know more about Enos."

"You need to speak with Aunt Lizzie. She can tell you as much as anyone about her parents."

"Aunt Lizzie is Madeleine and Enos's Elizabeth? Aunt Lizzie, the genealogist?"

Alma smiled. "Don't get too hopeful, Cara. The repeating of

the name Lehman doesn't have to mean a thing. And it certainly doesn't prove a thing."

I nodded. "I know." But it did. I knew it did. I felt it in my bones.

"Tell me about Madeleine's line of the family," I said. "What do you know of her parents?"

Alma traced her finger back a generation to Joshua and Lottie Biemsderfer. She tapped their names for a few minutes while I waited, trying to curb my impatience.

"Lottie was supposed to be a kind woman, and her pictures indicate she was quite lovely, made for the old-fashioned gowns and hairstyles. Joshua, on the other hand, was a stern man, the product of a strict German family, when *strict* meant rigid and unyielding. That he married the charming Lottie is amazing. I have some letters that he wrote to her when he went west for a time, trying to determine if he'd seek his fortune as a rancher. If he was intimidating in person, and everyone seems to agree that he was, on paper he was a true romantic. The letters are beautiful and full of genuine passion. She drew him back, the flame attracting the smitten moth, and he returned to claim her as his bride and settle here. They were married for fifty years before he died, a truly long marriage for those days.

"Family legend has it that he was besotted with daughter Madeleine because she was so like Lottie. He pampered her and loved her, but instead of growing up spoiled, she grew up as charming as her mother. If Madeleine was your great-grandmother, the pregnancy must have broken Joshua's heart. And his background, that old rigidity, and the mores of the day must have made it impossible to allow knowledge of the pregnancy to be public."

I sat mesmerized as Alma talked about these people who may have been my ancestors, my family, every bit as much as

122

they were hers. I kept swallowing, trying to control the teeming adrenaline attacking my stomach.

"Oh, Alma," I said, almost breathless with the speculation,
"what if Madeleine had Pop before she and Enos married?
What if Joshua didn't approve of them as a couple, and they
decided to take things into their own hands?"

Alma looked at me with kind, intelligent eyes. I knew she'd
already thought of several possible scenarios of her own.

"What if," I said, "he was marching off to war? After all, Pop
was born in the middle of this country's involvement in World
War I. It could have been one of those I-might-never-see-you-
again things, you know?"

"I've thought of that," Alma said. "It's definitely a possibility.
The other thing that was happening historically was the
influenza epidemic in which thousands of people died. I've
wondered if that somehow played into this situation, though I
haven't figured out how."

I had a scenario immediately. "Maybe Enos had a brother
who was Madeleine's first love, and he died of the flu before
they could marry." I could see the pathos of the scene as clearly
as if I were writing it—which was sometimes more clearly than
if I witnessed it. "Then she had to give away her baby, her only
real link to her true love. Enos, devastated by the death of his
brother, came alongside Madeleine to comfort her at the loss of
both her love and her child, and she fell deeply in love with
him. Happy ending."

"I can see why you're a successful novelist," Alma said,
laughing gently at my excitement. She handed me my glass of
watered-down Coke. "Take a drink, my dear."

I blushed, but I didn't back down on my imagined plots for
Madeleine. I wanted desperately for my great-grandmother to
have been happy. "I must visit Great-aunt Lizzie, I think."

Alma nodded. "She lives at Tel Hai Retirement Community in Honey Brook. I'll call her and tell her you'd like to visit. Then I'll call you and tell you what she says." She turned concerned eyes to me. "I don't think you should just show up, you understand. Aunt Lizzie is old and frail and has a bad heart."

I nodded. "I certainly don't want to give her a coronary."

Then I looked at Alma, my heart on my sleeve. She stared for a moment, trying to understand my expression. Then she nodded and pulled a cell phone from her purse.

I grinned happily as she dialed. Not wanting to seem too impolite in spite of the fact that I listened with clenched nerves to her entire conversation, I busied myself rolling up her marvelous chart.

Alma put her hand over the phone and said, "She'll see you any night but Friday."

"How about tonight?" I fluttered my hand over my heart. Nothing like being pushy.

Alma hung up and looked at me.

"Well?" I prompted. My lungs seemed unable to pull in air for the great paralysis that had taken possession of them.

Alma smiled at me. "Tonight about seven."

Air whooshed out as I recovered my ability to breathe again. "Thank you, thank you, thank you. You have no idea what this means to me."

She patted my hand. "I wish you well. And—" She paused and studied me. "I think I'd enjoy being your aunt or second cousin once removed or whatever it is we'd be to one another." She held the rolled document out to me.

I stared from it to her with shining eyes, stunned by her comment, suffused with affection for her and all the others I hadn't yet met. I reached for the family tree. "For me?"

"For you." She patted my hand again as I reached to take it.

"Just be careful, Cara. I don't want you to build too many castles in the clouds and then get hurt."

I nodded. I understood her concern though I wasn't certain I could prevent the castle building.

"You don't mind if I pray for you, do you?" Alma asked. "For God's leading and protection over you?"

"Not in the least. I've been praying about this search ever since I learned there was something to search for. I've even been praying that I'd find a family that prayed."

"Well," she said, "some of us pray anyway."

"The missionaries," I said.

"And a few others of us."

We walked out of the restaurant side by side, an easy camaraderie between us.

God, I want her to be my aunt or whatever she'd be. God, can't she be my aunt? Please?

When Alma stopped beside her car, I stopped with her.

She reached to give me a quick hug. "Let me know what you find out, even if we aren't the right family, okay?"

I nodded and stood watching as she drove away. Then I climbed into my car, putting the family tree—my family tree?—carefully on the passenger seat. My stomach was still teeming and my heart was still beating hard, but I was so encouraged. I knew I was on the right track. I couldn't wait to tell Todd. And Ward and Marnie, I thought belatedly.

I drove across the street from the Olive Garden to Park City Mall and went shopping for a dress suitable for a formal garden party. It didn't take long to realize that everything I was attracted to was beige, tan, cream, or champagne. My favorite dress was a soft cream silk that looked great on me, but I wouldn't allow myself to buy it. I finally settled on a coral column dress that fell from my shoulders to my ankles, skimming my body lightly

125

as it passed. I bought new dress sandals in black patent, not bone or taupe, and earrings of gold and coral that swayed and twisted below my ears. No little gold buttons for this night. I decided that I would carry the beautiful cream shawl that Pop and Mom had given me for my twenty-fifth birthday. Surely cream was okay for a shawl.

As I was leaving the store with my wild purchases, I passed the men's department. I wandered over to the ties and studied them. A wide splash of tans, browns, corals, and crimsons caught my eye. I thought of the monochromatic outfits Todd wore and the ties with the tiniest of patterns. I grabbed the wild one and bought it before I could change my mind. If I had to get rid of beige, he had to get rid of overly buttoned down. It was only fair.

As I drove toward home, I decided I couldn't wait until evening to tell Todd about my time with Alma. I grabbed my cell phone from my bag and dialed his office.

"Mrs. Smiley, this is Cara Bentley. May I speak to Todd, please? That is, if he's not with a client."

With a click of the tongue, Mrs. Smiley put me through.

"Cara, what's up?" Todd's voice was rich and vital, and I thought I'd rarely heard a more pleasant sound.

"I met with Alma Stoltzfus. And—"

"And you're vibrating," he interrupted.

"I am not."

He laughed. "Where are you calling from?"

"On 340. I just got off the 30 Bypass."

"Stop in and tell me what happened. It'd be much better in person."

"I'm not interrupting anything important?"

"I don't see another client for about an hour."

I was still grinning when I pulled into the parking area

behind his office. It was strange and wonderful that though I only knew one person in Bird-in-Hand and he was male, I not only felt free to call him, but he actually asked me to stop in to his office on a nonappointment basis.

It was obvious, though, that Mrs. Smiley didn't share my elation at the unscheduled visit.

"Miss Bentley, Mr. Reasoner doesn't receive visitors while at work," she informed me. "Only clients."

"I'm a client. Remember? Just tell him I'm here, okay?"

"Mr. Reasoner," she said as she unhappily ushered me into the office, "you must tell me when you change your schedule. How am I to keep the office running smoothly if I don't know your plans?"

"*Mea culpa*, Mrs. Smiley," he said, trying to look properly contrite. The fact that I was standing behind her smiling broadly at his groveling efforts didn't help his attempt to look apologetic. I wiggled my index finger back and forth at him, a silent reprimand.

When we were finally seated side by side on the alcove sofa, I opened the family tree that Alma had given me. I felt like an ancient Christian unrolling a letter from the apostle Paul, looking for and finding clues to a new life.

"Todd, I've got to tell you! I think I've found my family!"

Todd's mouth quirked in that half smile, and he shook his head. "You're definitely vibrating, woman."

I looked at him, exasperated. "I am not."

He raised an eyebrow.

My hand tapped against my collarbone and I relented a bit. "Okay, so maybe I'm excited."

"Vibrating and no maybe about it."

"Excited," I said with deliberation.

"Can't face the truth, can you?"

"Can't leave well enough alone, can you?"

We grinned at each other and kept staring long after the grins died away. His brown eyes captured mine, and I was trapped in their warmth just like a heroine in one of my novels. It was a ridiculous, wonderful moment.

Todd broke first, clearing his throat and saying, "So tell me all about it."

I blinked. "Right." And I showed him Madeleine who married Enos Lehman.

"Lehman, Todd! Lehman!" My finger trembled just a bit as it pointed out the name. "Just like Pop."

"But don't forget that Lehman is a relatively common name around this area." He bent forward over the chart, studying it seriously, giving the moment its due. "Just because your grandfather was called Lehman doesn't mean he's connected to Enos Lehman. Besides, when was your Pop born?"

"1917."

"And when were Madeleine and Enos married?"

"1920."

"Bit of a time discrepancy there. Isn't three years after the event a long time before a marriage between the principals would take place?"

I frowned at him. "I don't know. Maybe all it means is that we don't have the right explanation yet."

"Maybe." He looked at me carefully. "But Cara, it could mean a lot more than that." His voice was soft, but the point was hard. I knew he meant there could be no connection.

"Spoilsport," I said unhappily.

"Cara, look at me."

I tore my eyes from the family tree, my family tree. It had to be!

"Cara, don't set yourself up for disappointment by believing so strongly with so little information."

"Advice from my lawyer?"

"Advice from someone who cares, who also happens to be your attorney."

We sat quietly for a couple of minutes while I tried to deal with my conflicting emotions. I knew he was right when he said I was jumping ahead without any proof. I knew he was right when he said I was setting myself up to be hurt. I knew he was right when he said I didn't have enough information.

But I didn't want him to be right! I wanted God to answer my prayer and make these people mine. I wanted Alma to be my aunt. I wanted to be a Biemsderfer! The passion with which I wanted these things was unreasonable. I knew it. The need I felt was all out of proportion, and I knew that too. But the yearning remained, filling my mind and heart with a craving of extraordinary intensity.

While I sat and lectured myself, Todd continued over the chart, studying it with deep concentration. He followed the lines of descent from Madeleine and Enos down through the present time. Suddenly he tapped his finger against a name.

"I know an Amos Yost," Todd said. He was pointing to Amos Yost, son of Elizabeth Lehman Yost, daughter of Madeleine and Enos Lehman.

I turned, my eyes suddenly hopeful. "Will you introduce me to him? He would be Pop's nephew, my father's first cousin."

Todd was silent for a few seconds. "There are probably lots of Amos Yosts," he finally said. "Both Amos and Yost are common Dutch names."

"Yeah, but—"

"Yeah, but nothing," Todd said. "The truth is that I don't want this Amos to be yours. I don't like the man all that much."

"Then let me meet him so I can cross him off my list. He does live around here?"

"He lives around here."

"Come on, Todd." I wasn't quite begging, but I was very close to whining.

He cocked his head. "Let me think about it."

"Todd!"

"That's the best you're going to get for now."

And I could see that it was. But I knew I could talk him into introducing Amos and me, given time. After all, I always got what I wanted out of Pop, didn't I? I decided to take a slightly different tack.

"Do you remember when you were a kid—"

"I try not to," he said wryly.

I refused to be sidetracked. "Now listen to me and don't interrupt." I spoke the way a teacher might to her favorite ADD student.

Todd raised an eyebrow. "Bossy."

"Absolutely," I said. "Just ask Ward. Now, do you remember when you were a kid and you were going to do something very special and you got this agitated, uncomfortable feeling in your stomach? How it suddenly felt too full, almost sick?" I rested my palm on my chest and flapped my fingers up and down against my sternum. "Your heart got all fluttery and your chest got tight, like something was unfurling inside and forcing the oxygen out?"

He looked at me with an intensity that swirled about the room, a blazing energy that was directed at me. "I've gotten those feelings a lot."

He was not referring to any childhood experience. I knew that with certainty. Suddenly struck by the upset stomach, the fluttery heart, and the tight chest, I swallowed and tore my eyes from his penetrating gaze. I pointed a shaky finger at the family tree.

"That's how—" and my voice broke. I cleared my throat and swallowed again. "That's how I feel every time I learn information that might have something to do with Pop. I was proud that my voice barely shook though my insides trembled.

"Is that the only time?" he asked quietly.

"The only time?" I stared intently at the family tree.

"You feel that special way?"

I blinked. Did he mean what I thought he meant? "What?"

Todd stared at me a minute longer; I could feel it. Then he abruptly shook his head. "Forget I said that."

As if I could.

He took my hand. "Listen to me, Cara. Please." His voice was now entirely different, friendly, nothing more. Lawyer to client. "I'm worried about you. You're so intense about this search."

I took a deep breath to calm myself and turned my thoughts as he had turned his. How could I make him understand? "All I want to do is find the people who are bone of my bone and flesh of my flesh. I have no family but Ward." My throat closed and I had to swallow once more, this time against the pain. "I want more."

"I have no family but my father," he said quietly. "Oh, I have some distant cousins on my mother's side that I see every couple of years at a family reunion, but in reality all I have is my father. It doesn't make any difference whether I want more or not."

I stared at him, struck dumb. His loneliness was palpable, and my heart broke for the child he'd been and the man he'd become, alone, hurting, solitary. I pulled my hand free from his and quickly began rolling the family tree.

"I'm so sorry," I whispered. "I didn't mean for my selfish search to make you feel bad." I looked at him through a sheen of tears. "I never thought that I might be hurting you."

Todd pulled my hands from the chart and said, "Cara! That's not what I meant."

I shook my head, staring at my lap. Ward and Marnie had warned me about possible problems as I searched, but I'd never imagined one like this, one that hurt someone I was learning to care for, someone who could never find any "bone of my bone" to love him.

His voice was gentle. "Cara, look at me."

I couldn't; I wouldn't. I was embarrassed for my insensitivity.

He took my chin and lifted it, forcing my eyes up.

"You misapprehend," he said softly when my eyes finally met his. "I'm not worried about my lack of family. I'm worried about you. What will happen to you, in you, if all you have are Ward and Marnie? if none of this pans out?" He flicked a hand toward the chart. "I don't want to see you disillusioned and frustrated by what you don't have, when you've had so much, when you have so much. You've got love and support and people who care. Can't you let that be enough?"

"Oh, Todd." I reached out and rested my hand along the line of his jaw. I felt the hard strength of bone and the soft warmth of skin, a mixture much like what I saw in the man himself. Tough yet tender. "I'll be all right. I will. With you helping me, how can I be anything else?"

He studied me intently for another moment, then nodded his head as if accepting my comments.

With his nod, I suddenly felt awkward with my hand on his face in what I now saw as an unsuitably intimate gesture. I dropped it hastily to my lap and cast about for something to talk about to release the fizz of electricity in the atmosphere.

My eyes fell on my purse lying on the floor by the sofa and the flat package lying beside it.

"Oh," I said brightly, "I brought you a present."

He looked absolutely surprised, and I wondered when was the last time someone had bought him a gift. He took the flat box, its contents immediately obvious by its shape.

"Is this what I think it is?" he asked.

"Probably."

"You don't like this one?" And he fingered his tan tie with the thin, thin brown stripe.

"It's not that I don't like it. It's just that you tend to the monochromatic, and I'm offering a change."

"You, Miss Beige, are criticizing my wardrobe?" The smile took away any hint of reprimand.

"It's easier to do you than myself."

With an intensely cautious expression, Todd opened the box. When he saw the wild splashes of color lying within, the caution turned to incredulity.

"You actually expect me to wear this?"

I nodded. "You wouldn't want to hurt my feelings, would you?"

"Don't pout at me. I know manipulation when I see it."

"And I know a buttoned-down personality when I see one. Take that tan thing off."

He put a protecting hand over his tie. "Now?" He sounded like I'd asked him to strip in front of the ladies' missionary society.

"Now." I lifted an eyebrow and stared, daring him to be brave.

Slowly his hand went to his throat, and with a deep sigh, he loosened the knot and removed the tie. I lifted the new tie and held it out to him.

"How nice you wore your tan suit today." I beamed. "Just as though you knew to come prepared."

He rose and walked to the closed door to his washroom. He opened it, turned on the light, and stood in front of the mirror.

"Go on," I encouraged. "You can do it. If Mrs. Smiley can have wild nails, you can have a wild tie."

He looked daggers at me over his shoulder, but he slid the tie under his collar and began the ritual of making a Windsor knot. As he did that, I folded his old tie and slid it into the empty box.

He was looking at himself in the mirror, paralyzed at the rakish sight, when the buzzer on his desk announced his next appointment. He spun around, his tie fluttering with the abruptness of the move.

"Where's my real tie?" he asked, eyes searching the table where he'd dropped it.

I looked at the table, then at him with an innocent expression. "Looks to me like you're wearing the only tie I see. It looks very handsome."

And it did. The rich colors made the crisp, deep brown of his hair and eyes even more arresting. He, however, seemed to disagree.

"Cara." His voice was low and threatening.

"Want to take a trip to Tel Hai tonight to meet Great-aunt Lizzie?" I said, heading for the door with my purse and the tie box with its contraband contents clutched to my chest. "I'd love to have you go with me. See you at six?"

"Cara!" He took several steps toward me, and the glint in his eyes told me he couldn't wait to get me, or rather the item I held to me, in his hands.

I grabbed the doorknob at the same time Mrs. Smiley pulled the door open. I sailed cheerfully past her and a startled client.

"Don't you love his new tie, Mrs. Smiley?" I stage-whispered on my way by. "Matches your nails for style and pizzazz."

I glanced back over my shoulder and saw Todd, his flashy new tie swaying beneath his chin, shaking hands with his client as he glared over the man's shoulder at my retreating figure. I grinned, waved, and stuck up six fingers. His eyebrow rose, and he nodded. Then, as his client turned to sit, he glared at me, and I heard, "Look out, woman. I'll get you back," as clearly as if he'd actually said it.

Laughing happily, I went out to the parking lot.

EIGHT

The day was so lovely that I decided to wait for Todd on the front steps. Rainbow sat beside me eyeing the grass with alarm. With a sniff she walked to the door and stood, tail straight up, waiting to go in.

"Get down there on the lawn and be a good kitty, you coward," I told her and lifted her. She burrowed into me as I walked down the steps. When I leaned over to set her on the grass, she wrapped her paws around my arm, clinging to me, a difficult proposition for a declawed cat.

I put her in the middle of the lawn and stood back to watch. She looked at me in a panic and began walking as quickly as she could back to the porch. She lifted each foot high above the grass, which felt strange beneath her pads, giving herself the aspect of a prancing horse.

"She looks like Elam's Tennessee walker," Jake said as he wheeled around the corner. "He just got a new horse from a dealer that specializes in race horses, especially sulky trained ones. Bluegrass lifts her legs just like that."

As Jake spoke, Rainbow hit the bottom step and flew up to the porch. She sat in front of the door, casting a begging glance in my direction every couple of seconds. I decided she was safe there, and I turned my attention to Jake.

"How's your mother?"

"She's doing much better. She'll be coming home tomorrow."

"I'm sure she'll like that."

Jake looked unconvinced. "Not that she won't like coming home," he said. "She just won't like being confined to the bed-room. Mom's a doer, and she's going to go crazy with someone else taking care of her house, even someone as nice as Esther."

"I think Esther's got her eye on Elam," I said, thinking of Jake's dark-haired, gray-eyed, wiry, energetic younger brother.

"Poor Esther." Jake looked genuinely sad.

"Why do you say that? Does Elam have a girl?" I asked.

"He wishes. He's had a crush on Mary Clare Epp for years. I don't think he sees anyone but her."

"And Mary Clare doesn't return the favor?"

"I don't think so. You understand, I only know what I over-hear. Not hanging around in Amish circles these days, my sources are very limited. But the last I heard Mom and my sis-ter Ruth talking, it seemed Mary Clare was about to get engaged to Young Joe Lapp."

"Poor Elam. But maybe having Esther here will turn his attention to her." Ever the romantic, I didn't need much of a plotline to perk me up.

"Well, this setup should let them know whether they can stand each other well enough to get married." Jake rubbed absently at a spot on the front of his T-shirt. "I've decided that that's the most important thing anyway," he said with a decisive shake of the head. "You need to be able to stand being around each other."

I looked at him, laughing. "Ah, the bachelor who knows all about marriage from observation. Sort of like the childless expert on raising kids."

"I just speak the truth as I see it," he defended, but he grinned back.

"What about love?" I asked, unable to resist.

"What about it?"

"Doesn't a good marriage need love?"

He shrugged, his rugged shoulders rising and falling as though the question wasn't worth asking. "Maybe love is simply being able to stand each other with a little chemistry thrown in for good measure."

"Well, I can tell you one thing, guy. I don't want to miss the chemistry. Still I think you're right about the getting along part. It's the commonalities that make a marriage flow." Then I thought of Mom and Pop and Ward and Marnie and how dissimilar each of that pair was from the other. "I've noticed, though, that it's the differences that give a marriage its spice and excitement."

"You want spice and excitement?" He seemed surprised.

"Sure. Don't you?"

He was silent for a minute, his face shuttered. Then: "I don't let myself think too much about things like marriage in a personal sense. I choose to stay philosophical about it. It's safer."

"But dull," I said as I sat there in my boring tan slacks and tan-and-white striped shirt.

He smiled tightly. "Sometimes safer and dull are the way to go."

We were quiet for a couple of minutes while I wondered whether marriage was a possibility for him. I didn't know the extent of his injuries beyond the obvious, and maybe his thought patterns were to protect himself from what he saw as a solitary and lonely life stretching ahead of him. I'd have to ask Todd what he knew.

"Marriage is sort of expected in the Amish culture, isn't it?" I finally asked, reverting to Elam and Mary Clare and Esther.

"Definitely." Jake pulled his stare back from his contemplation of the shimmering haze over the fields across the street. "Church and family are all."

"How would they look at someone like me?" I asked. "If I were Amish, I mean."

"You mean because you're unmarried or because you're a writer?"

I shrugged. "How about both?"

"As an unmarried woman, you'd be treated politely, but you'd probably live with relatives. Since you're not a married woman, you'd sit with the unmarried folks at services, which in many districts means with the teens, even if you're much older than they."

I pulled a face. The idea of sitting with the teens forever didn't appeal to me, and I couldn't believe it appealed to any single Amish woman, no matter how obedient to the church she was.

"More and more unmarried women have jobs outside the home," Jake said, "but being a writer would still be very rare. And being a published writer would be almost unheard of, except for being published in the Amish newspapers."

"How about an unmarried man? Say that Elam decides to suffer for his lost love forever." I looked at Jake.

He shrugged. "Getting married's just the thing to do, and Elam would get married eventually in spite of Mary Clare's rejection. He'd just find someone else. It's what you do."

Jake's German shepherd, Hawk, ambled across the lawn and sat beside Jake. I glanced over my shoulder at Rainbow. She had seen Hawk, though he hadn't noticed her. Her back was arched and she looked panicky about the eyes.

"I think I'd better let the cat in before she has a heart attack," I said, getting up to open the door. At the last minute, Hawk saw her bushy tail zipping through the narrow opening to safety. He lunged up the porch steps and plastered his nose against the screen, whimpering. Rainbow was an orange-and-black blur as she dashed upstairs to our rooms and her hiding place under the bed.

I patted Hawk's head. "Sorry, guy. She's not very friendly."

Hawk looked up at me, and I realized I was making an assumption to suggest that friendship was what he wanted. Anabaptist pacifism did not appear to beat in his canine heart.

"Do the Amish adopt?" I asked Jake as I sat again on the steps.

"You thinking of your grandfather?"

I nodded.

Jake snapped his fingers at Hawk, and the dog regretfully left the door to come sit by his master. Jake's strong hands gently ruffled the animal's hair. "Certainly they would readily take in any child within the community who needed care. I don't know that they'd legalize it the way the English would, but the child would be raised as a member of the family. All the Amish value children, seeing them not only as hands to work the farm but as the future of the community."

Hawk raised up on his hind legs, front legs planted on the arm of the wheelchair, and kissed Jake wetly on the cheek. Jake made a face as he hugged the animal about the neck. "Ugh! Have you got bad breath! What have you been eating?"

The dog didn't answer, but he settled happily on the ground at Jake's feet.

Jake wiped at his slobbered-on face and continued the conversation as if Hawk hadn't interrupted. "As far as taking a child from outside goes, if they were approached, I'm sure they'd consider it. It's just not a usual circumstance to cross those cultural lines because the gulf is so wide, and they would raise the child never to cross that chasm."

Of course they would, I thought. Everyone who adopts raises the child to their beliefs and values. If you're from a cloistered community like the Amish, you raise the child to the cloister. If you're a Christian, the child's your own personal home missions project.

I tried to imagine how our lives would have been altered if Pop had been adopted into an Amish home. How would he have submerged that vibrant, authoritative personality in a peace-loving and submissive culture? What would he have done with that great business acumen of his? What would I be like as a third-generation Amish woman? The stretch was too great even for a creator of tales like me.

"You going out with Todd again tonight?" Jake asked, looking wickedly nosy.

I nodded. "We're going down to Tel Hai, wherever that is. Everyone says it's not too far. Do you know where it is?"

Jake nodded. "Yep. I'm all too familiar with that area. It's right down the street from where I had my accident. There are these two big hills south of Honey Brook, and in the low part between is the turn to Tel Hai." He sketched the hills with his hand, then looked at me. "That's the infamous intersection."

"How did it happen? A drunk driver?"

He shook his head. "Too much speed, some wet leaves, and someone who ran the stop sign. I braked, skidded, and ended up with my motorcycle on my back."

"Oh, Jake!"

He shrugged. "I survived."

"Jake?" It was Esther, standing in the doorway, pretty as could be with her rosy cheeks and thick hair. I'd noticed that many Amish women had thinning hair, a combination of inbreeding and the constant pulling of the hair into such severe lines, but Esther would never have that problem. Why didn't Elam realize how lovely she was?

"Jake, Cara already said she wouldn't be here for dinner. How about you?"

Jake shook his head. "I'm going into the hospital now to see Mom so I can get back and still have time to study. I'll pick at something when I get back. Don't worry about me."

Esther nodded. "There'll be extra chicken potpie, I'm sure. And I made a lemon chiffon pie."

After she went back into the house, Jake leaned toward me and whispered, "Lemon chiffon is Elam's favorite."

Forty-five minutes later Todd and I came to the intersection where Jake had lost his life as he had known it. It was just an ordinary country intersection with open fields on two corners, a house and business on the third and a tree farm on the fourth. Stop signs were in place to prevent drivers from coming off Beaver Dam Road onto Route 10 too quickly. But stop signs only achieved their purposes if people observed their command.

"It was a brutal accident," Todd said. "It's a wonder he didn't die. He probably would have, if it weren't for some nurse who lived in one of these houses by the crossroads. She sat with him in the rain until help came, keeping him from going into shock."

The little valley through which Beaver Dam Road wound spread out around us, golden in the slanting light of evening. Shortly Todd turned onto the beautifully landscaped campus that was Tel Hai with its cottages, apartments, medical facilities, and rising over all, a white spire pointing all residents heavenward.

"Did I mention my father lives here?"

"Here? At Tel Hai? Are we visiting him, too?"

"We could," Todd said with no enthusiasm.

"After Aunt Lizzie," I said. "Aunt Lizzie first."

Dear Lord, let this meeting go well! Let Great-aunt Lizzie give me some concrete information. Let me find the answers!

As we drove to the parking lot, we were separated from an Amish farm only by the thin strand of an electric fence dividing the properties. I could see the farmer standing on some piece of farm machinery as a six-horse team pulled it through a field, but the beauty of the scene barely registered. I was caught in the drama of my quest and the impending answers.

"Oh, Todd! This is so great!"

He misunderstood me and thought I meant the facility was great. "My father likes it here. He's got his own little cottage on the other side of the campus, and he can get as involved in the activities offered or be as solitary as he chooses." He paused, then continued in a flat tone. "And with him, it seems solitude wins every time."

I was pulled from my thoughts of Aunt Lizzie by the barely concealed distress in his voice. I looked at him with interest. "Do I detect a bit of disapproval here?"

Todd squirmed and ran a hand through his hair, a move I was learning to know meant agitation. The curls on the left side of his head sproinged free. "I know I'm being ridiculous. He's always been a man who kept his own counsel, who ignored people and emotion. Why should I expect him to change at this stage of his life? I just keep hoping that he'll get involved in the community activities, maybe even with people, since he lives right in the middle of them." He shrugged. *"Casus fortuitus non est supponenous."*

I waited for a translation, and when none came, I said, "Did anyone ever tell you that this Latin habit of yours is a bit frustrating, not to mention bizarre?"

He looked surprised at the acid in my voice. "A fortuitous event is not to be presumed."

"Thank you." I unsnapped my seat belt. "It sounded better in Latin. Then I didn't know it was in passive voice. We writers hate passive voice."

"Passive," Todd repeated. "That's just the word for Dad. He's a passive man. He's content to let life slide by without even attempting to grab hold of the things it has to offer. Wouldn't it bother you to watch that?"

"Probably, because I'm about as compulsive as you. But what's more important: that he be happy with his life or that you be happy with it?"

He looked at me from under a thoughtful frown. "Can you separate one from the other when it's family you're dealing with?"

Since I didn't know that answer any more than he did, I climbed out of the car. Time to find Aunt Lizzie.

After asking a couple of people for directions, we finally ended up in the partial care wing, third floor, talking with the woman in charge.

"You're the guest who's come to visit Elizabeth Yost, are you?" she asked.

I nodded. "Yes. Great-aunt Lizzie." I spoke like this relationship was definite, absolute, immutable, and I felt rather than saw Todd's unhappiness.

"Well," the woman said, and immediately I knew I had a problem. Surely this wouldn't be one of those so-near-and-yet-so-far situations, would it?

"I don't want to alarm you," the woman continued, "but we had to send Elizabeth to the hospital about thirty minutes ago."

"Oh, no!" My first thought was purely selfish. I'd lost my source, maybe forever! Hard on its coattails came more charitable and appropriate thoughts toward the woman herself. "What happened? Will she be all right?"

"She began having heart palpitations to the point that the nurses knew she needed more than we could do for her here. They were afraid of a full-blown heart episode, no small thing for a woman her age."

"No small thing for anyone at any age," I muttered.

The woman spread her hands in regret. "I'm sorry. I hope you didn't travel too far."

"That doesn't matter," I said.

"I know she was very excited about seeing you. She told everyone at dinner that she was having a special guest tonight."

A sudden thought chilled me. "You don't think I'm the reason she had the heart attack, do you?"

The woman looked at me strangely, but then she didn't know why I was here. I looked at Todd, my face bleak. Maybe my coming was a bad kind of exciting, distressing to her, upsetting.

He smiled briefly at me, took my arm, and turned me toward an exit. "Thank you for your help," he said to the woman. "Can you tell us what hospital Mrs. Yost is in?"

"Brandywine. It's the closest, and they've got a good trauma unit, too."

Todd nodded his thanks and led me outside.

I leaned against the side of his car, feeling the heat of the metal through my slacks. I put a hand to my forehead and rubbed the ache behind my left eye.

"What if it was my fault?" I whispered.

"Hey," he said, leaning against the car beside me, crossing one ankle over the other. "It wasn't your fault."

"You don't know that."

"True. But you don't know that it was, either."

His voice was soft but firm, and I looked at him gratefully. "You're right." The gentle breeze of his logic blew away my assumed guilt. I did not know for a fact that Aunt Lizzie's health difficulties were my fault, and until I did…

"Sufficient unto the day," I said.

He nodded. "Good girl. And we'll call the hospital to see how she is after they've had time to assess things. Okay?"

I studied him, my arms folded across my chest. *Lord, I can't believe this guy. He's so nice! I could like him, I mean really like him, so easily that it scares me.*

He stared back, his mouth quirked in a half smile. "Are you all right?"

I blinked. "Yeah." I stepped away from the car to face him and grabbed the first topic of conversation that occurred to me. "You know what? You need to run your hand through the other side of your hair."

He looked as though he couldn't quite believe what I was saying.

"Half of it's all free and curly," I explained. "The other half is still moussed within an inch of its life."

"What?" He grabbed the outside mirror in alarm and twisted it until he could see his reflection. "Oh, no!" His hand went immediately to the springy curls, and he tried to plaster them back to the rigidity of the controlled ones.

"No, no," I said, grabbing at his arm. "Free the other side."

He stared at me. "You can't be serious."

"Go on," I encouraged. "Let those beautiful curls spring to life. You have to, or you'll look lopsided for the rest of the evening."

"Isn't it enough that you make me wear atrocious ties? Do you have to make me look like a leftover hippie, too?"

I laughed. "Come on. Free those curls!"

With a groan he ran a hand through the restrained side of his hair. Immediately the curls sproinged to exuberant life.

147

"Look at me," I told him.

He did, his face lemon sour.

"You've got the most wonderful hair," I said. "Why do you keep it a secret? You could have all the girls lining up to run their fingers through it."

"Yeah, just what I want," he groused, but I could see a sparkle of pleasure at my comment peeking through his frown.

"Why do you dislike it? Do you think curls are for girls or something?"

"Well, they're not very professional looking. Do you think a jury or judge is going to listen to a frizzy-haired bozo?"

You, guy, will never be a bozo, I thought, but for once I was prudent enough to keep my mouth shut.

"You just like it because you don't have to live with it," he continued, enjoying his grump. "You have wonderful straight hair." And he indicated my hair, which tonight hung down my back from a barrette at my nape.

"I might not live with your curls, but I have to look at them. And I like to look at the freed curls. Now let's go visit your father."

That little sparkle of suppressed pleasure disappeared. Sighing, he opened my car door and walked around to his side.

"You know, Cara, how you talk about what family is? You think it's bone of my bone and flesh of my flesh? Well, you're about to meet bone of my bone. We've shared DNA, genes, and a house, but for as long as I can remember, at least since my mother died, we have not been what I think of as family. We've merely been related."

He looked at me over the roof of the car and repeated in a voice both melancholy and hard, "Merely related."

I don't know what I expected in Dr. Edward Reasoner after Todd's bleak comments broke my heart, but it wasn't the handsome, white-haired gentleman who eventually answered the door when Todd rang his cottage's doorbell.

"Well, Toddy." It was a statement, like Dr. Reasoner was pronouncing on the temperature. Seventy-eight degrees. Well, Toddy. No surprise, no pleasure, just acceptance.

"Hello, Dad."

The two men stared at each other through the screen while I slowly turned gray from the passage of time. Finally I could stand the silence no longer.

"Hello, Dr. Reasoner. I'm Cara Bentley." I wore my best smile and most scintillating manner.

Todd looked slightly pained, but he stepped belatedly into the breech. "Dad," he said, "I'd like to introduce Cara Bentley. She's a client."

"I'm pleased to meet you." Dr. Reasoner looked at me with a spark of interest deep in his eyes. At least I think there was a spark of interest. We were still standing on the porch talking to him through the screen, so it was hard to tell for certain.

Suddenly Dr. Reasoner came to himself. "Oh!" He reached for the door. "Please come in, Toddy. And bring your client." Did I imagine a slight pause before the word *client*?

Todd took the opened door from his father and Dr. Reasoner turned into the house. As he walked away, I bumped Todd's arm. He looked at me questioningly.

"Toddy?" I said softly but with as much malice as I could manage. After all, he'd introduced me as a mere client. He deserved to be tormented.

He glared at me. "If you ever tell anyone, so help me, I'll triple your billing."

"Nasty, nasty, Toddy," I said, wiggling my index finger in his face. He looked like he'd enjoy biting it off at the second knuckle.

We walked into a living room furnished with a sofa, a leather recliner, and books. Books were everywhere, on shelves that lined three walls, in piles on the completely uncarpeted floor, on the sofa, on a coffee table and on the end table by the recliner. They sat upright like soldiers at attention; they lay flat in high, haphazard stacks, children's block towers waiting the right vibration level to tumble them wildly. Big books, fat books, slim books. Leather covers, hard covers, soft covers. And all looked read, handled, and appreciated.

I wanted to stop and read titles, but with a firm hand on my back Todd hustled me toward a glassed-in back porch. On the way, I glimpsed a bedroom and a den, both rooms holding a minimum of furniture and a maximum of books. The porch was awash with more books piled helter-skelter, several open and laid on their faces, spines to the ceiling. The one nearest me was Lewis Carroll's *Alice Through the Looking Glass*. A glass-topped table that I was certain was meant for summer dining had become a repository for garishly colored paperbacks, mostly mysteries, espionage, and fantasy. I saw several Dick Francis titles, a smattering of Robert Ludlum and Helen MacInnes, and Stephen Lawhead's entire Pendragon Cycle. Facedown on the table beside what was obviously his reading chair was the first of Diana Gabaldon's Outlander series, a leather-bound copy of *Great Expectations,* and a much read paperback whose title I couldn't see from this angle.

"Oh, Dr. Reasoner," I said breathily. "You are a man after my own heart."

I hear a gurgling noise from Todd, half astonishment, half alarm. Dr. Reasoner himself looked at me, startled and uncertain.

"The books," I said, sweeping my arm wide. "The books!"

Dr. Reasoner gave a nod, relaxing now that he knew exactly

what I meant. "You love them, too?"

"I do. I can't imagine a worse fate than being somewhere without a book."

Dr. Reasoner turned to Todd. "You say she's a…client?"

Todd nodded. "We drove down on business to visit Elizabeth Yost."

I waited for the normal questions and comments, things like, do you know her, Dad? And no, Toddy, I don't or yes, I do. Or was it a good visit? But there was nothing.

Todd sat in a kitchen chair that he dragged to the porch, arms folded, face set. I sat in Dr. Reasoner's reading chair at his silent insistence as he waved a hand in its direction and bowed me toward it.

He took the only other chair on the porch, a webbed folding aluminum one, and proceeded to fold his arms exactly like Todd. The lines of his face weren't as set, though, because he was curious about me.

I immediately became engrossed in reading the title beside me.

"Beowulf?" I said in surprise. I picked up the book. "In the original?"

"I don't want to lose my Old English skills." He said it as if keeping such skills alive was as common and reasonable as crossing a street at the light.

"How about you?" I said to Todd, waving the book at him. "You ever read this?"

He shook his head. "Milton was about as dedicated as I ever got."

Again the men fell silent while I struggled to make sense of the text in my hands. I looked up, grinning. "How about if I read one of those Harry Krauss medical thrillers instead?" I pointed to a couple of paperbacks on the table, then nodded toward a couple others. "I've already read all those Peretti things."

"What did you think of Peretti?" Dr. Reasoner asked.

We plunged into a wonderful discussion of writing styles and plot versus character-driven fiction and which was best and why. Every so often one of us looked at Todd to give him a chance to enter the conversation, but he merely sat there looking stunned. Finally when I glanced at him for the hundredth time, he spoke.

"Cara's a writer," he said with all the enthusiasm of a fisherman confessing that they all got away. "Published, too."

After a moment of astonished silence that Todd had actually spoken, Dr. Reasoner turned back to me. "Did you always plan to write?" His brown eyes, so much like his son's, watched me.

I looked at Todd and found him staring at his father, astounded. He felt my eyes on him and turned to me. I winked, and he gave a little snort of surprise and a half smile.

"Everyone, including me, expected me to go into the family business," I said. "It wasn't until my senior year in college that I realized I didn't want that. I wanted to write. I was terrified when I told my grandfather, but he backed my decision. I've been writing romances ever since."

I looked quickly at Dr. Reasoner when I said the word *romances,* just the way I'd looked at Pop, though for different reasons. I'd been afraid of Pop's reaction because he was Pop and up to that point I'd always pleased him, always done exactly what he wanted, including majoring in business.

I was not exactly *afraid* of the reaction to my chosen field of a scholar like Dr. Reasoner, but I was slightly intimidated. A man who read *Beowulf* in the original wasn't likely to be impressed by romances. And I had to admit that I wanted Todd's father to like me.

"I'm sure your grandfather's very proud of you," Dr. Reasoner said. He glanced at Todd and spoke again. "I've always been so proud of Toddy."

Todd, who had been diligently studying his feet, jerked at that, head whipping up, mouth all but hanging open in shock. But Dr. Reasoner had turned back to me and didn't see the struggle between disbelief and joy on his son's face. I did, though, and I wanted to cry. How tragic that Dr. Reasoner saw fit to tell me this highly important fact instead of the man who desperately wanted to hear it.

"I'd like to read something you wrote," Dr. Reasoner said gallantly.

I pulled my eyes from Todd and smiled at the old gentleman's kindness. "I'll give a book to Todd to give you."

"Wait," Todd said, suddenly coming to life. "I've got one in the car." And he almost dashed from the room. In no time he was back with the copies of *As the Deer* and *So My Soul* that I'd given him.

I sighed a great mental sigh. It was painfully obvious that he had not even cracked the covers. Not that he'd had time to read them yet, but he could have at least taken them into his house instead of forgetting them in the car. He could have at least looked inside the covers, read the first page, even read the last page.

Todd glanced at me, then handed the books to his father who immediately began reading the cover blurbs. "We've got to go, Dad. It's a long trip back."

Dr. Reasoner walked to the door with us, reading as he walked. "The cover copy makes these sound wonderful, Cara. It's obvious you're not working a cash register anywhere these days."

I grinned. "Nope, not at all." I shook his proffered hand.

"It's been a pleasure meeting you," I said sincerely.

I had noticed that he and Todd hadn't touched when we arrived. Not that I expected a hug or anything overtly demonstrative, but they hadn't even shaken hands. Nor did they hug or shake hands good-bye. Todd sort of nodded in his father's general direction. Dr. Reasoner sort of smiled vaguely. And we were gone.

The car had barely begun to move when Todd looked at me, something close to excitement in his face.

"Did you see that?" he exclaimed. "Did you see that?"

"Uh, what?" I asked, looking all around me even though I knew what he was talking about.

"That visit! That was the best visit I've had with my father in years."

"I was afraid of that," I began, but he wasn't finished.

"And I have you to thank." He reached over and squeezed my hand as it lay in my lap. "Now tell me how you did it."

"How I did it?" I couldn't believe he was serious.

"Yeah. How did you get him to talk to you?"

"All I did was talk about something he likes."

"Books?"

"Books." I had a moment of panic. "You do read, don't you? I mean, if you don't, what do you do in the evenings in your house all alone?"

He turned off of Route 10 onto 340.

"Well," he said, "I work on the lawn. I watch the Phillies. I e-mail missionaries all over the world. I explore the Internet." He shrugged. "Stuff."

"But not reading."

He shook his head. "I read the Bible every day and the newspaper and of course I read lots of legal documents, but fun reading? Not a lot. I think the detail of the reading I have to do professionally has slowed my reading speed so much that reading's not a pleasure for me. It's a chore."

I stared at my hands, deeply disappointed. Can a writer have a meaningful relationship—now there was a trite phrase if ever I thought one—with a nonreader?

"I saw your face when I gave your books to Dad," he said. "Did you mind?"

"No, of course not," I said. "It was nice of you."

"Then it was the fact that I hadn't read them that upset you."

He was too perceptive. I took a deep breath. I knew I had to be completely honest.

"I admit that it hurt me that you hadn't even taken them in from the car." I was surprised at the tears that sprang to my eyes as I spoke. This man had too much of an effect on my heart.

He nodded. "I thought that was probably it."

We were silent for a few minutes, the only sound the soft wheeze of his air conditioner.

"Did Pop and Ward read your books?" Todd suddenly asked.

I shook my head. "That hurt me too, but I learned to live with it. At least Mom and Marnie read them."

He turned to me with a challenging expression. "How'd you like to read some of my legal opinions? I've got a great one I just finished on an obscure point of business law in MacKenzie vs. MacKenzie, Inc."

"Mmm," I said thoughtfully. I'd never considered that I was a prejudiced reader too. "Point taken."

He stretched out a hand palm up. "I won't make any promises about reading, Cara. I'm too afraid I'll break them. But I'll always defend your right to write and be proud of you for being published. Can you live with that?"

I looked at him, then at his hand. I nodded. "I can." *At least for now.* And I slipped my hand in his.

NINE

Esther and I brought Mary home from the hospital late Friday morning. I felt so sorry for her because I knew she was in severe pain, her leg in a cast, her cuts barely crusted with scabs. In fact there was a very deep gash on her right hip that they wouldn't let heal. They kept it open to wash it regularly with an antibiotic drip because of an infection in the bone that wouldn't go away.

"They say I probably got the infection from something on the cellar steps," Mary said. "But I keep a clean house!"

She was clearly more offended about the perceived lapse in her housekeeping skills than about the wound itself.

I thought of the manure that came into the house as an inevitable part of living on a farm. Maybe that had been the source of the infection. Who knew?

A visiting nurse would come daily to oversee the antibiotic drip as well as dress the cuts, and Mary was confined to bed for some time.

Elam and John had come in from the field and were waiting for us when we got home. They carried Mary inside and up to the bedroom she and John shared. She was barely settled when the visiting nurse showed up.

"Hi," she said when I came to the door. "I'm Rose."

"Rose!" I said in surprise as I let in the woman EMT, now dressed in the blue uniform of the Lancaster Home Health Group. "Do you moonlight as an emergency tech or as a visiting nurse?"

She smiled. "You remembered me."

I nodded. "The woman who knows but doesn't know Jake."

She grinned but didn't explain.

I liked her, with her curly brown hair and those sparkling hazel eyes beaming through her glasses.

"He's still at school right now," I said.

"School?"

"Millersville University. I'm not certain when he finishes classes today, but I'm sure he'll try to get home as soon as possible. Like all the rest of the family, he's concerned about Mary."

I led Rose upstairs and introduced her to Mary, John, Esther, and Elam. After speaking briefly to everyone, Rose firmly sent all of us but John from the room.

"I need to run the drip over the wound," she explained. "Mary doesn't need an audience."

As we left, I looked over my shoulder at Mary, so frail in the great bed. John sat beside her on the edge of the bed, his large calloused hand holding her smaller, work-reddened one. He reached out and pushed her long, unbound hair back from her face in a loving gesture that he would never normally let another see. It was a sign of his concern for his wife that he didn't even realize that he still had an audience.

Jake arrived while Elam, Esther, and I were at the table eating the ham loaf and whipped potatoes Esther had prepared for the noon meal.

"Is she okay?" he asked immediately. "Was the trip home too hard on her?"

"She's fine," said a voice behind him, and we all turned to find Rose at the foot of the stairs. "Esther? John asked that you bring up some broth to Mary and sit with her until she falls asleep. If you ask me, the trick will be to get some of the broth in her before she falls asleep. He'll come down as soon as you go up."

Esther jumped to do as she was asked, and I turned to Jake.

"Jake, this is Rose, your mother's visiting nurse."

"Rose." He nodded to her, and she smiled. Why, I wondered, does she know him but he doesn't know her?

I helped Esther prepare a tray for Mary, putting a dishcloth under the soup bowl to make the tray surface slip proof. I added a glass of ginger ale and some saltines while Esther ladled the now warm broth.

"Here, I'll carry that." Elam took the tray from Esther as she walked toward the steps.

Esther beamed, but I thought he offered more because he wanted to see for himself once more that his mother was all right than because he wanted to help Esther.

I turned from watching Elam and Esther go up the stairs to watch Jake and Rose talking by the front door.

"I'll be here about the same time every day," I heard her say.

He mumbled something in response that I couldn't make out, then reached out and pushed open the screen door for her. He rolled onto the front porch after her and watched as she climbed into her car with its Lancaster Home Health Group logo of a blue cross inside the black outline of a house.

Feeling a little unnecessary, I went up to my rooms and began working on the series proposal my agent wanted from me. I always enjoyed working up the bare bones of a plot and establishing the characters that lived within it. I worked happily for what seemed only a few minutes when I happened to look at my watch and saw that it was five-thirty already.

I flew around, getting ready for Ward and Marnie's visit. I was pulling my hair back into a wide gold barrette when my cell phone rang.

"Cara, it's Marnie. We're behind schedule, but we're coming! The baby-sitter was late. I'm going to blame it on her rather than my husband."

"Where are you?"

"On Route 100 not too far from Exton. We'll pick up Route 30 from there. What do you think? An hour from you?"

"Give or take a few minutes. Why don't you just meet us at the restaurant instead of coming to the farm first? I'll call and change the time of the reservation. We can come back here after dinner." I gave her direction.

"Sounds good," she said. "But tell me, what's this 'us'? Is he really coming with you?"

"Who?" I asked innocently. I could hear Ward in the background yelling, "What? The lawyer's actually coming? Cara's got a real date?"

"Don't give me that who stuff. You know who I mean," Marnie said.

"Oh, you mean my lawyer," I said, trying to sound offhand about the whole matter. "My real date?"

"I most certainly do. We're going to get to meet him?" Her voice was eager.

I watched a gray car turn into the drive. "He's pulling up out front as we speak."

"I can't wait," she said. "I told Ward the guy'd come. In fact we had a bet, and I won."

"You bet about me and Todd?"

"About whether you'd actually have the courage to invite him."

"Ah, I'd forgotten. Ward thinks I don't have any guts."

"Poor mistaken baby," Marnie said affectionately. She was probably looking at him as she spoke.

"Poor mistaken idiot, you mean," I said with a smile. "I love it when I prove him wrong."

"I know I should say something about you two being too old for sibling rivalry, but I love it when you get him, too."

"Marnie!" Ward said in the background. It was interesting how my brother couldn't resist taking part in any phone conversation he was around, whether he was an intended participant or not. "What about your wifely duty to be true to me?"

"My dearest heart," Marnie said to Ward, her voice so clear that I knew the comment was for me, too. I could almost hear her eyelashes fluttering as she spoke. "Never for one moment doubt my resolve to always fulfill my wifely duties. You are the king of my heart. But sometimes," and her voice lost all its honey in favor of vinegar, "it does the king good to get his ego knocked by one of those he perceives as his ladies-in-waiting!"

I laughed at my sister-in-law and thought again how much I cared for her. "We women must stick together," I agreed. "See you soon."

I went down to meet Todd, glad for some time alone with him. Tonight he was wearing an olive green sport shirt and olive green slacks two shades deeper. Mr. Monochromatic. I, for my part, was wearing a soft yellow dress that I had gotten the day I met Alma and bought my lovely coral gown. I hoped he noticed.

"Hello," Todd said when I opened the door to him. "Will you tell Cara I'm here?"

I blinked.

"Not that I would mind having dinner with someone as lovely as you and wearing yellow, no less. But I'm committed for the evening to a woman who wears beige. *Ipso facto*, she must still be inside somewhere."

I grinned as I let the screen fall shut behind me. "Cute. Now let's go buy you an aloha shirt so we can pep up your wardrobe, too."

He looked pained. "Over my dead body."

"I really do want to go shopping," I told him as he began to back out of the drive. "Marnie and Ward are going to be late so we have some time to kill. Let's go to Bentley Mart."

"Okay," he said. "I could pick up a few things myself."

The Lancaster Bentley Mart wasn't all that far from the farm, but it was a world apart. The road on which the farm was located was quiet and rural, lined with snarls of raspberry canes and honeysuckle or cleared to the edge so there was room for the six-horse or six-mule teams to turn without going on the road. Fields of golden winter wheat stood waiting harvest, and the rows of corn now reached to my thighs. Alfalfa grew almost tall enough for the cutting of the first of three crops grown over the season.

Amish women in bare feet mowed their lawns with push mowers while their children weeded the vegetable patch. Boys pushing scooters ran errands, and a girl who looked remarkably like Esther flew down the road toward us on inline skates. It wasn't until we were driving past her that I realized it actually was Esther, a pharmacy bag hanging from one hand. We waved as we passed.

By contrast, Bentley Mart sat on Route 30 just east of Lancaster City in a sprawling shopping area. "Discount" stores, entertainment complexes, and motels lined the highway, and traffic was heavy, requiring full concentration to navigate. Tour buses, travel trailers, out-of-state drivers, and locals who actually knew where they were going all vied for position. It was a relief to park in the Mart's vast parking lot, but I was very unhappy to look up at the sign and see that the second E in Bentley was burned out.

"Look at that," I said to Todd. "Disgusting."

He glanced at me, amused. "I wouldn't let it ruin my night," he said. "If it was a traffic light that was burned out, then we might have a problem."

"Mmm."

We went into the store, and I was struck with a feeling of clutter. I hate clutter. The interior layout of Bentley Marts was designed to avoid even the look of congestion. I shuddered. Something wasn't right here.

When I went to the film department, there was no one to help me.

"I used to work this counter," I said, irritated. "There's always supposed to be someone here because of the value of the cameras. It helps prevent shoplifting."

"You worked here?" Todd asked.

"Not this store. One in Cherry Hill, New Jersey, near home."

But there was one thing that made me very happy. I found a Choice Books rack, and there were *As the Deer* and *So My Soul*.

"At least they're doing something right," I said, patting my titles proprietarily.

I moved on, only to realize a few steps down the aisle that Todd wasn't with me. I turned and saw him reading the cover copy of *As the Deer*. Perhaps his father's perusal and comments had made him curious. At one point he looked up and frowned at me. I smiled back, especially cheered when he picked up *So My Soul*. He read some more, then opened to the back of the title page.

I came to stand next to him.

"It says here that you're a bestseller," he said, pointing to the words on the cover.

I nodded.

"It says here that you teach writing all over the country."

I nodded again. "At writers conferences."

"It says here that this book's in its tenth printing in less than two years."

"Twelfth by now," I said. "Over 100,000 copies sold."

"The review comments on the cover make you sound like the best thing since sliced bread."

I nodded. "People have been very nice about these books."

"They aren't fluff, are they?"

I shook my head. "No. Did you think they were?"

"But you said you wrote romances." He looked like I had been purposely deceiving him.

"A romance doesn't have to be shallow, you know. After all, isn't love the strongest and most noble of human emotions, an emotion that God himself feels toward us, the attribute of God that led him to send Christ for us?"

"Um." Todd read again for a moment, then looked up. "As the deer pants for streams of water, so my soul pants for you, O God," he said, quoting the psalm the titles came from.

I grinned. "You got it. Come on. I want to hit the computer aisle for a minute. I always check out the computer aisle at Bentley's."

But when we got there, my smile faded. I stood around waiting for someone to help me, and not one person materialized. I knew that when Pop and Ward decided to carry a choice selection of computers, they decided that the only way they could compete with the computer megastores was to offer unparalleled sales help. That's why I always checked the aisle. I wanted to be certain the help was truly available.

Todd stood beside me but paid no attention to me. He was reading chapter one of *As the Deer.*

"Excuse me," I called to a salesperson walking past two aisles over. "Can you help me?"

"That isn't my department, lady," he yelled back, not slowing his pace at all.

In an attack of pique, I began typing on a computer. Immediately a "Warning: you have performed an illegal act" sign lit the screen.

"An illegal act, my foot," I muttered. "I haven't had time to do anything illegal yet."

Suddenly Todd began to read aloud.

"Marci watched the moon's light fall across the heaving black waves. The lunar radiance burned a path to her feet, shimmering in the wet sand as each wave receded, the soft luminescence like a highway to God. She put out a foot to step on the light. But as she moved, so did the lambent stream, retreating so that she could never quite reach it, never quite touch it, never quite hold it.

"'O God!' she cried when she found herself waist deep in the midnight water, the shaft of light still floating just beyond her grasp. 'I can't reach you! You're just like the moonbeam. O God, you can't be! You can't!'"

He looked up and studied me as though he hadn't seen me before. I stared back, a slight smile on my lips. He shook his head slowly.

"You're a surprise every time I see you, Cara Bentley. And this is no exception." He waved the book in my face.

"Does that mean you're impressed?"

"Most definitely," he said. "Most definitely."

I feared I was vibrating again.

"Are you interested in a computer, lady?" asked a grouchy male voice just behind me. I jumped and spun to find an older man in a red Bentley Mart shirt staring resentfully at me.

I nodded yes, and the man did everything in his power to ruin the pleasure I felt in Todd's comment. He was rude, abrupt, ill informed, and seemed to feel he was doing me a great favor by deigning to speak with me. After he told me for the fifth time that 5.1 gigabytes meant a modem of great strength, I walked away.

"Lady, did you ever think about doing a little homework before you come in to make a purchase this size?" he called after me. "Then you'd know what you were doing."

"The man's an idiot," I hissed as I stalked toward the exit. "I can't stand incompetence!"

"Well, slow down and wait for me," Todd said. "I have to pay for the book."

"I'll give you another, for Pete's sake," I groused.

"Nope. I want the next printing to say 100,001."

I waited for him at the big exit doors. "Thanks," I said when he walked up with a little bag holding *As the Deer*.

He nodded. "My pleasure. Did you know that the moonbeam over the water to your feet is caused when the angle of incidence is equal to the angle of reflection?"

I looked at him. "No, I didn't know that, Mr. Physics Professor. Did you know that scientific explanations kill the romance of a scene?"

He draped his arm companionably over my shoulder. "No, I didn't know that. But then I always thought it was the company that made a situation romantic."

"Yeah," I said, my heart turning somersaults. "You have a point there."

We were barely seated at the restaurant before I started telling Ward all about my disastrous visit to the store. I had just worked myself up to full Bentley choleric steam when Todd leaned toward Ward.

"She's a little bent out of shape over an unqualified sales-clerk," he explained with just a touch of condescension. "And some clutter."

Fat lot you know. I gave him a look to scorch asbestos.

"He called me lady like it was the crudest epithet he could come up with," I snarled.

166

Todd and Ward exchanged a man-to-man glance that made me want to gnash my teeth. I could almost forgive Todd because he didn't know what was going on here, but Ward!

"And what did you say to him to rile him so?" Ward asked me with a smirk that was a very close relative to Todd's condescending expression.

"I told him gigabytes had nothing to do with modems! And they don't! Every idiot knows that."

"And your tone of voice?" Ward asked in an absolutely infuriating one of his own.

I decided I didn't want to answer that question. I was afraid I didn't meet the biblical standard of speech seasoned with grace. Then or now.

"Listen, Ward," I said instead, pointing my finger in his face. "If you're running all our stores the way that store is run, we're going to be out of business in no time! Pop must be rolling over in his grave."

"All our stores?" Todd asked, his condescension suddenly turning to alarm.

"I'll check on things tomorrow," Ward said, grabbing my finger and pushing it into his salad. It came up loaded with parmesan peppercorn dressing. "You know that's not the way we do business, Cara."

"Cara Bentley. Bentley Marts." Todd looked stunned. "Bentley Marts is you?"

"I hope it's not, Ward." I went to lick my finger, realized what a bad impression that might make on Todd, and wiped it on my napkin instead. "I think you should fire that store's manager and all the personnel. Send the human resources people and the industrial engineering people up from the Cherry Hill headquarters to give that store a thorough overhaul. And they need a new E."

"Consider it done," Ward said, eating his salad as if I hadn't just had a finger in it.

I nodded. "Good. Thanks."

"You guys are Bentley Marts?" Todd was still reeling.

"Yes," I mumbled around a mouthful of greens dashed with raspberry vinaigrette.

"And you never thought to tell me?" His surprise was quickly becoming pique.

"Ward made me promise not to."

"I'm your lawyer, for heaven's sake." He was definitely out of sorts.

Marnie entered the fray. "My husband was afraid of fortune hunters," she explained. "He was certain that Cara would fall in with unscrupulous villains who would take advantage of her and steal her money."

"Take advantage of Cara?" Todd looked at Marnie in disbelief. "Our Cara?"

I liked the sound of "our Cara."

"I know," Marnie said. "But in spite of overwhelming evidence to the contrary, he always thinks he knows best."

"I do," muttered Ward. "It was a good plan. I still say it's my job to protect her. Who knew what kind of people might suddenly claim to be related to us?"

Todd ate his Caesar salad in silence, the Romaine crunching beneath the strength of those wonderful jaws. He was deep in intense thought. "How many stores are there?" he finally said. "If I might ask."

Marnie saw his irritated expression and sympathized. "When I first realized that Bentley meant that Bentley, I was shocked too," she said. "And if it makes you feel better, Ward didn't tell me until we'd dated for almost a year."

"See," I said, patting Todd's hand. "Only a week. You're way ahead of the game."

Somehow that comment didn't seem to calm him as much as I thought it should.

"But don't let the money bother you," Marnie said, patting his other hand. "They're remarkably normal and nice for being so filthy rich."

"There are forty-five stores," I said, finally answering Todd's question.

"Soon to be forty-seven," Ward corrected me. "Two more open next month, one in Virginia and one in Rhode Island."

"Don't expand too rapidly, Ward," I cautioned around a sesame-seed roll. "You know what that can do to a business. I'd rather you moved a little cautiously until you're used to things without Pop. You don't want it to look like you're trying to prove something to the world now that you have the CEO's office."

For the first time Ward looked unhappy with me. "Cara, I say this with love and affection." He stuck his finger in my face. "Butt out."

"A bit outspoken," Marnie said to Todd, "and very Type A. But nice."

"Millionaires?" Todd asked.

Marnie nodded. "Several times over."

"She says she earns her living by writing," Todd said.

"I do," I snapped, mad at Ward's attitude.

Marnie grinned compassionately at Todd. "Paradigm shift time?"

"Big time," muttered Todd.

I leaned over and bit at Ward's finger, still waving under my nose.

"They hardly ever yell at me," Marnie said to Todd. "I don't think they'll yell much at you, either. And certainly neither Ward nor Cara has ever bitten my finger."

Ward suddenly grabbed Marnie's hand. "Never! Instead I kiss your hand, madame." And did so.

While Marnie giggled at Ward, Todd looked at me. "Why didn't you tell me who you were? Couldn't you trust me?"

I looked into his unhappy brown eyes, blinking so I wouldn't stare too hard and drown in their depths.

"It had nothing to do with trust," I said.

He looked unconvinced.

"It didn't! I honestly don't even think about Bentley Marts most of the time. The only reason we're talking about it now is because that store was so bad. If it had been up to snuff, I'd never even have thought about it at all."

He glanced at me briefly without saying anything, then looked away. I thought how much easier this explanation bit would be if I could just write it down and then rewrite and rewrite until I was saying what I wanted instead of what popped out.

"Todd, you know as well as I do that I have been consumed with this adoption search." I leaned toward him. "And then there's Mary's accident. And my book proposal." I leaned closer. "And you."

I wasn't even certain Todd heard me. He was staring, frowning, into his water glass as if he was looking for a clear thought within its crystalline depths.

I looked at him unhappily. I didn't know what to say to make him understand that I wasn't trying to deceive him about who I was. In my mind I was Cara Bentley, writer, not Cara Bentley of Bentley Marts. The one was me. The other was just something that had happened to me because of other people to whom I happened to be related.

"Come on, Todd," Ward finally said. "Don't be mad at her. I mean, look at her." He waved a hand in my direction, and Todd's eyes swung to me. I stared back, my heart in my eyes.

"She's beautiful and rich," Ward said. "I can't hide the one, but I can try and protect her from the other."

Todd sighed. "Well, she's beautiful all right," he said, his eyes still on me. "I knew that from the first. It'll just take a while to get used to the second."

"But you'll try to get used to it?" I asked. "Please?"

He shook his head at me, the corner of his mouth quirking up. "I'll try."

I beamed at him.

TEN

The Paddock looked like something from a fairy tale. The house, an early nineteenth century brick farmhouse restored to its original splendor, was hung with flowering baskets and planters of geraniums and ivy. Mature beeches, maples, and oaks shadowed the lawn, and evergreens stood sentinel as they had done four centuries ago when the first German settlers came to this abundant valley. A white split-rail fence edged the property.

The deep front lawn was filled with round tables covered with white linens, each set with silver and crystal for eight. Candles and flowers in a medley of summer colors blazed on the tables. White covers draping to the ground sheathed the chairs completely. To the left in front of an immaculate barn was a wooden dance floor beside which a quintet of musicians was playing.

"Oh, Todd!" I breathed as we walked up the drive. A teen in a tux jacket, dress shirt, bow tie, jeans, and white tennis shoes had taken our car, and we were able to appreciate the full effect of the setting as we walked.

I tucked my hand in the crook of Todd's elbow and thought again how handsome he looked in his tux. He'd even let his curls arrange themselves in a less rigid manner, a good sign, I thought, because it meant he listened to my suggestions and preferences. And he was willing to forgive me for being rich.

"Everything looks lovely," he agreed, surveying the grounds. "But not half as lovely as you."

I turned and found him looking at me in a way that made my breath catch. I was suddenly very glad I had spent the time and money to buy this coral dress. I wasn't boring tonight, though I wasn't sure I'd made it all the way to sophisticated or ever would. It had taken me forever just to successfully pull my hair back into a figure-eight chignon that actually stayed in place.

As I had told Rainbow while I brushed out yet another failed attempt with my hair, "Now I remember why I let it hang down my back or wear it braided. Elegance is too much work!"

But tonight it appeared worth all the effort, right down to the sprig of baby's breath in the chignon.

Todd spent most of the evening introducing me to people whose names I would never remember. The women blazed in sequins or shimmered in silk. The men looked substantial and well cared for in tuxes. I didn't realize there were so many lawyers to be had, let alone so many in one county.

"That's our host," Todd told me shortly after we arrived.

I looked where he indicated and saw a big man with a powerful voice. I could hear its boom even where we were, though I couldn't make out the words. He had a full head of dark hair with silver at the temples and a marvelous smile, which he used freely. He was obviously a man who liked his position as president of the county bar, talking to everyone, glad-handing, laughing easily, whispering compliments to the ladies and delighting in their blushes and simpers.

"I bet he could charm the birds from the trees," I muttered to Todd as I watched him lean over to whisper in the ear of a stout, well-corseted older woman. She listened for a moment, then leaned back and laughed like a young girl.

"Amos, you are a liar," she said, her upper register voice carrying. "But I love it. I love it."

"Judge Wallace Brubaker's wife," Todd whispered, pointing out the judge who was more than equal to his wife's girth and was busy talking to a slim, carefully coifed woman in a swirling sea green silk number. "And talking to the judge is Jessica, Amos's wife."

"Shall we go pay our respects?" I asked, turning in their direction.

"No rush," Todd said. And he led me to the bar where we each got a Perrier with a twist of lime.

We made a leisurely loop around the yard, enjoying the setting and watching the people. Amos's voice rolled over us wherever we were.

"He is a bit noisy, isn't he?" I asked.

Todd made a noncommittal sound in his throat just as Amos laughed raucously. The man he was with turned a brilliant shade of red, visible even from our distance.

"Does he often make people uncomfortable?" I asked.

"Only when he has a reason to. Otherwise he is, as you noted, a charmer."

When we finally reached Amos, he turned his charm on me.

"My, my, Todd," he said, taking my hand in his a little bit too enthusiastically. "Where have you been keeping this lovely young woman? You look absolutely beautiful, my dear, in that dress the color of sunrise."

The color of sunrise? Give me a break. But I simpered with the rest as he patted my hand and gave the impression I was the only woman in the world.

"May I present Cara Bentley," Todd said, standing at my shoulder and looking as frosty as January rime at the edge of a lake. "And Cara, this is our host, Amos Yost."

"Amos," I said and dipped my head politely while I tried to

reclaim my hand. Then his name registered. My breath caught in my throat and I spun to Todd.

My Amos Yost? I wanted to yell. *My maybe uncle/cousin? And you didn't tell me?*

Todd grasped my arm and smiled at me very sweetly. Too sweetly. He reached out, put a finger under my drooping jaw, and pushed my mouth gently closed. Then he turned back to Amos. "You've done yourself proud here tonight, you and Jessica. The place looks absolutely wonderful. I know Cara is impressed." And he squeezed my arm. Make that pinched.

It might have hurt, but it was a wise move on Todd's part. It brought me out of my stupor in short order. I shot him a look of pure venom before I turned back to Amos.

"I am most definitely impressed, sir. It looks like a fairyland, and I'm delighted to be here."

I let my anger at Todd simmer in the back of my mind while I looked at Amos with great interest. If he were my Amos Yost, Pop would be his uncle. Could I see any physical resemblance to Pop in him? Maybe they were somewhat alike in the barrel chest, but the biggest similarity wasn't so much in appearance as in manner. He shared with Pop—and with Ward, come to think of it—that indefinable but palpable charisma that made everyone listen when he spoke and act upon his suggestions with all due haste.

But that didn't mean he was related to me. Lots of people had charisma. Pop's hallmark was the affection for just about everyone that tempered the force of his great personality. And much as I groused about Ward, I could see that same respect for people developing more and more in him. I think it came from both of them appreciating people as the image of God. I must study Amos and see if he had that family trait.

"Jessica," Amos said to his wife. He reached out and

touched her arm to get her attention. She was again talking to Judge and Mrs. Brubaker. "You remember Todd Reasoner? And this is his guest, Cara Bentley."

Jessica Yost turned to me with a smile. Suddenly her expression congealed and she stared. In fact, she reacted to me about the same way I had probably reacted to Amos. Then she blinked and seemed to shake herself.

"How nice to meet you," she said, as cool and distant as Amos was in-your-face charming. She smiled vaguely at us, then turned with what looked to be relief to speak to some others who were wandering up to greet the host and hostess. With a nod of his head, Amos turned away, too.

Todd tucked my arm into his and started to walk. I didn't follow. I stood rooted, staring at my feet, trying to decide how one murdered one's date and got away with it.

"You louse!" I hissed when he turned to see why I wasn't following him. I didn't scream or raise my voice. We were surrounded, after all, by lots of well-dressed people, and I didn't want to embarrass myself in front of them. Mom would have been proud that her lessons in deportment had taken so well. "How could you do this to me?"

"Smile, woman," he returned, a phony grin pasted across his mouth. "We're having fun. And let's walk. We won't look quite so much like we're fighting if we move around a bit. We are fighting, aren't we?"

"We sure are," I said, but I let him take my arm and lead me in another circle of the yard.

He sighed. "I was afraid of that. But at least I'm learning to recognize the real thing. That's a hopeful sign for someone as repressed as I am, right?"

"Not repressed. Buttoned down," I corrected in a snarly voice.

"Ah, right."

I made the mistake of looking at Todd then. My eyes might be sparking with anger, but his were puppy dog worried—for me. I turned my head abruptly away. They affected me too much.

"I didn't tell you because I didn't want you to get your hopes up," he said. His voice was soft, caring, like the whisper of the breeze that floated in the trees above us.

"So instead you let me get hit across the head by a verbal two-by-four! You should have warned me!"

He nodded. "I probably should have, but I chose not to."

"You chose! You chose!" My voice shook. "You had no right, Todd! It's my family."

"I know. And I knew you'd probably be furious with me. But I'd do the same thing again." He glanced at me and saw my face. "At least I think I would," he said wryly.

"But why, Todd? Why would you do that to me? People don't hurt people they care for."

He cleared his throat self-consciously. "I was afraid you'd claim him as your own, and quite frankly, I don't want him to be yours."

"You don't want him to be mine?" I stopped to put my hands on my hips as I glared at him, but he took my elbow and pulled me along with him, completely ruining my desired effect. "Why? Are you jealous?"

He was suddenly genuinely smiling. In fact he was laughing his fool head off, something that did not make me feel any better, especially since I deserved the laughter after making such a inane comment.

"Jealous?" he repeated. "Oh, no. After all, he's probably a cousin or something. Besides, you've got better taste than to ever be hoodwinked by someone like him."

"Just by someone like you," I muttered.

He grinned and took my hand. "Cara, I know how important finding your family is to you and how much you want them to be nice people, but I've got to tell you that I just don't like the guy. I don't trust him. He's always got an angle. I've faced him often enough in court to know he's expedient instead of ethical, more interested in accruing billing hours than in giving solid legal services. He spends more time furthering his career than serving his clients."

"And yet he's president of the local bar association."

Todd nodded. "Politics."

I took a deep breath and studied Todd thoughtfully as the light from the torches flickered over his face. I was still angry that he hadn't told me about Amos, but there was an even more basic question at issue here. I had to answer about him the same question he had answered negatively about Amos. Did I trust him even when I disagreed with what he'd done? Did I trust his motives? His opinions? Did I trust his actions for me to be for my benefit, not his? Did I trust his advice? His obvious affection for me? Did I trust him with my future?

And how did I know I was right, whatever answer I came up with?

My staring must have made him uncomfortable, because he began fiddling with his bow tie. Then he ran his finger under his collar. "This shirt is slowly choking me to death. I must have gained weight since the last time I wore it."

"How long ago was that?"

"Five years. I told you I don't like chitchat. I usually avoid evenings like this."

"You've probably filled out a bit since then. Matured."

He nodded. "I used to be quite skinny."

I eyed his shoulders. "You're not skinny now." And I

grinned. Not broadly, but enough that he knew I wasn't about to bolt on him or burn him at the stake.

His sigh of relief reached all the way to his toes. He grabbed my hands. "Cara, I have nothing but my instincts when it comes to Amos. I have no evidence that I can present to you to encourage you to go slow with him, no evidence that proves he's really not a very nice man. I thought maybe if you saw him in action for a bit before you met him, before you knew who he might be, you'd be able to make a better judgment about how involved to get with him. Assuming he's the right Amos Yost."

I nodded. We had stopped walking and stood under a circle of giant hemlocks. From tiny cones and tinier seeds these giants had grown. From tiny trusts grew solid relationships.

"I can see that my actions look selfish to you," he continued. "And looking at them in hindsight, they look foolish to me. I shouldn't have let you get a shock like that. If the truth be known, I was probably just trying to protect myself."

"Protect yourself?"

"I don't want him in your life because if he is, then I have to deal with him, too. It seems that more and more anything that touches you touches me."

"Right," I said, mildly sarcastic. "As you never fail to tell everyone, I'm your client."

"That is not the alliance to which I refer, and you know it."

I glanced up at the towering evergreens, then looked at the intent face of the man before me. And I chose to trust.

"I accept what you say about how you see Amos, Todd. And because I'm coming to know you well, I accept that you're probably right in your judgment. He's not the greatest guy in the world, and I'm not going to be all that delighted to have him for a relative."

His shoulders relaxed, and he opened his mouth to speak. I held a hand up.

"But—and it's a big but, at least to me—I have to make my own judgments. You have to give me that freedom. You want me to trust your instincts. Well, you have to trust mine, too. You can't make my choices for me. You can't decide unilaterally what's good for me."

Todd stared at our clasped hands and was silent for a few minutes. Then he nodded slowly. "This trusting the other guy to make sound decisions isn't easy for a pair of controllers like us, is it?"

I looked up at the soaring hemlocks again. Little seeds. Little trusts. "No, but it's necessary. That is," and I swallowed hard, "if we want our friendship to go any further."

He looked me straight in the eye. "I want. I want very much."

My bones turned to liquid. "Me too," I whispered. "Me too."

His hug was warm and enveloping and over too soon. We walked slowly back toward the dinner tables and the other guests. As we were walking toward the bar for another Perrier, Judge Wallace Marley Brubaker grabbed Todd's arm.

"Son," the little man said, "I've been looking for you. I've got to tell you how impressed I was with your work on MacKenzie vs. MacKenzie, Inc. Your brief was a masterful presentation of your arguments, very cogent and well-written."

"Thank you, sir," Todd said, surprised. Pleasure oozed from his every pore. "Coming from you, that is a great compliment."

The men began talking shop, and I stood patiently, hoping dinner would be served soon. Late dinners might be elegant, but the sound of my growling stomach indicated how long ago lunch had been. It also shattered any illusion I might hold that I was as genteel as the setting.

"I'm afraid those two will be at it for some time, my dear. We might as well make the best of it."

I turned and found Mrs. Judge Brubaker, pouter pigeon body corseted and stuffed into a gown a lovely shade of blue. Her blond hair was fluffy and her gown too ruffled and froufrou, but her eyes were intelligent and aware.

"I'm Hannelore and he's Wally," she said, indicating the judge.

I smiled, delighted that Hannelore was rescuing me. Now I wouldn't have to look like Todd's not too bright appendage for the duration of his conversation. "I'm Cara Bentley."

"And what do you do, Cara? I assume you have a profession? All the young women do these days."

"I'm a writer."

"Of what?"

"Romances."

"Romances? I love romances." She got a faraway look in her eyes, not uncommon with romance readers. Suddenly her eyes widened. "Cara Bentley!"

I nodded.

"Oh, my dear!" She giggled. "This is so exciting. Stay right here," she ordered. "Don't move. I'll be right back."

When she returned, she had two women with her.

"Judy, Pat, this is Cara Bentley." She said it like I was some recently discovered but strange life form.

Judy and Pat immediately grabbed my hand and shook.

"It's a pleasure," Pat said.

"A real pleasure," Judy concurred.

"We belong to a book club," Hannelore explained.

Pat nodded. "There are five others of us, but they're not here."

"They're not in the legal professions," Judy said, obviously pitying them this lapse.

"We meet every month," Hannelore said. "And last month guess what book we discussed?"

"*As the Deer,*" all three women said in unison.

"And we all loved it," Judy said.

"All except Mindy," Pat said. "But Mindy never likes anything unless it's so dark and obscure that you can't understand it."

"I just finished *So My Soul* last week," Hannelore said.

"Me too," Pat said, a handsome women in her forties. "I want to know where you found the hero."

"You liked Scott?" I said. "Me too."

"But does he exist?" asked Pat. "Is there a Scott out there? I sure haven't found him if there is."

"Pat's single," Hannelore said. "She's a lawyer, a marvelous lawyer, and she scares most of the men away. Too strong."

"But I wouldn't scare Scott," Pat said, accepting Hannelore's assessment of her without batting an eye. "That's why I want to know if he even exists."

It was Hannelore who answered the question. "He exists," she said emphatically. "But he's already taken."

"Aren't they always," Judy said. Judy had hair so black it was almost blue and the most vivid and unusual blue eyes I'd ever seen, making her look somewhat like a husky minus the tan markings.

"Judy's a judge," Pat said. "She's been on the bench for five years now. She was married, but the jerk couldn't stand her success and left her for a beautician."

"A beautician twenty years younger than me," Judy said.

"So you see why," Pat said, "we want to know if Scott exists in real life."

I never know how to answer that question, especially when asked by mature, successful professional women who should know better. Heroes are larger than life, magnifications of all the qualities we want or dream of in our men. They are stronger, more resilient, more understanding and sensitive. They are braver, wiser, more loving. They never get killed because, obviously, if they did, they couldn't be the hero. And when the chips are down, they always come through for their women. In romances especially, heroes are way beyond mortal.

"I don't know if Scott exists or not," I said. At that moment Todd's arm brushed my back as he gestured about something to Judge Brubaker. I smiled. "Real men tend to be human with flaws that require trust and understanding on the part of their women. But I guess we never live up to the heroines either, come to think of it."

"I disagree," Hannelore said. We all looked at her. "Scott exists. I know he does." She swept her hand wide in her enthusiasm. "And there he is!"

We turned en masse to follow her pointing finger, and there stood portly Judge Brubaker.

"My Wally," Hannelore said. "Scott in the flesh."

Judge Brubaker flushed, though he had no idea why we were all staring at him. Hannelore went to him and kissed his cheek. Again he flushed, but he looked quite pleased with his wife as he slid his arm about her middle.

"Beauty is certainly in the eye of the beholder," whispered Pat in my ear. "But I'm still jealous that she even thinks he's Scott."

"Of course, there's Todd," Judy said, eyeing him speculatively.

"That there is," I said, smiling at him. "And he comes pretty close."

"But he's too young for us," Pat said with a sad sigh, grabbing Judy and pulling her away. Judy gave a small wave, and the two women disappeared in the crowd.

When it was finally time to sit down for dinner, Todd and I

found our table where we had a pleasant but uneventful meal making small talk. The only time things got really interesting was when one of the wives confessed to liking romances, and she and I had a pleasant conversation that clearly bored or appalled everyone else.

The candles on the tables and the torches flaring about the property, the women in formal dresses and the men in tuxes gave the illusion of a more gracious, genteel era when one dressed for dinner each evening, ate multiple course meals served by retainers in livery, and lingered over clever conversation instead of rushing away to the mall. I loved the glamour of it all and planned a scene in my next book where my heroine attended just such a gala.

The waiter removed my dinner plate with the remains of chicken topped with crab imperial, green beans seasoned with bacon and a sweet/sour sauce, julienne potatoes, and grilled tomatoes. Unfortunately he stepped back at precisely the same time as did the waiter at the table behind us. Their collision sent what was left of my dinner onto my lap.

"Ack!" I stared at the stain spreading over my beautiful sunrise dress and thought that I should have worn the old cream number I'd bought for last year's Romance Writers of America convention after all.

"I'm fine," I hastened to assure everyone, especially the young man who had deposited the food on me. He looked panic stricken. "It's okay. Really."

I mopped at the mess while Todd picked up my dish from the ground where it had bounced and swept the dinner debris off my lap back onto the plate. My romance reading friend dunked her napkin in her water glass and handed it across the table to me. I dabbed a bit at the ugly blotch, but in the dimness I couldn't see too clearly.

I stood. "I'll just go up to the house and see if I can get something to put on this to keep the stain from setting." Everyone nodded approval at this positive action, and I started across the lawn.

As I made my way through the company, I realized Todd was with me. He took my elbow and smiled at all the people we passed, as though it was normal for your date to have big stains running down the front of her dress. I noticed Amos and Jessica spot us and felt warmed by their look of consternation at my ill fortune.

"Will it come out?" Todd asked.

I looked down and made a sad face. "I doubt it."

"But it's such a beautiful dress." He was genuinely distressed for me.

"You just like it because it's not beige," I said.

"No," he said. "I like it because you're in it." And he tucked my arm tightly against his side.

We went inside where I asked the first person I saw the way to the bathroom.

"I think it's down there," the girl said vaguely. "But I've never been here before. I'm part of the caterer's staff."

"I'll find it," I said with more confidence than I felt.

"I'll wait right here," Todd said, sitting on a deacon's bench in the front hall.

After a couple of turns I found the powder room and went to work on my dress, not an easy task when the skirt was too slim to hold over the sink. By the time I was finished, I had a wet streak from waist to hem, sort of like a skunk's stripe, only down my front instead of my back, deep orange instead of white, and water instead of fur. I wasn't sure that the greasy blob from dinner wasn't preferable, especially since it was probably still there, buried under all the wet.

Shaking my head, I left the powder room and began my trek down the dimly lit hall back to the front of the house.

"Hey, Meaghan! What are you doing? We're waiting!"

The voice was that of a young man, and the tone indicated that he was not very happy with Meaghan.

"Yo, Meaghan! I'm talking to you, girl!"

I couldn't resist the impulse to glance over my shoulder and see who was yelling and whom he was yelling at.

A very large but considerably younger version of Amos Yost was stalking down the hall toward me. Obviously he was the yeller. The problem was that I saw no yellee. Unless he was yelling at me?

"What are you planning to do, crash the party?" His voice got nastier if anything.

I looked up and down the hall again, but there was no one in sight but me and him.

"Are you talking to me?" I asked hesitantly, pointing at myself.

He sneered at me. "Oh, that's cute. Just who else would I be talking to? Do you see anyone else?" And he grabbed for my arm.

I jerked back and frowned at him. "Just what do you think you're doing?" I asked in my best Bentley hauteur.

He reached for me again, and as his hand closed over my arm, he froze. His eyes narrowed and he stared at me, looking me over from head to toe. I took a step back, uncomfortable under his scrutiny.

"I don't believe it," he muttered.

"What?" I asked.

"Hey, Pip," he yelled suddenly. "Come here! You've got to see this!"

If he could call out reinforcements, so could I.

"Hey, Todd," I yelled. "Come here! Quick!"

Another young man, presumably Pip, appeared behind my captor. He didn't have the bulk or look of the one staring at me with unfriendly eyes. He had, in fact, a strong resemblance to Jessica Yost.

"Who's he?" I asked. "Your brother?"

I got no answer.

"What do you want, Mick?" asked the newcomer. "Oh, you found her. It's about time. Come on, Meaghan, you're holding us up! And what are you wearing that ridiculous dress for?"

"It's not ridiculous," I said, stung. "And I'm not Meaghan."

I looked pointedly at my arm where Mick had it in a death grip. My skin around the edges of his hand was white from the pressure, and I thought that tomorrow I might well have a hand-shaped bruise. "Don't you think it would be a good idea to let go of me?"

"Oh. Right." Mick released me just as Todd came into the hallway. He looked wonderful, my hero, though by now I didn't think I'd need rescuing. I'd figured out who I was talking to, thanks to the memorized family tree. Mick was undoubtedly Michael Yost and Pip was Philip. Meaghan was their sister.

"Who's he?" demanded Mick, looking at Todd. "What's he doing here? And who in the world are you?"

"Mick," Pip said, "just leave Meaghan there. If she doesn't want to come with us, there's no rule that says she has to. I'd rather go without her anyway." He looked at me like he expected me to complain about being abandoned. And I guess if I were Meaghan, I might. As it was, I looked from him to Mick and answered Mick's questions.

"He's Todd Reasoner, Esq. We're here for your father's dinner party. And I'm Cara."

"Anything wrong?" Todd rested a hand protectively on my shoulder.

"I don't think so," I said. "I think it's a case of mistaken identity."

By now Pip was staring at me over Mick's shoulder as if he couldn't believe his eyes. "It's not Meaghan, but it is." His voice was full of awe.

"Who's Meaghan?" Todd asked.

"Our sister," Mick said.

"And I must look like her. Right?" My heart was now tripping at a fantastic rate. I looked at Todd to see if he understood the possible ramifications of a resemblance here. He looked at me with a crooked eyebrow that said I understand, but don't jump to conclusions. He gave my shoulder a squeeze.

Suddenly a girl with long brown hair and long slim legs came barreling around the corner and down the hall behind Mick and Pip.

"What's keeping you two?" she demanded. "I've been waiting out back in the car. It's getting later by the moment, and I don't want to miss the beginning of the movie because you two are too dense to tell time."

Then she saw me. Her mouth made a small O and a little woof of sound emerged—as though someone had punched her in the stomach. I suspect that I looked exactly the same.

In fact, I did look exactly the same. Looking at Meaghan Yost was like looking in a mirror. Certainly there were slight differences, like the shape of our eyes wasn't quite the same and my hair appeared to be a little lighter than hers, though she had just washed hers and it hung long and dark with moisture down her back almost to her waist. And she was younger.

The five of us were clustered in the hall, staring, when suddenly Amos and Jessica were there, Amos swearing under his breath as they came up behind Todd and me.

"Who are you?" Meaghan asked me when she could finally talk.

I swallowed, trying to get enough moisture in my mouth to speak. "I think I might be your long-lost cousin several times removed," I said.

"Really?" Meaghan looked surprised.

"Neat!" Pip looked impressed.

"Rubbish!" Mick looked furious.

"Oh, dear." Jessica looked worried.

Amos snorted. "We will talk in my study." And he stalked off down the hall and around the corner, obviously expecting us to follow. We did. That family charisma.

The three kids sat on the navy blue-and-white checkered sofa in descending order by size—Mick, Pip, Meaghan. Jessica sat on a navy wing chair while I sat in an overstuffed white chair, piped in navy. Todd sat on the arm of my chair, a very comforting support. Amos sat behind his desk in an executive's chair covered in navy leather. The navy rug was deep and plush and had sweeper marks across its surface. A watercolor of a sleek Nittany lion hung over the sofa, and various service and award plaques hung in clusters on the walls. However, pride of place was given to a photo of Amos shaking hands with football coaching great Joe Paterno. It was a Penn State alumnus's dream office.

"I know all about you," Amos began, his eyes on me cold and accusing. "Tel Hai called. So did Alma."

"I was very sorry that your mother had to go to the hospital," I said. "I spoke with Alma too. She told me your mother's doing well and was expected back at Tel Hai today now that her heart is regulated. It was a matter of medication."

"Medication, my foot." He put his hands on his desk, palms down, and leaned forward. "It was you."

I jerked as though hit. Todd put a comforting hand on my shoulder.

"Amos, that's not true and you know it," he said.

"No, I don't know that," Amos said. "Mom had been doing quite well until she came along." And he pointed at me.

"She wanted to see me." I sounded desperate that he believe me.

"Hah! She's a senile old lady. She doesn't even understand why you were coming. But I know."

Suddenly something felt very strange here. "Why do you think I wanted to see your mother?"

He all but sneered. "Her money, of course."

"She's wealthy? I didn't know that."

This time he did sneer, looking amazingly like Elvis. "Do you honestly expect me to believe that?"

"You might try. It's true."

"Cara came to me as a client because she was looking for her family and needed advice on Pennsylvania law regarding adoptions," Todd said. "She has been following leads carefully since she's been here. She has not indicated in any way that she seeks anything from her family but acquaintance."

"Well, we're not her family, and if we were, we wouldn't want any acquaintance." Amos's voice was heavy and final.

"I don't know about not being her family, Daddy." Meaghan got up from the sofa and walked toward me, studying me intently.

I glanced at Amos, and while he didn't look happy with his daughter, neither was he going to stop her speaking.

"Look at her, Daddy. She's me. Or me in what? Fifteen-twenty years?"

I started. Thanks a lot, I thought, and could feel Todd's enjoyment of my response to the unintended barb.

"How old are you?" Meaghan asked.

"Thirty," I said. "How about you?"

191

"Eighteen. I graduated this year."

"Are you going to college next year?"

She nodded. "Penn State, main campus."

"What will you be studying?"

"English and journalism. I want to write."

My skin prickled. "I'm a writer."

"Really? What do you write? Are you published? How did you get published?"

"That's enough!" Amos roared.

I flinched, but Meaghan didn't. "We'll talk later," she said to me quietly.

I nodded and opened my evening purse. I pulled out a little gold case and extracted a business card. "Here. It's my cell-phone number and the address where I'm staying." I smiled at her. "I just made them today in case I saw anyone important tonight."

"Thanks," she said, and with a challenging look at her father put the card in her shorts pocket.

"Meaghan," Amos said in a taut voice. "You will not contact this woman. Do you understand me?"

Meaghan nodded but made no promises. Strong-willed parents breed strong-willed children, I thought.

"Dad, Meaghan's right," Pip said, also apparently not intimidated by his father. "There's some family something here. There has to be with a resemblance like theirs. Aren't you at all curious about it?"

"I already know about it," Amos said. "She claims she's the descendant of an illegitimate child of my grandmother."

"Yeah?" Pip looked intrigued. "So it's not you that was adopted?" he asked me. "You're not Mom or Dad's kid?"

My horror at such a thought was second only to that of Amos and Jessica. I tried not to shudder as I shook my head.

"Not me," I said. "My parents died when I was only two, but I wasn't adopted at that point. My grandparents raised me and my brother. It's my grandfather who's the one that was adopted. He's the one whose family I'm trying to trace."

"Are you having any luck?" asked Pip.

"I keep tracing everyone I can find who is or was a Biemsderfer."

Pip nodded. "Well, that's us a couple of generations back."

"Pip," Amos said, heavily authoritative. "We do not have illegitimacy in our family."

"Dad, who cares if your grandmother had a baby before she was married? She's been dead for years. Besides, it happens all the time."

"That does not make it right!" Amos all but shouted.

Somehow I didn't think the issue of having sex outside of marriage was what Amos saw as wrong. It was that his grandmother had gotten caught, that his family had had to deal then and was having to deal now with the ramifications, and, most importantly, that his reputation might get besmirched by this bit of family history—though I had to agree with Pip. Who cared at this point?

And I realized how overwhelmingly important appearances were to Amos. Expedient, Todd had called him.

Jessica had sat quietly through all the conversation so far. Now she spoke to me, her eyes hot with contained resentment. "When I was introduced to you, I was absolutely shocked. I knew you were out there." She waved her hand vaguely. "I knew you were looking. Alma had called us. She said there was an uncanny similarity between you and Meaghan. But when I turned around and saw you right here in my own yard…" She let the sentence trail away, the horror of my presence speaking for itself.

I nodded. "I can only imagine," I said. "We had no idea, of course."

Amos suddenly stood and with that movement took control of the conference once more. He walked out from behind his desk as Meaghan took her seat next to Pip. Jessica sank back into her chair looking sorry she had spoken.

Amos came to a stop a few feet in front of me, standing too close to my chair, trying to intimidate me and make me look up at him. I refused to cooperate, looking instead at my feet. I wasn't a Bentley for nothing.

Todd stood and moved to the front of the chair we occupied. When he turned sideways to offer me his hand to help me rise, his movement forced Amos to step back. I looked at Todd gratefully.

"Listen here, whoever you are," Amos said when we finally stood face-to-face, eyes level. "I forbid you to see my mother. I absolutely forbid it."

I looked from Amos to Jessica to the children, especially Meaghan. I felt a burning behind my eyes. I'd had such hopes. To have them dashed like this, especially after Alma had been so kind, was very painful.

"And one other thing," Amos said, his voice low and threatening. "If you ever try to insinuate yourself into my home or family again, you will regret it."

Todd bristled immediately, but I laid a hand on his arm. "Let's go," I whispered. "It doesn't matter."

But it did, it did, and I was desperate to get out of there before I began to weep.

ELEVEN

Todd was so gentle and kind to me both when he brought me home Saturday night and when he took me to church Sunday morning. There's something quite terrific about a man who supports you even when he doesn't necessarily support your objectives.

For church, Mr. Monochromatic was all in tans from the tan-and-white stripes of his knit shirt to his tan slacks. I had on tan too, so we sort of looked like a matched pair if you discounted height, hair, jawline, and gender. I had added some color to my cotton knit dress with a necklace of multihued wooden beads Marnie had given me.

"So you don't blend in with the woodwork completely," she'd told me with a loving smile when she gave them to me.

"We Bentleys don't blend," I'd told her as I hung the beads about my neck.

She'd laughed. "That's one of the truest things you've ever said!"

Smiling, I fingered the beads as I climbed out of Todd's car. Heart relatives like Marnie were so much nicer than blood relatives like Amos. So why did Amos and the rest of the Biemsderfer clan mean so much to me? And what was wrong with me that they did?

"I had a thought last night," Todd said as we walked across the parking lot toward the church.

I refrained from making a smart-mouth remark because he looked so serious.

"It occurred to me," he continued, "that God is a proponent of adoption."

I looked at him. "So am I."

He quirked an eyebrow. "Are you? Sometimes it seems you're almost trying to undo Pop's adoption with this great drive to find your blood family."

I gave his comment careful consideration before I answered. "No, I don't think so. That would say something negative and unfair and unjust about my great-grandparents, and I'd never want to do that. From everything I've heard, they were wonderful people. Great-grandfather Bentley was a doctor and Great-grandmother was an artist. I have some of the most beautiful hand-painted china that she did. Painting china was popular with ladies in those days, you know."

"Um, no, I didn't know." Todd's mouth twitched.

"Now why am I not surprised?" I grinned at him. "Most of the ladies who painted were no-talent dilettantes, but Great-grandmother Bentley's work is absolutely wonderful. If she lived today, she'd be an artist in great demand."

We stopped to avoid getting bowled over by three little stair-step brothers running for the door of the Sunday school wing. One ran so close that my skirt swayed in the breeze he created.

"I'm sorry," their mother panted as she ran after them with a fourth little boy in her arms. "But at least they like to come."

"See how much they look alike?" I said as I watched the boys disappear into the building. "That's genetics. Great-grandmother Bentley might have been talented, but it didn't rub off on me. What abilities did Pop's birth parents have that we know nothing about? That's one of the strange things about adoption: where do your abilities come from? Was there a Biemsderfer somewhere who liked to write?"

"Does it matter?" He shrugged.

"Doesn't it?"

"Well, think about this," Todd said. "Jesus was raised by an adoptive father."

I nodded. "Joseph. I've often thought raising the Son of God must have been a tall order. "

"Well, if it was good enough for Jesus, why isn't it good enough for you?"

"But Jesus knew his Father. He knew his eternal background."

Todd frowned. "Okay, I'll give you that. But how about this? When we believe in Jesus, the Bible refers to us as adopted children of our heavenly Father. I always liked the old King James phrase 'accepted in the Beloved.'"

"What are you trying to tell me, Todd? That Pop's adoption has a spiritual parallel, and because it does, I shouldn't be looking for birth family?"

He shook his head. "No. But maybe I'm suggesting that adopted family should be enough."

I thought about his comment all through the worship service. It was one of those Sundays when I heard little the pastor said, but I knew God was very close. I thought about Amos and Jessica and their rejection of me. I thought of Alma and her friendliness; I also thought of her not mentioning to me my resemblance to Meaghan, though she told Amos about it. I thought of Meaghan who wanted to be a writer and Pip who wondered if I were the child of one of his parents. I thought of Mick who didn't bother to talk to me after his initial response in the hallway. I thought of the branch of the Biemsderfers who no longer lived in Lancaster County but were scattered around the world. And I thought of Mom and Pop and Ward and Marnie and little Johnny.

And I realized that generation to generation doesn't have to be blood generations. In theory, family should be bone of my bone as well as heart of my heart. But if you had to choose, maybe love and acceptance were more important than DNA.

I was still mulling over these ideas as Todd and I stopped for something to eat on the way home following the service.

"It's like Pop's a coin with two sides," I said to him over a burger and fries. "I know the Bentley side. I'd like to know the Biemsderfer side, too. I think for some who search, there is a driving need to find where they've come from, an intensity that is painful and overwhelming and utterly compelling. The need for roots is an unhealthy compulsion for some because they think it will fix all the problems in their lives—and of course it won't. Locating the Biemsderfers isn't that all-consuming for me, probably for two reasons—I'm not the adopted person, and I love my family. I'm not looking to replace them. But I can't deny a compulsion to find out about the Biemsderfers, even the ones that are all over the globe."

"In spite of the fact that an omnipotent God allowed the Bentley side of Pop's coin?"

"I'm not denying our side of the coin. Truly I'm not. I love my family too much to do that. It's just that I can't deny the other side, either."

I was swallowing my last fry when my cell phone in my purse rang.

"This is Elizabeth Yost," a voice told me when I answered.

"Oh, Mrs. Yost," I breathed, looking at Todd with excitement.

"Jessica?" Todd said in surprise.

I shook my head and mouthed, "Aunt Lizzie."

"I want you to come and visit me," she said. "I was so disappointed we missed each other on Thursday. Sometimes this old

198

heart gives me such trouble, and at the most inconvenient times."

"I'd love to come, Mrs. Yost. But Amos asked me not to." Now that was a kind way of explaining his uncompromising order.

"I'm Aunt Lizzie to you, child. And I don't care what Amos says."

I liked this woman already.

"He's always trying to tell me what to do," she continued. "I'm not senile yet, and I'll make my own choices. So please come. I want to meet you. And I want to tell you a story."

"When do you want me?"

"How about later this afternoon?"

"Later this afternoon?" I repeated with a look at Todd. It didn't strike either him or me as odd that I expected him to come along. He nodded. "We'll see you then," I told her.

"I think," I said to Todd as we drove to the farm, "that it's okay if I look for family if I don't need them, if I can function without them. If I find them and they accept me, I'll know a fuller life. If I find them and they reject me, as Amos did, I'll know sadness, but it's not the end of the world. I keep thinking of what St. Paul wrote: 'We are hard pressed on every side, but not crushed; perplexed, but not in despair; persecuted, but not abandoned; struck down, but not destroyed.' That's me and how I feel about Amos."

I felt tears rising again as I had frequently since we'd left Amos's last night. "I feel struck down by last night's events, but I'm not destroyed. I realize more strongly than ever that if I'm looking for my birth family to make me whole, I'm looking in the wrong place. Only God can fill my deepest longings because only he understands them. People come and go, but God is forever."

"He's there when you don't know who your family is," Todd agreed. "And he's there when you do, but they don't give you much emotionally."

I looked at him sharply, ready to give sympathy since he was obviously speaking of his situation, but he was already distracted.

"Would you look at that!"

I looked and saw the entire Zook drive full of buggies.

Todd pulled to the side of the road. "I'll have to let you out here," he said. "I don't want to get in the middle of all that. But I'll be back in a couple of hours. Why not try to get a nap?" He looked at the circles under my eyes. "I'd say you didn't sleep very well last night."

"I'd say you're right, and I'd also say my cover-up stick isn't working as well as it should."

I climbed out of the car and watched him drive away. Then I threaded my way up the drive and went inside. The large open room that filled the downstairs was full of people, some of whom, I'm sorry to say, weren't using deodorant on this very hot June day. The men in their black Sunday suits and white shirts occupied the living room end of the house, talking in Pennsylvania Dutch. The women occupied the kitchen end, fussing over food and talking in Pennsylvania Dutch.

When I came in, everyone fell silent, the hush sounding terribly loud to my embarrassed ears. Everyone smiled and nodded politely to me, and Elam gave a little wave before returning to his conversation with two other young men. Esther walked over.

"They're here to visit Mary," she explained. "They're taking turns going upstairs."

"I see all the buggies," I semiwhispered. "But where are the horses?"

She giggled and answered in the same *sotto voce* manner. "They're tied behind the barn at a special hitching rail Elam and John set up."

"Ah." I nodded sagely. "You guys are so practical!"

Just then an older woman in a royal purple dress, black apron, black shoes and hose, and white kapp appeared at the bottom of the steps.

"She needs a nap," the woman announced, and everyone nodded. "We should eat."

I slipped upstairs to my rooms as the men began filing into the kitchen to fill their plates with the cold food prepared yesterday, since cooking on the Sabbath was prohibited. I wondered if Elam's Mary Clare or his rival Young Joe Lapp were here, but the only one I could ask was Jake, and he seemed to be hiding out in his apartment.

I changed into khaki slacks and was sitting in front of my fan reading this month's *Christian Communicator* when I heard a knock at my door. It was Esther, looking worried and unsure of herself.

"Come in, Esther. What's wrong?"

"Cara, Mary's in a lot of pain today, and she's run out of medicine. Could you call her doctor and ask for more? It'd save me running down to the phone shanty at the end of the road."

"Sure." I pulled out my cell phone and dialed the number Esther gave me. In a remarkably short time, the doctor returned my call and agreed to contact the pharmacy for a refill. When I hung up, I asked, "Who's going to go pick this up?"

"I can skate down for it," she said.

"But it's Sunday! Should you skate on Sunday? Besides you're caring for the guests. Let me go get it, okay? You don't want to go to the store on Sunday anyway, do you?" Surely that was anti-*Ordnung*.

"I'd do it for Mary."

"I'll go," I said, putting my magazine aside, and Esther smiled her thanks.

I was afraid that I wouldn't be able to get my car out of the drive with all the buggies that were here, but they had graciously left room for either Jake or me to get around. I walked to my car and reached for the door handle. I missed on my first grab. I had just extended my hand again when I realized something was very strange about my car. The handle was lower than it should be.

I stepped back and looked and with a gasp realized all my tires were flat. All of them!

I bent and looked more closely, and my skin crawled. On each tire were long slash marks where someone had taken a knife and cut and cut and cut.

I stared in shock. My tires! Someone had purposely sliced my tires. Why? Who? I looked at all the buggies but quickly dismissed that idea. Not one of the Zooks's guests. Aside from the fact that they were peaceable folks, there was no privacy. Surely slashers liked privacy.

I looked back at my car and was overwhelmed. Why me? Why my car?

I turned to Jake's van, but his tires were fine. No one had done anything to him. Just to me. To my tires. And whoever it was hadn't been satisfied with a single cut. Far from it. I shivered in the shimmering June heat.

I pulled out my cell phone and made two calls. First I called the police. Then I called the automobile club.

"Tell whoever comes to bring four new tires," I told the dispatcher.

"Four?" Disbelief edged her voice.

"Four."

The police came quickly, and I stood by my wounded car answering questions for their report surrounded by men in black suits and broad-brimmed hats. Jake sat supportively by my side.

"Don't worry about Mom's medicine," he told me. "I'll go get it as soon as we're finished here."

I nodded gratefully and smiled my thanks. I had discovered that if I spoke, I was having trouble controlling the quaver that insisted on wobbling uninvited through my words.

"I don't know, Miss Bentley," the officer told me. "Finding perpetrators of random nastiness like this is very difficult."

I nodded. "I understand."

"You're sure you don't know anyone who has a grudge against you or anything?"

I shook my head. I felt very tired. "I just moved to Bird-in-Hand a little over a week ago. The only people I know are the Zooks; Todd Reasoner, my lawyer; and Amos Yost, a lawyer in Lancaster. Not much in the way of suspects, I'm afraid."

The police were preparing to leave when the AAA service truck pulled into the drive. Jake, the Amishmen, and I watched as the service man began work on the first tire.

"Wow," he whistled. "Somebody did a number on this!"

Somehow his awe at the cowardly attack made me feel ill. I turned and walked down the drive, down the street, and into the woods until I came to the stream. I sat on one of the rocks and felt vulnerable. It was an uncomfortable feeling, and I didn't like it.

I also didn't like the idea of violence on the Zooks's farm. They were pacifists, and nothing so evil should happen near them, especially because of my presence.

Was it me, God? Did someone want to hurt me? I know Amos doesn't like me, but this is not the work of a man like him. Maybe it was just random violence. My car was just a handy target for some kids who had no sense and a streak of malice.

I don't know how long I sat staring at the burbling stream, the chattering rush of the water somehow comforting. I do know how glad I was to hear a concerned voice just behind me.

"Hey. Are you all right?" Todd sat on the rock beside me and reached for my hand.

"Where'd you come from?" I asked.

"Jake called me."

Now that I had someone to sympathize, I went to pieces. Tears burned my eyes, breached my lower lids, and fell. Todd put his arm around me and pulled me to him until my head rested on his shoulder.

"Shush. It's okay," he whispered as he patted me gently on the back. "It's okay."

"Yeah, right," I snuffled. "Someone slashes my tires and you say it's okay. Some lawyer you are."

I felt as much as heard his little burst of laughter. "A smart remark. Why am I not surprised? I knew you were a gutsy lady. You're going to be okay."

I didn't feel very gutsy. I took a deep quavery breath. "Why would someone do that to my tires, Todd?"

His arm tightened around me. "It wasn't you, Cara. Never think it was you."

"But it was my car!"

"Just because it was there."

"Do you really think so?"

"What else could it be? So don't cry, sweetheart. Don't cry."

I nodded. "I won't." But I did. Buckets. All over his blue shirt, turning one side into a mass of wrinkles. I looked at him apologetically. "I think I'm crying as much over Amos's nastiness as I am over the tires," I sniffed. "Up until now I was trying to be brave about it. But it hurts! I'm not used to people not liking me."

I sat up, sniffed, and wiped at my face in a mostly futile effort to erase the tears. My cheeks felt hot and puffy. I knelt and leaned over the stream. I took a handful of water and splashed my eyes, my cheeks. The coolness felt good. I took a quick drink.

I sat back on my rock and pulled my sandals off. I rolled up my slacks and lowered my feet into the stream.

"Yo! Cold!" I pulled my feet out of the water, then tried again.

Todd reached forward and lowered his hand into the water. "It's not cold."

"Oh, sure. You're only sticking your hand under. Hands are tough. They can take it. It's feet that complain."

"Not mine." And having so said, he took off his shoes and stuck his feet into the water. "Yo! Cold!"

We grinned at each other as we sat on the rocks with our feet dangling in the creek, slowly turning purple.

Todd cleared his throat. "I had an idea after I left you today," he said. He fell silent and watched his feet slowly paddling.

I turned to him. "Do you think you'll share it?"

He looked at me, then back to the stream.

"It's about the adoption, isn't it?" I said. "And you're not sure you want to tell me?"

"What if acting on it somehow brings you another unpleasant episode like last night?" His eyes were bright with concern for me. "Or is that yours to decide?"

"What do you think?"

He sighed. "That's what I was afraid of."

I reached over and caught a handful of water. I flicked it in his direction. "Come on. Spill it."

He looked with great interest at the deep blue splash mark on his jeans leg. His eyebrow quirked and his jaw hardened. "I don't know after treatment like that." And he sent a cascade of water my way with his foot.

I gasped as the deluge caught me in the chest. My shirt was drenched and clung wetly to me.

"Sorry," Todd said with a huge grin, obviously as sorry as a bully who has tripped a poor innocent child. "I didn't mean to kick quite that much."

"Why, you!" I made my hand a scoop and gave him a face full. I was pleased to see him choke and sputter, but my pleasure turned to consternation as he sent another great spray my way. Now it was my turn to choke and splutter.

I jumped into the creek so I could aim head on, cupped my hands and threw, water flying. I got him square in the chest and crowed with pleasure. How did pacifists feel about water battles, I wondered as I tried unsuccessfully to duck his retaliatory measures. And on a Sunday?

Next thing I knew we were both in the stream dashing water at each other at a furious pace. We were wet and laughing, and my tears were forgotten. I never even saw the mossy rock that brought me down, but I felt myself start to fall.

"Ack!" To keep from tumbling I grabbed the nearest object, which was Todd. Suddenly both of us were sitting in water to our armpits.

"My wallet!" Todd moaned as he felt his back pocket.

"Look at it this way," I suggested. "You're just laundering your money."

"A great activity for a lawyer!" He pulled his wallet out of his pocket and tossed it onto the rock where it leaked a steady stream.

"I don't know." I smirked. "I've read in the papers about numerous lawyers who might launder money."

"Attacking a whole profession just because of a few. Unfair and unjust." He dipped into the stream with joined hands and poured the captured water over my head like he was ladling soup. Water dripped from my nose and ran off my chin. "Why, I might as well say all writers are plagiarists."

"A scurrilous attack!" I cried, laughing so hard I could barely get the words out. I cupped my hand and slid it along the surface of the stream, sending a great arc of water into Todd's face. It happened to get him with his mouth open in laughter and on an indrawn breath. He began to cough and wheeze.

"Serves you right!" I yelled. I clambered to my feet, waded around him, fell to my knees, and began clapping him on the back. The pats were pretty weak because of my laughter, but they helped curb his coughing.

I fell back on my seat and leaned back on my hands, out of breath and exhilarated. My braid trailed behind me in the stream. I couldn't remember the last time I'd done something so absolutely foolish and fun.

Todd slowly rotated until he was facing me, and I knew he had great plans for revenge. He reached around me and grabbed my braid.

"Dunk me and you're a dead man!" I reached out and grabbed his hand.

I expected him to try to pull me under, but instead he pulled me slowly toward him. I looked up, surprised. Our eyes met and held.

In a flash the frivolity dissipated and the atmosphere between us was as laden with electricity as the air is with ozone after a lightning strike. I couldn't have moved if my life depended on it. As it was, I could barely breathe. It was as if all the oxygen had been burned off by the atmospheric charge, and there was nothing left to draw into my lungs.

A fly buzzed between us and Todd blinked, reluctantly letting go of my hair. "Come on, Cara," he said softly. "We'd better get out of the water before we catch pneumonia."

He stood and pulled me to my feet. We climbed onto our rocks, brightly lit and warmed by a shaft of sunlight streaming through an opening in the canopy of leaves. Water ran from our clothes, forming pools that flowed into rivulets that became little waterfalls that fell back into the creek.

I was conscious of Todd's every movement even without looking directly at him. I pulled my braid over my shoulder with assumed nonchalance and squeezed. Water poured in a little torrent. I began working the rubber band that bound the plait, but it was wound about by hair and snarls. I felt myself go cross-eyed as I tried to unravel the tangled mess.

"Here, let me." Todd pulled my braid back over my shoulder. "Turn sideways," he ordered. I did and he sat behind me. He began struggling with my hair.

"Now tell me what you were going to tell me before we got sidetracked," I said. We definitely needed something ordinary to talk about to diffuse the intense reaction between us.

He cleared his throat. "Well, I was thinking about adoption papers and—Ow!" I heard the smack as the rubber band snapped him. "And you'd better not be smiling," he said grouchily.

I wiped the grin from my face. "I'm not."

"Umph." He went back to wrestling with the rubber band. "In the earlier part of the century, adoptions weren't sealed like they are today."

"No safes? No locks and keys?"

"Nope. There's a possibility that Pop's papers might be filed

208

along with all the other civil records from 1917 or 1918 in the prothonotary's office."

"You mean I could just walk in and ask to see the papers from 1917 or 1918 and find Pop's birth and adoption records?" I was floored.

"Maybe," Todd said. "I don't know. It's just something that occurred to me. You'd have to go and find out."

"Where?" I tried to turn to look at him, but my braid in his hands prevented it.

"The prothonotary is in the courthouse in Lancaster."

I nodded. I knew where that was. "What in the world is a prothonotary? I never even heard that word before."

"Don't you have prothonotaries in New Jersey?"

"If we do, I never knew it."

"We elect them here in Pennsylvania."

"Good for you staunch citizens, but what in the world is one?"

"It's the person who watches over all the civil records." With a satisfied grunt he finally pulled the rubber band free. He began carefully unbraiding my hair.

"Then why don't they call it the Civil Records Office?" I grumbled. "It's as bad as Orphan's Court."

"Thank you, Todd," said Todd. "That was very nice of you to come up with such a wonderful idea for me."

I could feel him spreading my hair out to the sun. I smiled. "Thank you, Todd. It was very nice of you to come up with such a wonderful idea for me. You are absolutely the best lawyer a woman could want. I will go to the courthouse tomorrow and check it out."

"Mmm," he said. His strong fingers combed my hair, catching every so often on knots, but it felt wonderful regardless. Mom had often combed my hair for me when I was a child, and few things meant love and security more. I closed my eyes and gave myself up to the pleasant sensation.

The sun fell warm on my face. The leaves hung hot and still above us, and the stream frolicked beside. I looked up into the branches overhead and saw a catbird land on a branch. His melodious trill filled the air as he sang with great joy. I smiled and my eyes slid shut again.

I woke when the sun had moved off me. I wasn't chilled; it was impossible to be chilled in the heat. I was just aware that time had passed, though I had no idea how much. I was also aware of Todd's touch still on my hair and of my head resting against his knee as he sat with his legs bracketing me.

"Enjoy your nap?" he asked softly as he brushed my hair back from my forehead.

I nodded. "Was I asleep long?"

"Only a few minutes. Maybe it'll get rid of those bruises under your eyes."

"I think I need more than a few minutes for that."

A honeybee hummed beside me and flew on; a mosquito buzzed next to my ear. I reached up and brushed it away.

I sighed with contentment. "Do you treat all your clients with such excellent care?"

Immediately his hands stilled. "No," he said. "Only the special ones." But just like that, in spite of his nice words, the magic mood was gone.

I sighed, this time at my stupidity. I should have kept my mouth shut. I sat up straight, feeling the weight of my hair fall over my shoulders and back.

"I guess we'd better get going if we want to see Great-aunt Lizzie," I said.

Todd glanced at his wrist and nodded. "My fortunately waterproof watch tells me you're right."

We walked down the quiet road back toward the house. We weren't dripping too badly by now, but we were a sight, clothes wrinkled, my hair wild and all over the place, Todd's curls in a riot of unruly brown all over his head.

I stopped walking abruptly. "The company! I can't walk through the living room looking like this. They'll stare and think terrible things about me."

Todd eyed me. "I don't know. I think you look kind of cute."

I grinned. "Thanks, but I probably look like a reprobate to them. What am I going to do? I have to change my clothes. I can't go visit Lizzie like this."

When we reached the edge of the yard, I had an inspiration. "Come on." I grabbed his hand and dragged him toward Jake's door.

Jake's expression was priceless when he saw us.

"We fell in the stream," I explained.

"Obviously."

"And I don't want to walk through the living room in front of everyone."

"I don't blame you. It is, after all, Sunday, and you both look very un-Sabbath."

"So I thought you could get Esther."

"And she?"

"Could get some clothes for me."

In a minute Jake had Esther, who took one look at Todd and me and was torn between laughter at how bedraggled we looked and horror that we participated in such activities on Sunday. But she was sweet and helpful, and in a short time I had dry clothes in hand. I shut myself in Jake's bathroom and changed. I pulled my hair back in a loose ponytail and wrapped it with a scrunchie I found in the purse she also brought for me.

By the time I finally emerged from Jake's bathroom, I looked quite presentable, but I couldn't say the same for my date.

"Jake, have you got a shirt Todd can borrow?" I asked. The blue one he had on was a woven cotton, and the water had done a number on it.

The men eyed each other and decided that a large knit polo shirt would do as well on one as the other. As far as jeans, Todd would just have to dry out as he went. He went to Jake's room to change, and I heard a cry of anguish.

"His hair, I bet," I said to Jake. "The curls are out of control."

"Makes him look less buttoned down," Jake said.

"My feeling exactly. But," and I grinned sympathetically as Todd strode into the room looking grumpy, "he doesn't agree."

Jake had given Todd a red shirt, and between the bright color and the unchecked curls, he looked better than ever. He turned as red as his shirt when I told him so, but he didn't stop grinning from Bird-in-Hand to Tel Hai.

TWELVE

I was very nervous about meeting Great-aunt Lizzie. I kept replaying Amos's words, feeling their heat and fury. *"I forbid you to see my mother. I absolutely forbid it."*

"Am I making a mistake?" I asked Todd as we drove past the peaceful Amish farms on Beaver Dam Road. "Should I have listened to Amos?"

"I think you're doing the right thing," he said as he slowed for the turn into Tel Hai. "Mrs. Yost wants to see you. She invited you to come, and she has every right to select her own company." He reached over and squeezed my hand. "Don't worry."

Father God, it's not that I want to worry; it's just that I do. Please calm my fears and help us to have a good visit!

Once again we made our way to the third-floor partial-care area, but this time the attendant led us directly to Lizzie's room.

"She's been looking forward to your visit all day," the attendant said with a smile. "I'm just glad for someone visiting her! It makes me angry that her family ignores her like they do. There's a niece who visits her every so often, but she lives up in Camp Hill. That's a pretty good trip, so she doesn't come as often as Lizzie would like. But she comes more frequently than the son."

That's Alma, I thought. She comes, but Amos and Jessica don't.

"Lizzie is one of my favorite people," the attendant said. "In fact, everyone here loves her. But then I'm sure you know how wonderful she is."

I merely smiled, thinking an explanation would be much too complicated.

"Come in," a tremulous voice called when we knocked.

We walked into a large room filled with furniture, personal treasures, books, and Aunt Lizzie. The overall effect was of too much stuff for the confined space, but even so, it was a pleasant place to live.

A love seat and an easy chair sat at right angles near the door, ready for company. A bookcase hugged one wall, and she could have won a competition with Dr. Reasoner for getting the most books into a limited area. Her bed was against the back wall of the room, and a dresser faced it. Photos sat on the bookcase and the dresser, and what looked to me to be original watercolors hung on the walls. Several beautiful petit point pillows sat on the chairs and the bed, and I wondered if she had done them. A rug in fragile creams, roses, and greens was echoed in the window treatments, bedspread, and slipcovers.

Lizzie sat in a rocking chair beside the window, and she had been reading a *Reader's Digest* condensation. She put it down and rose slowly to her feet.

"I read lots of these any more," she said, pointing to the book. "I don't have enough time left to read the unabridged versions, you see. I'm seventy-seven, and there's so much more to squeeze in!"

She walked across her room on feet slightly unsteady, but her eyes were keenly alert as they looked Todd and me over.

"Now I know you must be Cara Bentley," she said to me. "And Alma was right. You do have the look of Meaghan about you. But who's this?"

I introduced Todd.

"Your lawyer?" Aunt Lizzie said. "My, my. I don't know many people who come to call with their lawyer in tow."

"I'm not here tonight as her lawyer," Todd said as he took the old woman's proffered hand and shook it. The smile he gave her would have stolen my breath, and it tickled me that Aunt Lizzie wasn't entirely immune either as she preened at his attention. "I'm here tonight as Cara's special friend."

"Ah," Aunt Lizzie said knowingly as she indicated we should sit on the love seat. "I know all about special friends. That's how Harlan used to describe himself until the day we married. After that he said he was a privileged friend, a very privileged friend." And she sank into the easy chair and smiled. "I miss that man. I truly do."

I studied Aunt Lizzie. If we were related, as I believed we were, she was Pop's sister. I was seized by a feeling of disbelief. All my life or at least as far back as I could remember, our family had been the four of us, five when Marnie joined us. To think that there was a woman out there who would have expanded that circle was almost beyond comprehension.

But if I looked like Meaghan, Aunt Lizzie did not look like Pop. She was small to his huge, even considering the fact that she had undoubtedly shrunk with age. She had delicate features to his strong ones. And she was a reader to his doer. I was somewhat disappointed at the lack of family resemblance.

Then she put out her hand in a gesture that was so Pop that my heart stopped.

"Do that again," I whispered.

"What?"

"That hand movement. Please."

And she did it again, just the same. The hand was considerably smaller, the nails delicate and cared for as his never were, but the movement was all Pop.

"My mother used to make that gesture all the time," Lizzie said.

"So did Pop," I said. "And so does Ward."

"Who is Ward, my dear?"

"My younger brother." And I began talking about my family, telling her stories, making her laugh and, when I told of Pop's death just a few months ago, making her cry.

When I finally ran out of steam, she smiled at me. "I have wondered for years if my brother was happy." She looked at me through misty eyes. "It is a great joy to hear just how happy he was."

"You believe Pop was your brother?"

"I have no doubt, my dear. No doubt. I know it. And now I will tell you my story." She leaned back in her chair and stared at the middle distance, seeing her own mental pictures, her own scenes as she recounted her tale.

"My brother Josh and I had a happy home. Mom and Dad loved each other and us very much. We laughed a lot, but I always thought there was a touch of sorrow about Mom that I couldn't understand. One time when I was about nineteen, old enough to be brave and young enough to be foolish, I asked her what made her sad, especially around the same dates every November. She wouldn't tell me. All I knew was what we all observed: the beginning of that month was always very difficult for her, but by Thanksgiving she was usually back to her normal self."

I leaned forward. "Pop was born in the beginning of November."

Lizzie nodded. "I eventually learned that, but not for many years. In fact, I was fifty-five when I finally learned Mom's story. My father was already several years gone, and she was dying. It was the beginning of November…"

"Sit down, Liz," Madeleine said. "Stop fussing over me."

Liz sat. "I'm only trying to help, Mom."

216

Madeleine smiled the best she could for November. "I know. But it drives me crazy."

Liz nodded and watched her mother. The older woman lay on her pillows, looking weak, fragile, brittle enough to break into pieces if touched. Her weight had dropped precipitously in recent days and she was having trouble keeping anything down. She was dying rapidly and with no possibility of reversal.

The thought of losing her mother made Liz want to weep. No, to wail. Her mother was her friend, her confidant, her sounding board.

"This is my last November," Madeleine said in a voice that was stronger than it had been in recent weeks.

Liz made a disclaiming sound, a quick hand movement of denial.

"Yes, it is, Liz. But it's all right. I don't mind. Novembers have always been a time of deep pain for me. Enos tried his best to help me, and I loved him for trying. He'd hold me and love me and whisper soothingly in my ear. But he never understood how or why I felt such pain year after year even though he knew its cause. Always my heart breaking. Always a bit of me dying."

Liz looked at her mother and dared to ask again, "What causes you such hurt, Mom? What is it that tears you away from us at this time every year? What is it that breaks your heart?"

"It's your brother, my dear."

"Josh?" Liz couldn't have been more surprised. Josh was a wonderful person. In fact he was the person she admired most in the world. He set a standard of Christian living that was without peer, and his wonderful sense of humor prevented her or anyone from thinking him too holy, too pure for real folks to like.

"No dear. Not Josh. Lehman."

"Lehman?" Liz stared at her mother. "I have another brother? And his name is Lehman? But that's our last name. How can this be?" She began working dates in her mind, but try as she would, she couldn't see when another child had been born to her parents. "Was

he stillborn? Is he in an institution somewhere? Why do you never talk about him?"

"One doesn't talk about illegitimacy, Liz, especially not to one's daughter."

Liz felt the world tilt under her. Her mother, that paragon of Christian virtue, that gracious example of a woman worth far more than rubies, was saying she was involved in an illegitimate birth? Madeleine Biemsderfer Lehman? The Pope might as well announce he had become a Baptist. The Soviet Union might as well say it considered the United States its closest and most prized ally. Her husband might as well say he'd welcome liver for dinner.

Madeleine smiled sadly. "You should see your face, Liz. Then you'd understand why you don't know about Lehman. But it's my last November, and someone has to know about him! Someone has to keep his memory alive!" The last was a whisper.

Madeleine lay back on her pillows, her eyes closed, her breathing labored. Liz studied her mother and tried to comprehend a brother besides Josh. And the ramifications!

The thought of Madeleine with another man besides Enos was too fantastic, too terrible to even consider. They had loved each other with such commitment and passion. Yet there was an out-of-wedlock child.

"It was World War I," Madeleine suddenly said, eyes still shut. "Enos was to go to Europe. A doughboy who would save the world from the Kaiser. We were already very much in love, and the thought of the separation was a knife in our hearts."

"How old were you?" Liz asked.

"I was sixteen and Enos was nineteen. And we ignored God and took what we wanted, which was each other."

Even at fifty-five it was hard for Liz to imagine her parents in bed together within the bonds of holy matrimony. Trying to imagine them as hormonally driven teenage kids desperate over an impending separation and the possibility of death on a foreign battlefield was beyond her limited imaginings. But at least there was no other man. For that she was intensely grateful.

Madeleine's lips curved in a sad smile. "I finally understood that I was pregnant a month after Enos had shipped out. My parents were understandably upset." Madeleine fell silent as she pondered the massive understatement she had just made. "They took me out of school and kept me home for the remaining five months of my pregnancy. They refused to let me write Enos, and they wouldn't give me any of the letters he wrote."

Even now Madeleine's voice shook as she remembered the anguish of those days.

Due to the added brilliance of the elderly recalling far memory, the agony was a burning coal searing her heart.

"I was so distraught with worry for Enos, for his safety and for what he must think of me for not writing. And I was eaten up by guilt that we had done things out of God's order. We knew, we knew, and we had willfully disobeyed. How could God forgive us? It's a wonder I didn't miscarry from the emotional stresses alone. But I delivered a healthy baby boy on November 1. I saw the baby only twice. Of course adoption was the only possible way to deal with the situation, and I was too weary and frightened to offer any protest. My one independent action was selecting the name for the birth certificate. Lehman Biemsderfer. Enos and me."

Liz stared out the hospital room window. "So I have a brother out there somewhere? A full blood brother?" What was he like? Was he happy? Had nice people raised him? How had he survived the Depression? World War II? Had he survived? Was he married? Did he have children, grandchildren? Would she ever know any of these answers?

Madeleine saw the questions in Liz and nodded her understanding. She was all too familiar with them, had asked them daily for *almost sixty years.* "Open my Bible to Proverbs 3, will you?"

Liz did so and found a picture of a chubby baby boy propped up on a blanket embroidered with baskets of flowers.

"Lehman," Madeleine said. "It's the only proof I have that he even exists beyond my imagination."

Liz looked at the sepia print and her heart turned over. This adorable child was her brother! No wonder November was hell for Mom.

"When he was almost six months old," Madeleine continued, "I went to the agency that had placed him. I was absolutely desperate. Enos was still somewhere in Europe, and I hadn't heard from him for so long that I doubted he could still love me. I knew he was probably still alive only because I hadn't read of his death in the paper, but that was all I knew of him. Mother and Father were still reeling from what I had done to them, and my baby was gone. I had nothing! Please, I pleaded with the people at the agency. Please get me a picture of my baby or I shall surely go insane. They took one look at me and believed. A month later this photo arrived for me."

Madeleine reached out and ran a gentle hand over the cracked and faded print. "As long as I had the picture, I knew I wouldn't go insane. I knew I wouldn't forget. I knew God would care for him. That's why it's in Proverbs 3. 'Trust in the Lord with all your heart.' I did that every day for Lehman. I did it for you and Josh too, but I saw what was happening in your lives. I talked with you, prayed with you. Lehman I could only trust to God."

Liz, herself the mother of a son who was ignoring God, knew all about trusting to God those who, for whatever reason, you cannot influence.

"Mom," she whispered, eyes full of tears. "I love you."

Madeleine laid a frail hand on Liz's strong one. "Thank you, Liz."

The women sat quietly for a while, thinking, praying, wondering.

When she felt strong enough, Madeleine took up her story once again. "When Enos finally came home from the war, my parents forbade me to see him. I was barely eighteen, sheltered, living with the consequences of the one great rebellion of my life. But I knew I loved Enos and sent him messages through my brother Harold. Enos sent love letters back, so I knew he loved me and felt anguish over Lehman too, especially over the fact that he hadn't known, hadn't been here for me. When I turned twenty-one, we ran off and married. My parents were furious, especially Father."

Liz thought of her grandfather, a German in the old tradition, fierce, strict, unemotional. What must it have been like for Madeleine to defy him?

"The first Christmas we were married, my parents refused even to accept a gift from us. By the second Christmas you were born, and you were the one who broke the barriers. They loved you, Liz. And Josh. And one day when you were five, Mother cried and told me she prayed every single day for Lehman. We wept together that day, she and I, a mother and a grandmother sorrowing over a boy we would never know but would always love."

"How many years older than I is Lehman?" Liz asked.

"Four years. He was born November 1, 1917. And I still pray every single day for him, just like I do for you and Josh. And I pray for his family, just like I do for yours and Josh's."

Madeleine turned to Liz and grasped her hand in desperation. "Liz, you must keep praying for them." It was both an order and a plea. "Someone has to keep praying for them because we don't know who raised Lehman. We don't know if anyone taught him about Jesus. Promise me, Liz, that you will pray for your brother and his family every single day of your life. Promise me that he won't be forgotten. Promise me, Liz. Promise me!"

Liz was shaking with fear for Madeleine. "Mom, calm down. You're making yourself sick!"

"I am sick. And it's November. And Enos isn't here to help me. My one hope is that I am forgiven in Christ. I have at least learned that over the years. When I sorrow now, it's only loss, not guilt, that fuels my pain. Christ has borne my guilt, and he helps me with my pain." A slight smile touched her pale face momentarily.

Liz leaned over and kissed her mother. No wonder there was such depth to her walk with God. Great pain had forged that relationship.

"Liz, you must promise me." Madeleine's voice was a hoarse whisper but all the more compelling for it.

"I promise, Mom," Liz said, tears falling onto Madeleine's pillow, Madeleine's face, Madeleine's nightgown. *"I promise that every day for the rest of my life I will pray for Lehman and his family."*

"Thank you." Exhausted, Madeleine fell back on her pillow and went to sleep.

"She never woke up," Lizzie said, smiling sadly at Todd and me.

The three of us sat silently in the gathering dusk. My heart broke for Madeleine and her years of sorrow, and I found myself swallowing, trying to control my emotions. What she had missed by not knowing Pop!

Finally Lizzie spoke. "I kept my promise. I have prayed for Lehman and his family every day for more than twenty years."

"That means you've been praying for me." I leaned forward and laid my hand on hers. "Thank you, Aunt Liz. Thank you. And from now on, I shall pray daily for you and your family."

Aunt Lizzie smiled sweetly. "Thank you. It will be nice to have someone praying for me." She leaned forward and tried to rise from her chair, but her legs seemed to have trouble bearing her weight.

"Is there something I can get for you?" I asked, rising myself.

"Over there on the end table by the window. My Bible."

I handed her the requested book and sat down. Aunt Lizzie riffled through the pages.

"Proverbs 3," she said and took out an old photograph. She passed it to me.

I stared at the chubby baby on the embroidered blanket, holding it so Todd could see, too. Once again I had to blink back tears. Todd's arm slid around my shoulders and pressed comfortingly.

"Aunt Lizzie," I said through a throat tight with emotion. "I know this picture. Mom had a copy of it on her bureau for as long as I can remember. 'For when John gets too big for his britches,' she always said. 'Then I can remind him that he's nothing but a grown-up baby, just like the rest of us.'"

I traced the baskets of flowers with my index finger. "And we still have the blanket. It's a family treasure. Great-grandmother Bentley did the needlework on it, and she and Great-grandfather Bentley brought Pop home from the adoption agency wrapped in it. Since then, each generation of Bentleys has brought their children home in the blanket. Trey and Caroline brought Ward and me. Ward and Marnie brought Johnny home in it. I've always thought that someday I'll use it for that same purpose myself."

"You've actually seen the same picture and have the blanket?" Aunt Lizzie said.

I nodded. "The background is cream, the baskets are a soft aqua, and the flowers are worked in pinks and roses with light green leaves. I'm sure the colors have faded over eighty years, but it's still very beautiful. And the moths have never gotten it. I'll bring it next time I visit so that you can see it."

"You're coming to see me again?" Aunt Lizzie said, her eyes bright with hope. It broke my heart that there was such surprise in her voice.

"Of course." I nodded while I thought dark thoughts about Amos and his lack of interest in his mother. Then I recalled that not ten minutes ago, I had promised to pray for him daily. Well, my first prayer would be that he become a loving and dutiful son. His sweet mother deserved nothing less.

Todd and I didn't talk until we pulled into the drive at his dad's cottage.

"I have a question for you, Cara," Todd finally said as he put the car in park. He was thoughtful, and I knew he had been almost as moved as I was by Lizzie's story. "Why do you think Pop never tried to find his family? From what you've told me, you have a drive to know and understand your genetic heritage. Why didn't he have the same compulsion?"

"I've wondered about that myself. And I can only come up with one answer. He didn't care where he came from."

Todd frowned. "But he was a creative and imaginative person. Why wouldn't he be curious about his birth family?"

"I don't know exactly." I searched for the right words. "Pop was very secure in himself. He was born confident. Most people have gaps in their self-confidence, some little chinks, some gigantic holes as big as the Grand Canyon. Some few, though, seem born without that internal uncertainty. They take life and mold it to their dreams without questioning their right to do so and without questioning their ability. Pop was one of those. He never debated with himself about who he was. He always knew."

"Doesn't that make them terribly difficult to live with?"

"It can. They can become controlling and assume they know what's best for the whole world. If these people don't develop a heart for others and a heart for God, they can be very intimidating and controlling. If they don't have people who are strong enough to challenge them on their attitudes and behavior, they can overwhelm others and not even recognize the pain they've caused. But they don't need the holes in their lives filled because they don't have holes."

"And adoption searches are often ventures in hole filling?"

"Uh-huh. At least this search is for me. But Pop was confident that being a Bentley was great. He was confident that opening the first Bentley's was great. And he was confident that expanding to the chain was great. Ward's the same way. He doesn't understand why I want to know about the Biemsderfers. He doesn't feel the holes."

"I thought that was because he saw family in terms of heart, not body and bone."

I pushed some straggling hair back into my ponytail. "I see family in terms of heart too, but I also think it's body and bone. And I feel the body and bone holes. Ward doesn't. Apparently Pop didn't either."

Todd opened his car door and climbed reluctantly out. "Well, let's go visit some body and bone."

"Todd." I laid a hand on his arm as we walked up the sidewalk. "There's heart here too. You just need to learn how to see it."

He looked at me skeptically but said nothing.

We knocked on Dr. Reasoner's door just as we had a few nights ago. A slow steady shuffle sounded, and Dr. Reasoner appeared on the other side of the screen.

"Toddy."

"Dad."

I poked Todd in the ribs.

"Oh. Dad, you remember Cara Bentley, my client?"

"Ah," he said. "Of course I remember the…client. Come in. Come in." He turned to walk back into the house, assuming we would follow.

I poked Todd in the ribs again. "You've got to stop introducing me as your client," I hissed. "I'm beginning to think I'm going to get billed for all the extra hours we spend together."

He turned a broad grin on me. "Of course you're getting billed for all those hours. How else can I ever afford the cabin I want on that lake in Canada?"

I quirked an eyebrow. "If you think I'm paying so you can flee the country to get away from me, you're much mistaken, guy."

Suddenly Todd's grin faded and his eyes darkened. He slipped his arm around my waist and bumped his hip against mine, lifting me clean off my feet. I made a little squeak of surprise. He spun me effortlessly until I was standing with my back against the side of the cottage. I could feel the bricks through my cream knit shirt. He placed a hand against the wall on either side of my head, trapping me. Not that I was trying to escape.

"Todd," I said breathlessly. "Your father's waiting."

He ignored me. Well, he actually ignored what I said. Me he paid lots of attention to as he leaned over and kissed me.

As kisses go, I don't know how it would rate on a scale of one to ten. I haven't had lots of experience, so I can't make a sound judgment. But I do know that as far as I was concerned, and I am, after all, the one who counts, I felt it all the way to my toes. I also realized very quickly that I had been underwriting my heroines' responses to my heroes.

Todd drew back and gave a devastating smile. "I've been

wanting to do that for some time now, probably since the day you gave me that ridiculous tie."

"Really?" It was all I could do to get that one word out.

His wonderful eyes glommed onto mine, and I saw all sorts of possibilities written there. "Really."

I looked at him a minute longer, then threw myself into his arms. "Again."

It was a discreet cough that pulled us apart. Arms still wrapped about each other, we turned to see Dr. Reasoner standing at the door watching us.

"Toddy," he said conversationally, "I must insist you stop ravishing your…client on my front porch. What will my neighbors think? I have a reputation to consider." And he turned and walked inside.

I felt Todd stiffen, and glancing at him, realized he thought his father was criticizing us.

"Todd, he was teasing," I said softly.

Todd frowned. "Teasing?"

"Didn't you see the twinkle in his eye?"

"Twinkle? In Dad's eye?" He looked through the screen at his father's retreating figure, trying to wrap his mind about this alien thought.

"Trust me on this," I said, going up on tiptoe and kissing his cheek. "You'll see."

We sat in the same seats on the glassed-in porch that we had occupied on our last visit. I glanced with great interest at the end table beside my chair and saw that *Beowulf* was gone. So were *Great Expectations* and *Through the Looking Glass*. In their places and obviously read were *As the Deer, So My Soul*, and George Eliot's *Silas Marner*.

"Wow," I said, pointing. "You've got me in excellent company."

"I must tell you, Cara, that I enjoyed your books very

much. You have a distinctive and delightful style."

If I weren't already glowing like an incandescent bulb from Todd's kiss, I would have from the compliment.

"Marci and Scott are memorable characters," said Dr. Reasoner, professor of English and authority on literature who liked my books! "And you show their development as both humans and believers very realistically. You also develop their love in a delightful, thoughtful progression."

"You have no idea what your words mean to me, Dr. Reasoner." I hugged them to myself, metaphorically spinning like a top or, better yet, like Maria as she serenaded the sky in *The Sound of Music*. I really wanted to ask him to write the wonderful words down so I'd have them forever, but it seemed a bit premature in our acquaintance to ask for potential cover copy. "Thank you very much."

He nodded his head. "I made one very interesting observation." He glanced from me to Todd, who was following the conversation with great interest, and back to me. "You write about love as if you are acquainted with it."

I felt myself blush, sitting here in front of Todd and under his father's obviously assessing eye. "I've lived all my life observing it," I managed.

Dr. Reasoner quirked an eyebrow in question, an expression I'd seen on his son's face many times.

"My grandparents who raised me," I said. "Theirs was a great love affair."

"So by observation you've been able to capture both the emotional and volitional aspects of love. I find that amazing."

I blinked. "You do?"

"I do. Love is so difficult to define, to portray. You have captured the essence of what I think of as love." He glanced hesitantly at Todd, as if he weren't certain about speaking his mind in front of his son. "I know that while I was reading, I realized I hadn't missed Catherine so much in years. You made me yearn again for what I thought I had forgotten."

I must have looked distressed because he hurried to say, "It was a good missing, my dear, a bringing to mind of all the joy we shared."

His eyes grew misty with reminiscence. "Catherine taught me that sharing love makes you more than you are alone. That's how I know you got your characters right. They made each other more than they were alone." He smiled. "Catherine taught me laughter, something I hadn't known before her—or after for that matter. When she died, my life lost its joy. I became the morose and melancholy man she had prevented me from becoming."

He glanced again at Todd, but he turned to speak to me. "I think it was hard on Toddy, the lack of laughter. I tried for his sake, but I didn't know how to be other than I was, than I am. I'm afraid his growing up was shadows instead of sunshine, and I regret that more than I can possibly say." He smiled sadly at me, as though asking my forgiveness.

Together he and I turned to Todd who was sitting with his mouth hanging open, staring at his father. In a reversal of last night, I reached over and pushed his jaw shut. He blinked and looked at me. I rested my hand along his jaw for a moment, smiling at him, reminding him from my heart that there was much more than body and bone between him and his father. It was just that neither of them knew how to see it yet.

Again Dr. Reasoner turned from Todd to speak to me. "From the day Catherine died, I have prayed that Toddy would find his sunshine. I see his mother's laughter in him, but I've never known how to release it. I can't even talk with him, much less make him laugh. Perhaps, Cara," he said hopefully, "in you I'm seeing the answer to my prayers."

"Oh, Dr. Reasoner!" I was overwhelmed by his words. I stole a glance at Todd and saw he was as confounded as I.

"And now," Dr. Reasoner said, slapping his legs briskly. "Let me get you two a bowl of ice cream." And he rose and left the porch.

Todd watched his father leave, his face a study in conflicting emotions. Hope, disbelief, wonder, anger, bemusement, affection all flashed through his eyes. He looked at me and shook his head, unable to articulate what he was feeling. He reached for my hand and gripped it fiercely between both his.

Ah, Lord, teach this man about heart and family. In fact, and I glanced toward the kitchen, *teach both of them.*

"He prays for me!" Todd's voice and face were full of wonder. "Like Madeleine and Lizzie prayed for Pop. I never knew he did that, never would have imagined it in a million years."

I nodded. "One of the things I've grieved over most since Mom's and Pop's deaths is knowing that no one is praying for me with the same concern and commitment I'd taken for granted all my life."

"You want someone to pray for you?" He ran a hand gently down my cheek. "I'll pray for you."

"Don't say that lightly," I said. "It's too precious a promise."

"And not one to be broken," he agreed. "But praying for you will be easy. You're the one with the hard job. You promised to pray for Amos and Jessica."

"I know. I think it's going to force me to stretch myself spiritually in ways I never foresaw."

We sat silently for a few minutes. I could hear Dr. Reasoner opening and shutting the refrigerator and the cupboards. I heard the chink of dishes and the schuss of pretzels being poured into a basket.

"Cara, why did he tell you all those things instead of me?"

Todd asked suddenly. There was hurt and a slight edge of anger in his tone.

I shrugged. "Because he knows me better?"

"What? He's only seen you twice!"

"But he read my books. He's seen into my heart."

Todd looked at me skeptically.

"You'll see what I mean if you ever get around to reading my stuff."

"I am reading your stuff," he said in a huff. "I'm halfway through *As the Deer.*"

"And don't you feel you know me better by reading it?"

He thought, obviously trying to find an answer. "Well, I guess I know that you like Coke better than Pepsi because your characters always drink Coke."

A burst of air escaped me, half amusement, half frustration.

"Isn't that what you meant?" he asked, his eyebrows drawn together.

"Not quite. But knowing me isn't the real issue here, is it? It's how can you and your dad get to know each other."

His shoulders dipped. "I haven't figured that one out in thirty years."

"Well, we'll just have to work on that, won't we?"

He raised his eyebrow and smiled. "We will?"

I raised my own eyebrow and smiled back. "We will. I'll ask your father a question. He'll answer. Then all you have to do is ask why. Now go help him carry the ice cream out."

He blinked.

I jerked my head toward the door to the house. "Two hands, three bowls. Go."

To my surprise, he went. To Dr. Reasoner's surprise too, if the look on his face when they returned to the porch was any indication.

When we were eating our ice cream, I asked innocently, "Dr. Reasoner, aside from *As the Deer* and *So My Soul,* what has been your favorite book you've recently read?"

When he answered, I looked at Todd. For a minute he stared blankly back. Then he sat up straight and looked at his father.

"Why?"

Dr Reasoner looked at him in surprise. "Why is it my favorite?"

Todd looked at me in a slight panic. I inclined my head ever so slightly.

"Yes," Todd said. "Why is it your favorite?"

"Well…" Dr. Reasoner began.

The conversation lasted thirty minutes, and I was very proud of Todd. His eyes didn't glaze over once.

THIRTEEN

I woke up Monday morning tense and irritable. As I lurched into the bathroom and turned on the shower, I tried to analyze my bad mood. It didn't take long until I had the answer. In a word: change.

Three months ago I was safe and secure in Pop's house, writing away as I'd done for the past eight years. Then *poof!* Pop was gone.

Three weeks ago I was safe and secure in what was now my house, writing away as I'd done for the past eight years. Then *poof!* I finished the novel and had to face the reality of being alone.

Three weeks ago I was safe and secure, a Bentley with a proud and wonderful heritage. Then *poof!* I wasn't a Bentley. None of us were from Pop down.

Three weeks ago I slept in my own bed in the bedroom that had been mine for essentially my whole life. Then *poof!* I was living on an Amish farm in a little village that was schizophrenic, half of its citizens living in a parallel universe, the other half enjoying the prosperity the fantasy half generated in tourist dollars.

Three weeks ago I had a small family I'd known and loved all my life. Then *poof!* I had relatives coming out my ears, and a significant number of them didn't like me.

Three weeks ago, I was Cara Bentley, spinster, not exactly happy over my single state but not losing any sleep over it either. Then *poof!* I got a new lawyer, and suddenly I was enamored with brown curls and strong jawlines.

I adjusted the shower temperature and told God a few of the things that were simmering in the back of my mind.

How come I have to deal with so many changes of such magnitude? You know I hate change! Couldn't we have dealt with one, maybe two, at a time?

But I recognized quickly that I couldn't have any one of them without the others. They were a package, and they were giving me a headache!

Except for Todd. He made me smile.

I let the water beat on my head and slide down over my face and shoulders and race away down the drain. I felt a significant amount of my stress slip away with it. I turned my back to the spray and lowered my head, pulling my hair aside. The sharp needles of spray massaged my neck, easing the tension in my taut muscles.

As I shampooed my hair, I had a most electrifying thought, an epiphany of sorts. The notion appeared out of the blue between squeezing a blob of Pert in my palm and massaging it into my hair. I raised my hands to my head in a daze. As I worked the shampoo to the tips of my hair, I pondered and wondered.

What if Pop's adoption papers weren't just for the purpose of discovering where we came from? What if they were for the purpose of teaching me lessons I'd never learn any other way? Lessons like letting go of the past, moving on, adapting to change? Lessons like reaching out even when it was uncomfortable and stretching way beyond my boundaries?

I'd glibly told Todd that Pop had never searched because he wasn't interested in his heritage. He was secure in himself with things as they were. While I still thought that was right, maybe there was more to it than that. Maybe God knew that three generations later I would need something drastic to get my life out of the comfortable rut it had fallen into, something so dramatic that I'd make changes in spite of my predilections.

Maybe God knew these things? No maybe about it. This was God I was thinking about. If I was right, God had planned that I find those papers, papers that shouldn't even have been in that box of photographs but in Mr. Havens's office with the rest of Pop's things. Papers that would turn my life upside-down.

Another snippet of a psalm floated through my mind. "I will instruct you and teach you in the way which you shall go."

I pondered this radical idea of mine as I dressed in my tan denim skirt and white scoop-neck knit shirt with a brown leather belt and sandals. I wondered about it as I sat at my desk and stared at the crisp, clear view out my window. A cool front had blown in over night, and the humidity was temporarily gone. The sky was a brilliant blue, and the far fields were as crisp and green as the leaves on the great maple in the front yard.

Maybe my narrow view of what I will accept in my life is clearing some, Lord, just like the atmosphere outside. Please help me with these changes, the wonderful ones like Todd and Aunt Lizzie and the difficult ones like Pop and Mom being gone and Amos not liking me.

By the time I went down for breakfast, I was feeling excited about life's possibilities once again. So much for my prescience.

The first thing I saw was a pair of hens lying on the kitchen counter. Their throats had been slit and they were lying there waiting to be cleaned. I knew full well that the family killed the poultry they ate, but I hadn't been on the farm long enough to witness this particular farm reality before. I turned my back on the gruesome sight as Esther came down the stairs from Mary's room.

"Dinner?" I said, gesturing to the hens.

"I guess so," Esther said. "There's not much choice."

Something in her voice made me look at her closely. "What do you mean? Is something wrong?"

"Elam found them lying on the front porch with their throats slit when he went out to milk the cows this morning."

It felt like ice slid down my back. "Another act of vandalism?"

Esther shrugged, her great eyes wide, her normally rosy cheeks pale. "I guess. I don't know about vandalism. I've never seen anything like this before."

"Except for my slashed tires," I said grimly.

If possible, Esther's eyes got bigger.

The front door slammed, and Elam walked in. He took one look at Esther and frowned. "What's wrong?"

She sighed and shook her head. "Your mother keeps asking what's troubling me. I try to act natural, but it's hard when I'm upset. And I can't lie and say everything's fine."

"Is she okay?" He looked toward the stairs.

Esther nodded. "She's sleeping. Yesterday all the company wore her out. She'll sleep until Rose comes."

Elam nodded.

"Do you think the hens have any connection to my slashed tires?" I asked him.

He shrugged, but it was obvious the idea had crossed his mind.

"Should we report it to the police?" I asked.

"No." He was emphatic. "Father and I don't want to do that. We'd rather just accept the loss." He placed some mail on the table.

"Turn the other cheek?" I asked. "Give him your cloak?"

"Exactly," Elam said. "If you're okay, Esther, I have to get back to work."

Suddenly her pale cheeks flooded with color. He had come to see how she was doing. "I'm fine," she said, eyes aglow. But he was looking at the mail.

236

You're an idiot, Elam. I don't care how nice Mary Clare is. Esther's just the girl for you.

"Couple of letters for you, Cara," he said, holding them out to me. "And one for you, Esther. From Ammon Stoltzfus?"

Esther grabbed her letter, blushing furiously. "It's from my mother!"

"How do you know? You haven't opened it yet. Maybe it is from Ammon."

"I recognize the handwriting." Her voice was breathless.

"Then Ammon is even dumber than I thought," Elam said as he let the screen door slam behind him.

Since Esther was a brilliant red, I decided the kindest thing I could do would be to read my mail and make believe I didn't notice the effect Elam had on her.

I slid my finger under the flap and opened a card from Marnie. *Sometimes life throws curve balls,* it read on the cover. An absolute harridan stood at the plate as the ball whizzed by. *But you managed a home run anyway,* read the inside. The harridan wore a giant grin as she ran the bases.

We like him, Marnie wrote. *Definitely a home run.*

I was still grinning when I opened my second letter.

You were told not to visit her. You were warned. Now you will suffer. Like the chickens.

I stared at the block printing on lined paper torn from a spiral notebook and felt like spiders were crawling all over me. I threw the letter down and started rubbing my arms like I was brushing the insects away.

Don't look! But my eyes went of their own volition to the hens. They had been thoroughly bled, but in my imagination, I saw red welling up and spilling from the wounds at their throats.

God, am I that lousy a relative?

I picked up my threatening letter and went to my rooms. I got my cell phone and called Todd's office. If I ever needed advice from my lawyer, it was now.

"Mrs. Smiley, this is Cara Bentley. May I speak to Todd, please?"

A slight clearing of her throat was her only sign of disapproval. I wondered in passing what color her fingernails were this week. "I'm sorry, Miss Bentley. Mr. Reasoner is not available."

"It's really important, Mrs. Smiley. How can I reach him? Does he have a beeper? Or is he in conference?"

"He's in court and cannot be interrupted."

I glanced at the clock. 11:15. "They do break for lunch, don't they?"

"Well, yes."

"I'll find him then." I clicked off and gathered my things. I wanted to go to the courthouse anyway to visit the prothonotary's office. Not that I needed more proof of Pop's origins than Meaghan's and my amazing resemblance and Aunt Lizzie's picture, but Amos needed hard evidence.

I glanced at the threatening note. Much as I had trouble believing he could stoop to something like this, I knew he was somehow involved. Too few knew about his order to me.

Well, I'd show him. I'd give him legal proof he couldn't refute. I wanted him to know in a manner that meant something to him that I was not an aberration. I was not a fortune hunter. I was a genuine relative with proof positive of that tie.

Lancaster County Court House was in the middle of downtown Lancaster at the intersection of Duke and Orange Streets. I had been there before, so I knew about the parking garage down the street. I took my ticket from the machine and found a slot for my car on the third level.

Approaching the main entrance of the courthouse, I glanced across the street at the graceful colonnade of St. James Episcopal Church. It was such a nonurban sight in the midst of concrete and brick, a delight to the eye.

I turned and reached for the door of the courthouse only to have someone rudely grab it out of my hand and move to barge through. I jumped and was face-to-face with Amos Yost.

I inclined my head slightly, the barest politeness I could imagine.

"What are you doing here?" he hissed with no attempt at civility.

I felt like saying, "None of your beeswax," but I remembered about speech being seasoned with grace and kept my mouth shut. I even kept silent about the letter currently burning a hole in my purse.

"I told you not to visit her." Amos's voice was like tiny pellets of hail beating on me, cold and stinging, but ultimately ineffective and not damaging.

I squared my shoulders. "She invited me." I regretted my compulsion to answer as soon as I spoke. I should have ignored him completely. I should have been smart enough not to try to defend myself to him and so begin a he-said, she-said exchange.

"She's a senile old lady," he said in a brutally dismissive tone. "She undoubtedly told you the strange story of my grandmother's baby. I bet she even showed you a picture, didn't she? Ah, I can see by your face that she did. And you thought you found the perfect way into her affections by claiming the baby in the picture was your grandfather."

I stared at him for a minute, wondering what it was like to

be so nasty and to speak of your own mother so cruelly. The affection in our family had been so genuine that people like Amos were hard for me to comprehend.

"Excuse me." I tried to reach around him for the door, but he shifted just enough to block me.

"You think I'm kidding when I tell you to leave my mother alone, do you? Ever hear of a restraining order?"

I looked at him in stunned disbelief. He saw me as that dangerous? That greedy? That threatening?

I heard a group of people walking up behind me. I waited until they had almost reached us, then I said very loudly, "Excuse me, sir. You're blocking my way."

Since five new people seemed to feel the same way about him, Amos had no choice but to move. I walked into the court-house with a calm I didn't feel and turned left. I was walking blindly, going anywhere to get away from Amos. When I felt a hand on my arm, I spun around, furious.

"Don't touch me!" I hissed.

"Okay," Todd said, slightly taken aback. "If you feel that strongly about it."

"Todd!" I grabbed his arm to hold me up. Now that he was beside me, I was shaking like the proverbial leaf. "I thought you were Amos."

He studied my face for a brief moment, then slipped his hand under my elbow. "Come on." He led me to the cafeteria where he found a table in a corner. He seated me facing the wall.

"All right. Give. What happened?"

Willing my chin not to tremble, I reached into my purse and pulled out the letter. Silently Todd read it. When he looked up, his eyes were hard and angry.

"What's this about chickens?"

"Two had their throats slit this morning. Elam found them on the front porch."

He looked at the letter again. "It's hard to believe that someone like Amos would write threatening letters and slit hens' throats." He ran his hand through his curls, but they were so naturally combed that they barely showed the strain. "A man of his position surely wouldn't stoop so low. It'd be professional suicide if it ever got out."

I shivered and said, "He doesn't mind verbal threats. He just threatened me with a restraining order to prevent me from visiting Lizzie again."

Todd nodded. "That's more what I would expect from him." He patted my hand. "Don't let the threat bother you. I'll take care of it."

I smiled my thanks. "But he still gives me the willies."

Todd glanced at his watch. "Oops! I have to be back in court in five minutes. I'll stop at the farm as soon as I'm finished, okay?" He pushed back his chair and grabbed his briefcase. "Will you be all right?" His face showed his concern.

"I'm fine," I said. "Now." I smiled my best smile.

The smile must have worked because he suddenly leaned down and kissed my cheek, looked surprised at himself, and left.

I bought myself a bottle of iced tea and a bagel and cream cheese. I munched as I thought. When I was finished, I had no more answers than I'd had when I began eating, but I was ready to visit the prothonotary's office.

Back in the lobby I found a directory that sent me to the second floor, almost to the end of the hall. I passed Orphan's Court and the Register of Deeds and came to the Prothonotary. I entered and waited my turn for assistance before a long counter.

"How can I help you?" asked a pleasant woman in wire-framed glasses.

"I'd like to look at papers from 1917," I said.

The woman blinked. "1917?"

I nodded.

"You'll have to go to Archives for them," she said. Though why I should want papers that old was clearly beyond her.

"Ah, where is Archives?"

She sent me down the hall and down some stairs, down another hall and down some more stairs.

"At the bottom of the stairs you can go right or left," the woman said. "I don't know which way will give you the material you want, but there will be people there to help you."

I thanked her and followed her directions, going from the new courthouse to the old in the process. I eventually found Archives. At the bottom of the last stairs was a T, just as the woman had said. I looked right and left and saw no one. I turned right.

I came to a large room full of bookshelves rising rank upon rank from wall to wall. The shelves were full of books of bound legal documents. *1887 Orphans Court. 1916 Orphans Court. 1901–1905 Marriages. 1926 Marriages.*

Marriages, I thought. I searched the shelves for 1921. I found the heavy book I wanted and slid it from its resting place over rollers that allowed easy access to the ungainly records. I carried the book to a counter and started leafing through it.

The legal record of long-ago love was fascinating to me. Widowed farmers, young clerks, thirty-year-old spinsters, divorced seamstresses—their personal stories were reduced to the equivalent of name, rank, and serial number. Every so often in the margins were the signatures of parents giving permission for underage children to marry. Apparently underage meant through twenty.

Some of the questions raised more questions in my mind.

Is the applicant an imbecile, epileptic, of unsound mind or under guardianship as a person of unsound mind or under the influence of intoxicating liquor or narcotic drugs?

If you were any of these things, would you admit it?

What is the relationship of parties making this application, if any, either by blood or marriage?

If the wrong answer meant you couldn't get a license, would you answer truthfully?

I flipped page after page until suddenly, there it was:

Statement of Male:

Full name: Enos Adam Lehman

Statement of Female:

Full name: Madeleine Elizabeth Biemsderfer

I traced Madeleine's name with my forefinger. Three years after Pop's birth, she and her Enos had finally married. It was overwhelming to try to imagine the heartache of those three years, pain beyond measure for Madeleine and Enos as well as for her parents, Joshua and Lottie. And, I thought for the first time, for Enos's parents—if they ever knew about Pop.

I closed the marriage license book and rolled it back into place. I found the 1917 Orphan's Court book on a high shelf. I had to look at it even though everyone had told me Orphan's Court meant estates. I found a stool and stepped up to slide the book from its place. The cover was torn and dusty. I lugged the heavy volume to the counter and started leafing through.

With no great surprise, I saw that the book did indeed contain records of estates in which the legatee was a minor and the estate was placed under the financial guardianship of an adult. I sighed, but I was glad I'd double-checked. It wasn't that I didn't trust Todd and all the other people I'd talked to at the courthouse. It was just that I liked to see things for myself.

After I climbed back on the step stool and slid the bound journal back into place, I decided there was nothing more for me in this room. I went back to the foot of the stairs and turned left. A lady saw me coming and met me in the doorway.

"May I help you?" she asked. Her name tag read Annabelle.

"I'm looking for the adoption record of my grandfather."

Immediately Annabelle looked distressed. "I'm sorry," she said, and I could tell she really was. "All adoption records are sealed. It's impossible to gain access to them without a judge's order, and such an order is difficult to obtain. I'm afraid I can't help you."

"I know all about the sealed records," I said. "But I'm looking for records from 1917 and 1918. I was told that adoption records going back that far may not be sealed."

Annabelle looked at me with interest. Her eyes narrowed as she considered my comment.

"You may be right," she said. "I think records of all adoption documentation going back to 1928 were purged under judge's orders. But adoption papers before that may still be in the public records."

I tried to still the flutter of anticipation in my stomach. I couldn't let myself get excited yet. Still, in spite of my stern self-lecture, I found myself holding my breath expectantly.

"If there is anything still available, it would be in the Trust Books," Annabelle said.

"What are they?"

"They're the bound prothonotary records. And they would be locked in a storeroom down the hall."

She turned back to her desk and got a handful of keys. She searched through them with quick fingers, selecting a silver-colored one. She walked up the last flight of stairs I'd come down, and I followed. Halfway down a hall, she stopped before a door and inserted the key. She turned it and the door swung inward. She reached around the corner and touched a light switch. A weak light shone over multiple file cabinets and more shelves full of books of bound documents.

"Have you worked in Archives long?" I asked.

"Ten years," Annabelle said.

I was very grateful for her longevity on the job. A new person wouldn't have known about these records, or if she did, wouldn't have been able to walk unerringly to the right shelf. In no time I had a volume in my hands that included papers from 1914 to 1920.

"Bring it out to my room where you'll have better light," Annabelle said.

"Really? I can just sit and read it as long as I want?"

"Sure," she said, leading the way back to the hall. She shut off the light and relocked the door. I trailed her down the steps, the heavy book under my arm.

Soon I was settled on a stool under a strong light, flipping pages. Everything in the book was written in old-fashioned longhand by a pen with a thin nub and a person with a neat hand. Once in a while I saw an ink blot, but whoever had recorded these papers was very particular and precise, a good civil servant.

As I read, Annabelle and the world receded, and decisions and petitions made almost a century ago took center stage. I was fascinated by the declarations of dementia and insanity that gave the care of property and money into the hands of another. I read bills of divorcement. And I found adoption records.

There was no careful wording of things, no protecting of the innocent. All the pertinent facts were spelled out clearly for anyone and everyone to read.

In re Adoption of Jonathan David Brewer.

In re Adoption of Eliza Tansy Duncan.

In re Adoption of Lehman Biemsderfer.

I sat stone still for a minute, one hand on my heart and the other on the page before me. Even though I knew already where Pop had come from, was totally convinced I had met his family for both good and ill, seeing the actual legal document moved me. I blinked the tears away lest any splash onto the page and blur the spiky handwriting.

June 15, 1918. Petition of John Seward Bentley and Mabel Brooks Bentley his wife of Lancaster City, Pennsylvania, setting forth that they are desirous of adopting as one of their heirs Lehman Biemsderfer, the minor child of Madeleine Biemsderfer of Lancaster City. He was born on November 1, 1917. That the child is now in their home and has been there since February 4, 1918 and was placed there by The Children's Home Society of the City of Lancaster. That they will perform all the duties of parents toward said minor, and that the mother of the said Lehman Biemsderfer has consented to said adoption. Affidavits of said consent attached to the petition.

And now August 20, 1918, upon consideration of the foregoing petition and statement and it appearing to the said court that the welfare of the said minor will be promoted by the said adoption and the Society in whose hands the child was originally placed consents thereto, the prayer of the petitioners is granted and it is ordered and decreed that the said Lehman Biemsderfer shall assume the name of John Seward Bentley, Jr. and herefore shall have all the rights of a child and heir of the said John Seward Bentley and Mabel Brooks Bentley respectively, and he shall be subject to the duties of such a child.

Attest Herman F. Walton, Prothy.

Such cold legalese. Such far reaching ramifications. Such changed lives.

Pop, it's all here. Here's your birth mother's name and your adoptive parents' names and both of your given names. All the ties, all the people who made you what you were, all except Enos. Do you know that I've met several of the family living today? Do you care? You wouldn't like Amos—you never had much time for unkind people or people full of their own importance—but you'd love your sister, Lizzie. She and Mom would have enjoyed each other so much.

But just like Ward and I never knew Trey and Caroline, Pop didn't know Madeleine and Lizzie and the others. Life's like that, full of absolutes that we can't change.

I became conscious of Annabelle standing beside me.

"Did you find what you were looking for?" she asked.

I nodded. "My grandfather. He raised me." Like she really cared.

She leaned over and scanned the page. "Amazing. Right there for all to see. I'm glad you found it."

"Me too." Massive understatement. "Can you make me some copies?"

"Sure." She picked up the book and carried it to a copy machine at the foot of the stairs. Soon I had five copies in my hand, and Annabelle was carrying the Trust Book back to the locked room where she'd gotten it.

By the time I got back to the farm, I was desperate for someone to talk to about my discovery. I was so delighted to see Jake and Rose that I almost ran from the car to them. Rose sat on the second step of the front porch and Jake was in his chair beside her.

"Look," I said, thrusting my papers under their noses. "I found it."

Then it dawned on me that they had been having a serious discussion and I had interrupted.

"I'm sorry," I said, pulling the papers back just as each had put a hand on them. "You were probably discussing Mary."

"We weren't," Jake said. "But I think it's a good time to be interrupted." He gave Rose a look that was half challenge, half tease.

She nodded agreement, then looked calmly at me. "So, Cara, what were you trying to show us?"

Grinning, I held out the papers again. "Pop's adoption papers!"

"I thought you already had them," Jake said as he bent for a look.

"I have a set given to my great-grandparents, but these are different. These are the court documents that have everyone's names in them, even Pop's mother. This is the absolute proof that Pop was born to Madeleine Biemsderfer."

"And?" Jake said.

"And now we know where he came from. Now we have a family."

"And you didn't before?"

I looked at him, exasperated. "A genetic family. DNA and all that."

"Ignore him, Cara," Rose said with a smile. "He likes to play devil's advocate."

Jake looked at her in surprise. "I do?"

Rose rolled her eyes. "Have you ever listened to yourself? You're the one that challenges everything, including my care of your mother."

"Well, it's just that I've been around hospitals a lot."

"Um. And you're an expert now."

Jake scowled. "I've learned how important it is to ask questions."

Rose scowled back. "Tell me about it." But her mouth quirked up and ruined the scowl. She turned to me. "So what will you do now that you have this information?"

"I can prove to a major skeptic that the relationship is real.

That will be a satisfying experience."

"Have the family members you've met been nice?" Rose asked.

"Most have. The skeptic hasn't."

"Is he responsible for the slashed tires and the dead hens?" Jake asked.

I frowned. "I don't know. But I find it hard to believe an adult would do things that are so juvenile."

"So who are the juveniles?" Rose asked.

I stared at her, appalled. "Surely not one of Amos's kids."

Jake looked at me like I wasn't too bright. "Why not?"

I thought about it a minute. Why not indeed. "Mick wasn't very pleasant to me," I said. "In fact he was cold and threatening." I thought of his hand on my arm and could almost feel the pressure.

"See?" Jake said. "A suspect already."

Rose stood. "I've got to get going. I have a couple more stops before my day's finished. But Jake, I still say that you can't claim Jesus was a nice man." And she left.

"You can't say Jesus was a nice man?" I stared after Rose. "Of course he was nice."

Jake gave a huff that was as close to a laugh as he got. "You've come in at the middle of the conversation. Somehow we got talking about what we believed. Rose believes Jesus is the Savior of the world."

"Me too," I said.

He nodded. "Them too." And he waved toward the house. "But I'm not certain. I said maybe he was just a nice man. Rose says he can't be. Did you know that she's a very opinionated woman?"

"Rose?" I thought of her sweet demeanor and gentle care of Mary.

He snorted. "See? She's fooled you too. She says that if Jesus wasn't God, then he was a maniac. He made too many claims about himself to be normal."

I nodded. "I agree."

He scowled, but I refused to let his bad mood affect me. I smiled brightly and watched his scowl deepen in response. "Careful," I muttered. "Your face'll freeze that way."

"Cute," he snarled, but I saw a bit of a smile tug at his mouth.

"Have you always believed differently than your family?" I asked.

"I don't remember a time when I didn't question all the rules and the hairsplitting and the separation from all that's 'worldly.' I decided that if I had to follow the *Ordnung* to be a Christian, then I wouldn't be one."

"Who says you have to follow the *Ordnung* to be a Christian?"

"All my DNA relatives." He looked at me in challenge. "I've known my blood family all my life, Cara, but I've never fit in. I've never really belonged. DNA doesn't guarantee anything. I don't know if Rose is right about Jesus, but I know I'm right about DNA. Don't hold your breath over your new relatives. Blood isn't necessarily thicker than water."

And he wheeled around and rolled to his apartment.

I sat on the steps for several minutes, thinking about Jake and his heritage. I knew he had broken free of the belief system, but he hadn't left the family. Was that because his disability forced him to stay dependent? Or was it because he loved them in spite of their disagreements? I knew how his mother felt. She loved him dearly even as he broke her heart.

If Jake could leave, would he? Certainly he'd have his own home, but would he break the emotional ties? Somehow I didn't think so. I'd seen the respect he had for his parents and his camaraderie with Elam.

I looked up at the sound of a motor and watched a FedEx truck pull into the drive.

The driver got out and walked toward me.

"Is there a Cara Bentley here?" he asked.

"That's me." I met him halfway up the walk.

I loved getting packages. Since a large part of my business was transacted through the mail, they were usually work related and contained page proofs or new covers or reviews. Maybe this was the new contract? I looked at the envelope with anticipation.

I rushed to my room and grabbed scissors from the pencil caddy on my desk. I slit the envelope and slid out the contents. And felt my heart contract with horror.

Lying on my desk were the mutilated pages of *As the Deer.*

FOURTEEN

I stared at the carnage in front of me. All the pages of *As the Deer* had been ripped from the binding. Some had been further torn in half, some crumpled into tight balls, some torn into confetti. Several of the tiny pieces fluttered to the floor, and Rainbow came running, thinking we were going to play a new game. She was quickly disappointed as I could do nothing but stare in shock.

Even the cover had been defaced. The back cover had been cut into tiny pieces about the size of my little fingernail. On the front the letters were colored in with a black permanent marker, obliterating the title. The beautiful forest scene in soft greens and golds had ugly, drooling monsters with lolling tongues, nasty eyes, and spiky horns added to it. And from each letter of my name dripped red drops of blood, forming a large puddle at the bottom of the page. At the edge of the puddle lay two dead chickens.

I don't know how long I stared at the destroyed book. Even if my tires hadn't been slashed, the hens killed, and the note delivered, I'd have felt threatened and incredibly vulnerable by the sheer nastiness of this attack. The cumulative effect of all the hate was overwhelming. I didn't know what to do, what to think. The audacity and spite made my mouth go dry and my insides clench.

Eventually I became aware of conscious thought and realized that I was convinced Amos had not done this terrible deed. The sheer amount of time required to accomplish this literary mutilation as well as the other attacks precluded his involvement. He was a man with things to do and places to go. He didn't have hours to sit around and plot and destroy books page by page.

Which left the kids. Angry Mick, talkative Pip, and lovely Meaghan.

With shaking hands I gathered all the pieces of paper into the FedEx envelope. I knew what I had to do. Much as I disliked the idea, I had to go talk with Amos and Jessica. And I had to go this evening. Whoever was committing this petty crime wave had to be stopped before it accelerated into actions that were truly dangerous.

I also wanted this flurry of nastiness stopped for the sake of Mary and John. I disliked intensely having any ugliness strike their farm because of me. It wasn't fair. They had enough to deal with due to Mary's fall. They didn't need a vandal with a vendetta against me.

By the time Todd arrived at five-thirty, I had calmed down quite a bit. In fact, I felt almost normal, whatever that was. Still I didn't doubt for a moment that my feeling of security was due largely to his general presence in my life and specific presence here at the farm this very minute. I ran down the stairs with Pop's paper in one hand and the FedEx envelope in the other. I needed to tell him about both, but which should I tell him first?

When I got outside, I stopped abruptly, my eyes drawn to the sky. It had that roiling, boiling look that presaged a momentous storm. To the west, the sun was already hidden behind banks of steel gray clouds, and they were moving rapidly in our direction.

Todd looked up and nodded. "Big storm coming." A roll of thunder in the distance punctuated his comment. He gave me

254

a quick kiss. "Let's go grab something to eat. I've got to be back at the office by seven. I'm seeing clients all evening."

Disappointed at the brevity of his visit, I decided to hold the slaughtered book until dinner was over. It would undoubtedly be better for our digestion that way. We ate at the Bird-in-Hand Restaurant, and over turkey and filling I described in great detail my trip to the Archives. Between bites of cranberry sauce, I passed him the copy of Pop's court record, which he read thoroughly.

"And I owe it all to you," I said. "If you hadn't thought of said prothonotary, I wouldn't have said proof that even said Amos can't contest."

He looked up from the document, grinning. "They did go a bit crazy on the saids, didn't they?"

"Ad nauseum," I agreed. "It's a good thing legal documents are so much easier to understand today." I even managed to say it with a straight face.

"Ouch," he said. "It's just that some things are *pro forma.*"

"If scientists said things were just the way they are, there wouldn't be any inventions or discoveries." I looked at him sternly.

"I liked it better when you were grateful for my help."

"Thanks, Todd," I said obediently. "The prothonotary was a brilliant idea."

"Then I can count on your vote for Lawyer of the Year?"

"I'll stuff the ballot box." I ate my shoofly pie with joy. There was something so wonderful about being with this man.

When we left the restaurant, the black clouds had taken up residence overhead, and the wind was whipping like a malevolent fury, but it wasn't yet raining. Gusts buffeted the car as we drove to the farm, and when we saw an Amish buggy approaching, horse trotting urgently, I was glad for the sturdiness of our vehicle. A flash of lightning lit the dimness, and a crack of thunder sounded like it was in our backseat. The horse, eyes wide and nostrils flared with fear, shied and tossed his head. The woman driving fought for control. I was relieved to see her turn into a farm lane as we drove past.

We were parked in the drive when I pulled out the FedEx envelope.

"I had another interesting experience today," I said.

"Saving the best till last?"

"Hardly." I grimaced. "Someone sent me this."

I handed the envelope to him. He looked at me questioningly, then peered inside. "What in the world?"

He dumped the contents in my lap. The pages, half pages, crumpled pages and confetti looked just as obscene against my tan skirt as they had on my desk.

"Someone knew how to stick a knife in a writer's heart without actually committing that particular crime," I said in an attempt at humor that missed the mark and then some. I think it was the catch in my voice.

Todd was clearly angry on my behalf. "I can't believe Amos would stoop to something like this."

"I don't think he did," I said. "I think it was one of his kids."

Todd's eyebrow rose and he nodded. "Of course. But which one and how do we prove it?"

"I really don't care which one," I said. "I just care that it stops. I thought I'd go to The Paddock this evening and talk to Amos. I've got my proof of relationship." I patted my purse, which held Pop's paper. "And I've got the note and what's left of my book." I began carefully slipping the wreckage back into the envelope.

"Don't go over there tonight," Todd said.

"Yeah, I want to," I said. "I want this settled."

"But I can't go with you. I've got hours."

I nodded. "I know and I feel badly about that. I'd like you with me." I patted his arm. "But I've managed for thirty years on my own. I can manage for one more night." I smiled wanly at him, then went back to collecting the scraps on my lap.

"Don't go, Cara. Amos isn't the nicest person at the best of times. Tonight he'll be even more unhappy, especially toward you."

"Why especially toward me? You mean because of the adoption?"

"You were with me the last time he saw you."

"And he doesn't like you?"

"Well, he doesn't for some reason, but that's not what I'm referring to."

"You're a threat to him."

"What?" He looked surprised.

"You're a threat. You're an up-and-coming lawyer whom judges congratulate on your work. People respect you. I saw that the other night. You're honest and more than capable." I shrugged. "You're a threat."

He obviously wasn't convinced, but I was. Amos didn't like competition, and Todd was competition whether he meant to be or not.

"Amos and I faced off in court today," he said. "The judge's ruling was in my client's favor. Amos can't stand losing, and he hasn't done it enough to have learned to deal with it well. I think it'd be better if you stayed away from him tonight."

I thought for a minute. "I think I'll go anyway." I dropped the last of the confetti in the envelope. "I don't think there's any good time as far as he and I are concerned."

"Cara." There was an edge to Todd's voice. "Don't go over there tonight."

"Don't worry. I'll be fine. I've just got to get this settled, or it'll drive me crazy." I glanced up from the envelope and saw his face. "What's wrong?"

"I don't want you to go to Amos's house."

"Todd," I said quietly. "It's my choice to make."

"Not this time," he said slowly and distinctly. "I'm telling you: don't go."

I looked at him, my eyes turning flinty at his dictatorial manner. "You can't stand it if someone chooses to differ with you, can you?" If my icy tone were any measure of climate, it would start to snow momentarily instead of rain, June or no.

"And you can't stand to take advice from anyone, can you?" His anger was hot enough to melt the polar ice cap.

"I think it's time to go," I said as I reached for the door handle. "It's 6:50. You're going to be late for your client."

"Cara!" He grabbed my arm. "Don't. Go. To. Yosts'!"

I narrowed my eyes and spat, "What gives you the right to tell me what I can and can't do?" I pulled my arm free and slid from the car, already fishing my keys from my purse. He wasn't going to order me around!

"If you don't know what gives me the right," he said, his voice low and hard, "then I can't explain it to you."

I slammed my door and he threw the car in reverse. I stalked to my car and he stormed out of the drive. I jammed my key in the ignition and he roared down the road. I stared out my windshield and wondered what had just happened.

The Paddock looked as lovely under this evening's threatening skies as it had when I was here with Todd. The tables were gone, the dance floor disassembled, the lanterns extinguished, but the beauty of the graceful estate was undiminished.

Only I was different. I was alone and remorseful instead of with Todd and full of dreams. I sighed for the millionth time. Gone was my anger both at Todd and at myself. Despair filled me in its place.

God, can two highly opinionated people with sinfully strong wills make it? Oh, God, please tell me they can! I'll even work at becoming a woman of a quiet and gentle spirit. I will. I promise.

I parked outside the garage and walked slowly to the front door. The air was now still and heavy, the quiet before the storm. I shivered in spite of the heat. Todd was right. I shouldn't have come here alone. Another person would be a witness to what was said, if nothing else. That he also might be comfort, strength, support, encouragement—the list went on—only made me feel more alone.

As I stood hesitantly on the front doorstep, lightning flashed and immediately a great crack of thunder ripped the night. I jumped.

I didn't need to talk to Amos tonight, I decided suddenly. I'd face him another time. Solving the crimes suddenly didn't have the immediacy I'd thought. I turned to leave.

Before I took a step off the porch, the skies opened, releasing a wall of water that fell in great sheets. One minute it was dry, the next the air was a river. Great drops fell straight down, so dense that I was surprised that there was oxygen enough to breathe.

My choices were reduced to facing Amos or drowning. Resigned, I turned and rang the doorbell.

Pip answered the door. "Hey, look who's here!" he cried. "Come on in!"

Well, I thought. At least one person's glad to see me.

Pip ushered me into the front hall. He grinned at me, then leaned his head back and bellowed, "Mom, Dad, company!"

He lowered his voice to a whisper and said, "I won't tell them who's here. They might not come if they knew." His eyes twinkled and he rocked back and forth on his toes, delighted with his own humor.

I couldn't help grinning back at him. There was something irrepressible and delightful about him. He wasn't as bulky as his father and Mick, and his lean attractiveness appealed to me. He had a wonderful smile, and his gray eyes were guileless and full of wonder, even with the great dark circles beneath them.

Heavy footsteps sounded in the hall and Mick appeared. He took one look at me and his handsome face soured. "Oh, it's you."

"Pleased to see you too, Mick," I said.

"Guess what?" Pip asked me, undeterred by his brother's ill humor. "Meaghan bought one of your books."

"Oh, yeah?" I said carefully. "Which one?"

"There's more than one?" He seemed surprised.

"Several more," I said. "I'm a writer, remember? To make a living at the profession, you need to keep producing."

More footsteps sounded in the hall, light and quick, and Jessica and Meaghan approached. Jessica froze when she saw me, but Meaghan rushed forward.

"I bought one of your books," she said. *As the Deer.* If I'm going to be a writer, I thought I ought to read what a successful author is writing." And she grinned.

As the Deer, I thought, and shivered.

"The weird thing is," Meaghan continued, "I can't find it anyplace. When I do, will you autograph it?"

"Sure," I said, all the while thinking that I had the book right here in the FedEx pouch. I studied her, trying to see if she was being clever or just being honest. I couldn't tell.

"Mom," Pip said, bouncing around the hall with an energy

that made me feel weary, "we haven't been very polite to Cara. We need to ask her into the living room."

Jessica looked trapped by Pip's comment. "Of course," she said without enthusiasm. "Please, Cara. Have a seat." She led the way and gestured to a wing chair.

I looked around the living room. At least I wasn't trapped in a paean of praise to Penn State. The greens and roses were lovely, though the room had the look of a showplace rather than a lived-in space. Jessica and the children sat stiffly, clearly unused to the room.

"So what have you been doing since you were here Saturday?" asked Pip, all excitement. "Anything interesting?"

"When your dad gets here, I'll tell all of you at the same time." I smiled at him so the answer didn't sound too brusque.

He nodded and jumped to his feet. "I'll go get Dad." And he dashed from the room.

I turned to Jessica. "He must wear you out with his energy."

She smiled like she'd just eaten a particularly sour lemon and said nothing. I became aware that Mick was watching her closely. When he felt my eyes on him, he looked at me in anger.

An awkward silence fell over the room, and it was a relief to finally hear two sets of footsteps approaching, even if one belonged to Amos.

When he walked into the room and saw me, he froze. It was obvious that Pip hadn't told him that I was his guest.

Jessica, Mick, and Meaghan all watched him nervously. Pip watched me.

Amos finally found his voice. "When I told you to stay away from my mother, I never imagined I'd have to tell you to stay away from us as well."

I tried not to cringe under the lash of his words.

"Dad." Pip laid a hand on his father's arm. "She's a guest here. We need to be polite." He turned to Jessica. "Right, Mom?"

Jessica opened her mouth but no sound came out.

"Be quiet, Pip," Amos ordered. "She is not a guest, and I will not be polite."

Praying like crazy, I stood up to face Amos on a more equal footing. "I won't stay long," I said. "I just have two things for you."

Amos didn't ask what they were, but he didn't throw me out, either.

"The first is this copy of a legal document that I found in the archives at the courthouse today." I held out a copy of Pop's adoption decree.

Amos made no move to take it, but Pip eagerly grabbed it. He looked it over quickly and said, "She's a Biemsderfer, Dad. It says here that Great-grandmother Madeleine had a baby boy who was adopted. See?" He held the paper to his father. "Here's Madeleine's name. And here's Cara's grandfather's name."

Amos shut his eyes for a moment, distress and distrust warring in his expression. He took a deep breath as if to steel himself and reached for the paper. He read it quickly and swore.

"I just wanted you to know that there is proof that Pop was Madeleine and Enos's son," I said.

"How did you know to look in the Archives?" Pip asked, his eyes bright with curiosity. "Dad said adoption records were sealed."

"My lawyer suggested it," I said, not mentioning Todd's name on purpose. If Amos was upset about the outcome of today's hearing, there was no sense in making things worse than they already were.

"Is that Todd Reasoner?" Pip asked innocently. "The guy you were here with the other night?"

I nodded while Amos glowered.

"There will be no money for you," Amos said suddenly, the chill in his voice lowering the room temperature several degrees.

"I don't want any money," I said.

Amos snorted. "I have power of attorney. I will never let Mother change her will."

"Nor should you," I agreed. "I don't—" I stopped, realizing that I could protest all night, and he wouldn't believe me. I scanned the others in the room and saw they didn't accept my protestations, either. I sighed and reached into my purse. I pulled out my threatening letter and handed it to Amos.

"This came in the mail this morning," I said.

He scanned it and went white.

"What's it say, Dad?" asked Pip, all innocent curiosity. The rest of the room's occupants showed no interest in the contents of the letter at all.

Amos cleared his throat and read. "You were told not to visit her. You were warned. Now you will suffer. Like the chickens."

"Like the chickens?" Mick asked in a tight voice. "What does that mean?"

"Someone slit the throats of two hens on the farm where I live. They were lying on the front porch this morning."

Pip stared at me, eyes wide. "Someone killed them?"

"Whoever wrote this note knew about it." Amos wasn't asking a question but making a statement.

I nodded. "There's more."

Mick flinched, and I noticed he was beginning to look scared.

"The tires on my car were all slashed Saturday night. I can't prove that incident is tied to the dead hens, but common sense says the two are connected. And then there's this." I upended the FedEx envelope onto the green carpet.

All five Yosts watched transfixed as the single pages floated, the crumpled pages tumbled, and the confetti showered until all rested about my feet.

Meaghan was out of her chair and on her knees in the debris in an instant. "Is that my book? Is it?" She sounded slightly panicked. "I bet it is!" She raised fearful eyes to her mother.

Mick suddenly staggered to his feet, took half a step, then collapsed into his chair again. He put his face in his hands and groaned. Jessica went deathly pale and began to cry, tears running unchecked down her face. Amos turned scarlet with fury. The only one unmoved was Pip. He grinned and bounced some more.

"How dare you disrupt our family like this!" Amos raged at me. "How dare you distress my wife! How dare you!"

I stared at him in disbelief.

"Amos." Jessica rose timidly from her chair. She sniffed and dashed a hand at her tears. "You know it's not her fau—"

Amos cut her off. "Get out!" he screamed at me.

With trembling legs I walked toward the front hall. I turned just before I left the room.

"No more," I said, gesturing to the envelope and note. "Or I tell the police."

"Out!" Amos roared.

I looked at the people who were my blood relatives but far from me in heart. Mick stared at the floor, agony in every line of his face. Meaghan watched her mother in uncertainty and fear. Jessica stood by her chair, hopeless and defeated. Amos was rigid with anger and despair. Pip looked from one person to the other, trying to gauge their feelings, trying to assess his own response.

And suddenly something clicked, and I thought I understood what was happening. Sorrow filled me as I turned into the front hall. These people were being torn apart by something they couldn't control.

I walked to the door and was reaching for the knob when Mick rushed into the hall.

"I'm sorry," he blurted. "I never meant—"

"It's all right," I said.

"No, it's not." He looked at me out of weary eyes. "I never should have—I didn't think—I didn't mean—" His shoulders slumped. "I'm sorry."

"It's not your fault."

"Yes, it is. I should have seen."

"You can't see everything."

"That's kind of you. But I should have. I'm sorry."

Pip came flying out to the hall. He punched Mick on the shoulder and said, "Don't apologize to her. Why should you apologize to her? She should apologize to us!"

"How long has he been sick?" I asked.

"Four years," Mick answered.

"Who's sick?" Pip's voice became strident. "She's sick! Barging in here and claiming to be family so she can take Dad's money! Well, she can't have it! It's ours!"

"Your father's in denial?"

Mick nodded. "A blot on the family."

"And you've tried to take care of Pip in his place?"

Mick shrugged. "Someone has to."

"No one has to take care of me! We should just take care of her." And he glared at me. Gone completely was the charming young man who had welcomed me and conned his family into talking with me.

"How long has it been since you've taken your lithium?" I asked Pip.

"I don't take medicine!" he yelled. "I'm not sick! I don't need lithium! I'm not bipolar! I'm not manic-depressive! Do you see a depressed person here? I'm healthier than all of you put together!"

Amos came into the hallway. He hesitated when he heard his younger son ranting, but he turned on me. "Are you still here? I thought I told you to leave!"

"You tell her, Dad!" Pip punched Amos in the shoulder hard enough to make him stagger.

"Come on, Pip," Mick said, throwing an arm about his brother's shoulders. "Let's go into the living room. Mom's waiting."

"Like I care." But he let Mick lead him away.

A loud knock sounded just as I turned the knob. I pulled the door open to find a tall, wet, unhappy man.

I ran straight into his arms. "You came!"

"I had to." He rested his cheek on my head.

"Reasoner! Just what I need!" Amos spat and slammed the front door in our faces.

We stood on the porch watching the deluge.

"What about your clients?" I asked.

"I finished with one early and left before the next ones came. Mrs. Smiley will just have to keep them happy until I get back."

"Poor Mrs. Smiley."

"Poor clients," Todd said.

I tried to smile, and suddenly the emotions of the night caught up with me, and I started to shake.

"You were right. I shouldn't have come alone," I said. I felt tears build. "And all I wanted was a body-and-bone family!"

Todd held me until I stopped crying.

"As if you're not wet enough from the rain, I have to weep all over you."

266

"Don't let it worry you. I'm about to get even wetter."

We both were soaked by the time we dashed into Todd's office. Mrs. Smiley sniffed mightily at our disreputable appearance.

"The Turleys got tired of waiting," she announced with satisfaction.

Todd nodded, unperturbed. "Buzz when the Rineers get here."

He led me past her desk and into his *sanctum sanctorum,* his hand solicitously resting on the small of my back. He put me in the leather chair opposite his desk.

"Are you all right?" he asked as he automatically took his seat behind his desk.

"Sure," I said "Maybe. Some day. Never."

Suddenly Amos's hostility and Pip's cruelty slapped me again. Even though I understood that illness was behind their actions, I felt bruised by the emotional toll.

"I'm too used to people being nice to me," I said, my chin wobbling. "Mom was always so kind, and Pop hugged us all the time. And Ward protected me. Everyone said I love you and meant it. I lived in a warm, wonderful cocoon, and I didn't realize how blessed I was until recently." I clenched my hands in my lap. "I miss it all so much."

I blinked wildly. I would not cry. I'd already wept too much. Besides, I looked terrible when I cried. I got a red nose and dark circles under my eyes. I swallowed and straightened my shoulders, but it didn't help, at least not enough.

I dropped my head to my hands and sobbed. "I'm s-sorry," I managed and cried harder.

Suddenly Todd was on his knees in front of me, his hands covering mine.

"Cara, sweetheart, don't cry." He reached out and pushed

my hair back. "They don't matter. You know that. The Yosts don't matter!"

I nodded. "I know that here," and lifted a hand to my head. "But—" and a fresh season of tears took me.

Todd spread his arms for me and, desperate, I fell into them. Somehow as we met, we lost our balance and ended up on the floor in an unexpected but most satisfying attorney-client huddle. He sat cross-legged with his back against his desk, and I sat sideways in the well between his knees. His arms were wrapped about me and he held me and stroked my hair and whispered soothing noises to me while I sobbed against his starched shirt front and silk tie. He didn't even try to move his tie out of harm's way. I had never felt safer in my life.

Eventually my storm of tears wore itself out, and I rested, spent, my head cradled on his shoulder. That's when I realized my arms were clutching him, one across his chest, the other his back. I forced myself to release my death grip, but since I couldn't figure out where else to put my arms, and in truth didn't want to put them anywhere else, I left them right where they were.

I felt Todd lower his head. "Feeling better?" he said to my cheek, and I felt the softest of kisses.

I nodded against his shoulder. For a bony surface, it cushioned me with amazing comfort. I gave a great sniff.

He jumped and I realized I had sniffed right in his ear. I sighed. My heroines would never have done a gauche thing like that. I could see that I needed to take lessons from them.

"Let me get my handkerchief," Todd said, and leaned in my direction as he reached into his far pocket.

The physics of our new position was too much for gravity's pull, and we lost our balance. I ended up on my back on the carpet and he ended up leaning over me, his weight held on one elbow-stiffened arm. I couldn't tear my eyes from his face.

"Sweetheart," he said in a gruff voice, "don't look at me like that."

I nodded and blinked a few times. I had no idea how I was looking at him, but if my emotions were as obvious on my face as his were, we were a dangerous pair.

Then I couldn't help it; I sniffed again. And again.

He grinned, raised his eyebrow, and shook his head. "And you're a romance writer."

He took the handkerchief he'd finally retrieved and wiped my eyes. He handed it to me. I stared at it.

"It's ironed. How can I dirty your ironed handkerchief?"

"The cleaners did it once, they can do it again."

"That's a good thing," I muttered. "I don't do handker-chiefs."

With barely a blink or a missed beat, Todd spoke. "Then we'll have to keep sending them to the cleaners, won't we?"

Nodding, I took his handkerchief and blew my nose, not an easy thing to do on your back.

He reached out his free hand to trace my eyebrows, my nose, my lips. "You are beautiful, absolutely beautiful."

I closed my eyes at his feather touch, knowing nothing I'd ever written came close to the sensation of someone you love loving you back. I ached all over from the sweetness of it.

Vaguely I heard a buzz somewhere in the real world, then a quick knock and the opening of a door. Mrs. Smiley's gasp was more than audible.

"I-I knocked," she sputtered.

"I know," Todd said without moving. His fingers were on my mouth. I wanted to nibble them.

Mrs. Smiley swallowed. "Your next client is here."

Todd nodded. "Give me five minutes."

The door closed.

I couldn't help but laugh. "She'll never respect you again," I said, taking his hand and pressing it against my cheek. "Your image has been ruined forever."

"At least I'm not lying on the floor like some people I know," he said. He took both my hands and pulled me back into the circle of his knees. Our faces were so close I couldn't even focus. His hand gripped the back of my neck, his thumb caressed my cheek.

"Cara, my beautiful Cara, what are you doing to me?" And he kissed me. That's when I knew that the heart-stopping, toe-curling kiss on his father's porch had been no aberration.

I drew back first, though very reluctantly. My nose was still stopped up from all the crying, and I desperately needed to breathe. While I gasped, Todd kissed away any remaining traces of my tears.

"I'd better go," I said.

He nodded and we picked ourselves up. Arms about each other's waists, we walked toward the door. We saw ourselves in the mirror on the side wall at the same time, and we both gasped.

I was all eyes and wild hair. I had great dark circles from crying, my nose was still slightly red, and my hair flew all about my face as if it were energized with static electricity.

"You need glasses," I blurted.

"What?" he asked, running his hands madly over his curls, seeking order.

"You told me I was beautiful. Attorneys aren't supposed to lie."

He looked at my reflection in the mirror and laughed at my long face. His hands dropped from his hair to rest on my shoulders as he stood behind me.

"Cara, tonight when you went off to Amos's all alone and I found myself trapped here with clients, I regretted what I'd said so much. Especially how I'd left you. I knew I had to get there to be with you, to stand by you. My heart broke for you there alone. And I knew I loved you." He slid his hand beneath my hair, grasping my neck. "I knew I loved your courage, your passion for things that matter to you, even your philosophical discussions about body and bone versus heart. I knew I'd love you forever."

"Oh, Todd!" I started to cry again.

"Sweetheart," he said, concern in his voice.

"Good crying," I said quickly. "Good crying."

He looked at me like I was crazy, but he nodded.

"I love you too," I said. "You are the only sure thing in my life apart from the Lord. You are the one who has been there for me, who has helped me when everyone else thought I should let well enough alone. You stood by me. You're my rock." I smiled. "And I love you. Always. Forever."

EPILOGUE

Two years later

I lay in my hospital bed, bruised and broken but happier than I'd ever been in my life. I looked down at Madeleine Elizabeth Reasoner held snug against my breast. A little knitted cap covered her newborn head, and her red, wrinkled face was beautiful.

Bone of my bone, born of my body, but child of my heart, our hearts.

I rested against her father who sat on the bed beside me, my back against his strong side and my head against his shoulder. One of his hands lay gently on my head and the other cupped our baby's skull. His look of utter infatuation as he stared at his daughter made me smile.

The last twelve hours had been terrible for him as he watched my pain and couldn't relieve it. His eyes were shadowed by purple and his strong jaw sported dark stubble, but he'd been there the whole time, as he'd always been there for me.

We had married the fall after we met and settled happily if sometimes argumentatively into Todd's house. He continued as a sole practitioner in his office in Bird-in-Hand, supervised by Mrs. Smiley who eventually forgave him his one evening of unprofessional behavior. I continued writing, and when I felt I had the energy, I was scheduled to begin the third volume in my first trilogy.

While Amos continued to be hostile to us, and Jessica followed his lead, Mick and Meaghan came to see us periodically. Pip never did. He still fought his medication, and the resulting emotional chaos continued to wrack the family. He never bothered me again in any way. I kept my promise to Aunt Lizzie and prayed for all of them regularly.

From my hospital bed, I looked across the room to the two who sat in the visitors' chairs. Dad Reasoner and Aunt Lizzie reminded me of the little wobbly-headed dolls that people sometimes put in their cars, smiling, smiling as their heads shook slightly on their ancient necks. Their delight in Madeleine was a joy to me.

"She looks like the Reasoners," Dad said. "Just like Catherine."

"Pshaw," Aunt Lizzie said. "She's all Biemsderfer."

"You always have to disagree with me, don't you, Liz?"

"Only because you always think you're right."

I looked at my husband and smiled. "Do they remind you of anyone?"

"*Res ipsa loquitor*," he said. "Some things just speak for themselves."

I grinned as a nurse walked in with a huge bouquet. Todd reached among the roses, lilies, and irises for the card and passed it to me.

With all our love, Marnie, Ward, Johnny, and Tess. We'll save all Tess's clothes for Madeleine.

"I can see that having a cousin a year older than Maddy will be a great benefit," I said. I ran a finger gently down Maddy's small cheek. My baby. I started to cry.

Todd leaned over and kissed me.

"I love you, Cara," he whispered. "Heart of my heart."

I fell asleep smiling.

Dear Reader:

I am the daughter of an adopted person and the mother of two adopted sons. Obviously the topic of adoption is one that has long interested me. The discussion in *The Document* about what makes family—bone and blood, DNA, and genes or affection, acceptance, and heart—are ideas I have long considered.

But beyond these issues, *The Document* is special to me because it is based on my mother's adoption papers. The document of the title, Pop's adoption certificate, is word for word my mother's adoption certificate with the exception of changing her name to his and Philadelphia County to Lancaster County. Like Pop, my mother cost six dollars. Like the picture of Pop requested by Madeleine, a picture of my mother was requested by my birth grandmother.

Unlike in the book, I do not know whether my grandmother ever sent a picture to my birth grandmother. I never saw the letter making the request until two years ago when my mother died. By then it was years too late to ask about the requested picture. I certainly hope Grandmom sent it.

We have never tried to search for Mom's family. Like Pop, Mom never felt a need to find them. She was content to be part of the family she was raised in, accepting heart and affection as sufficient. I've never felt the need to search, either. Sometimes when people tell me I remind them of someone they know, I wonder if it's someone I'm related to, someone I've not met, someone who may not even know there's a step-branch of the family out there. I do, after all, still live in the general geographic area in which my mother was born and raised.

My sons have looked for their mothers. We always told the boys we would support this action when they were old enough to handle the emotional ramifications, whatever they might be.

We also always refused to put ourselves in competition for the boys' affection with these women for whom I have a great deal of respect. They did not, after all, have to carry my sons to term, yet they were brave enough to do so.

One son had a successful and pleasant meeting with his mother, but no lasting relationship has developed. Our other son has not yet made contact with his mother at her request. Maybe some day. I hope so, for both of them.

Every time I hear someone denigrate adoption, I feel genuine sorrow. I think not only of Mom and my sons but also of the high view God has of adoption. I think of my position as an adopted child of the King. Where would I be without my Father? Where would I be if He weren't willing to take in a foundling and make her a daughter? It's heart, after all, that makes the difference, the heart of God that loved me enough to accept me—and you—in the Beloved.

Gayle Roper

PALISADES...PURE ROMANCE

⟨ PALISADES ⟩

Reunion, Karen Ball
Refuge, Lisa Tawn Bergren
Torchlight, Lisa Tawn Bergren
Treasure, Lisa Tawn Bergren
Chosen, Lisa Tawn Bergren
Firestorm, Lisa Tawn Bergren
Surrender, Lynn Bulock
Dalton's Dilemma, Lynn Bulock
Island Breeze, Lynn Bulock (February 1999)
Wise Man's House, Melody Carlson
Heartland Skies, Melody Carlson
Shades of Light, Melody Carlson
Cherish, Constance Colson
Chase the Dream, Constance Colson
Angel Valley, Peggy Darty
Sundance, Peggy Darty
Moonglow, Peggy Darty
Promises, Peggy Darty
Memories, Peggy Darty
Spirits, Peggy Darty
Remembering the Roses, Marion Duckworth
Love Song, Sharon Gillenwater
Antiques, Sharon Gillenwater
Texas Tender, Sharon Gillenwater
Secrets, Robin Jones Gunn
Whispers, Robin Jones Gunn
Echoes, Robin Jones Gunn
Sunsets, Robin Jones Gunn

Clouds, Robin Jones Gunn
Waterfalls, Robin Jones Gunn
Coming Home, Barbara Jean Hicks
Snow Swan, Barbara Jean Hicks
China Doll, Barbara Jean Hicks
Angel in the Senate, Kristen Johnson Ingram
Irish Eyes, Annie Jones
Father by Faith, Annie Jones
Irish Rogue, Annie Jones
Beloved, Deb Kastner
Glory, Marilyn Kok
On Assignment, Marilyn Kok
Sierra, Shari MacDonald
Forget-Me-Not, Shari MacDonald
Diamonds, Shari MacDonald
Stardust, Shari MacDonald
Westward, Amanda MacLean
Stonehaven, Amanda MacLean
Everlasting, Amanda MacLean
Kingdom Come, Amanda MacLean
Betrayed, Lorena McCourtney
Escape, Lorena McCourtney
Dear Silver, Lorena McCourtney
Forgotten, Lorena McCourtney
Canyon, Lorena McCourtney
Rustlers, Karen Rispin
Summit, Karen Rispin (February 1999)
Enough! Gayle Roper
The Key, Gayle Roper
The Document, Gayle Roper
Voyage, Elaine Schulte
Daddy's Home, Linda Windsor (February 1999)

Anthologies

A Christmas Joy, Darty, Gillenwater, MacLean
Mistletoe, Ball, Hicks, McCourtney
A Mother's Love, Bergren, Colson, MacLean
Silver Bells, Bergren, Krause, MacDonald
Heart's Delight, Ball, Hicks, Noble
Fools for Love, Ball, Brooks, Jones